OMAR HENRY

OMAR HENRY

THE MAN IN THE MIDDLE

Omar Henry

with
Keith Graham

Queen Anne Press

QUEEN ANNE PRESS
a division of Lennard Associates Limited
Mackerye End
Harpenden
Herts AL5 5DR

First published in Great Britain in 1994

British Library Cataloguing in Publication
is available

ISBN 1 85291 542 0

Typeset in New Baskerville and Univers Condensed
Editor: Caroline North
Editorial: Assistant Jacky Cleaver
Index: Mark Stephenson
Statistics: Richard Lockwood and Frank Heydenrych
Cover design and styling: Cooper Wilson

Cover photographs
Front: Allsport (Joe Mann)
Back: Allsport (Mike Hewitt)

Reproduced, printed and bound by
Butler and Tanner Limited,
Frome and London

PICTURE ACKNOWLEDGEMENTS
The publishers are grateful to Argus Newspapers (South Africa),
Keith Graham, Bill Smith and Allsport (Mike Hewitt) for their
contributions to the picture sections in this book.

CONTENTS

FOREWORD

Today is April 28th 1994. The new South Africa has been born – a fitting day on which to write a foreword for the book about Omar Henry's life. He, and he alone, was the one person who, because of his colour, became a symbol in South African cricket... of all that was wrong and, ultimately, all that was right.

I first met him when he was a young boy, back in 1967, and somehow our paths have been inextricably intertwined ever since. Omar Henry was a 'natural' cricketer then and all our predictions about him eventually became reality. Regrettably the rewards for him came late in his life but, nonetheless, he finally made it to the top and at last enjoyed a deserved international career.

Never one to shirk his responsibilities, on or off the field, Omar also always spoke his mind. He has been a fierce competitor and a fine team man, and Omar Henry will undoubtedly go down in South Africa's history not only for his cricket skills but for the unique position he occupied – the pawn who went across the chessboard of South African cricket history and eventually became a king.

It has been a pleasure to have Omar as a friend. May his story find that happy niche in the world of cricket – and beyond – that he himself should have enjoyed for much longer. I know that he and I will both find our own happy niche in the new South Africa.

EDDIE BARLOW
April 1994

A MOST UNLIKELY LAD

There are, I suppose, highlights in every cricketer's career. I've certainly had my moments; I've also had my failures and disappointments. But nothing will live longer in my memory than the day I walked out to the middle at my beloved Newlands in January 1980 to become the first non-white ever to represent Western Province against Transvaal.

This beautiful ground, sheltering in the shadow of Table Mountain, had been my personal shrine – my Mecca – ever since I was a small boy of five when my father took me to see such great cricketers as England's Mike Smith and New Zealand's John Reid. But my real hero, not surprisingly, was a South African. Trevor Goddard, because he, like me, was left-handed with both bat and ball, captured my imagination. I couldn't take my eyes off him. Most youngsters who want to become good cricketers have their heroes – their idols – and I was no different, except perhaps that as I was a coloured boy, it may surprise some to learn that my personal idol was a white South African – especially since when I was taken to see my hero and all the other great cricketers who played for and against South Africa in those days before the international doors closed upon the country, I was automatically consigned to watching them from the small section of the ground devoted to non-whites. In street 'test matches', played with a tennis ball, a bat fashioned out of a plank and using trees as wickets (they happened to be about 22 yards apart), I *was* Trevor Goddard.

Thus in 1980, when I took the field with my new team-mates at

Western Province, actually trod the turf that Goddard and so many other greats had walked on at Newlands, you can imagine that I felt pretty emotional. That match was a pinnacle, the fulfilment of a dream. Perhaps if I had died after that first Currie Cup game, I would have died happy. It represented the bridging of what at one time had been unbridgeable gaps for someone from the coloured section of the South African community. As a kid I had one ambition in my life and that was to play cricket at Newlands, and even though I knew that I was definitely not from the privileged section of the community, I held that dream within my heart. During my teenage years, that goal seemed always to be retreating before me as I began to understand more about the great human divide which has been the story of South Africa and almost its downfall. Yet I never, ever gave up on that dream. If over the years I have had to surmount what seemed to be unscalable barriers to achieve the various cricketing and indeed personal goals in my life, if I have had to battle every inch of the way, take risks and sometimes court unpopularity on a scale it might be difficult to imagine in societies in which there are no great divides according to race, I have few regrets on the difficult choices I sometimes had to make.

Where I have been, others now will assuredly follow. In 1994, if enormous changes have taken place in South Africa, there is still a long way to go, many more battles to be fought before there is the kind of equality of opportunity that was denied to me, my generation and succeeding generations of black and coloured South Africans. If I have achieved impossible dreams then I am realistic enough to know that I owe many debts of gratitude to people from all sections of the community and not least to my family, who supported me through thick and thin, were always there during the difficult times and were unstinting in their support. Their part, and indeed the part played by many other people in my progress from schoolboy cricketer to Test match player has been vital. Equally, the fighting qualities I inherited through my genes, from my religious convictions and from my family background, have been central to my life and central to whatever successes I have managed to achieve.

And yet after that first Currie Cup match there were other pinnacles. In so many respects, the climax of it all came at the end of the 1992-93

South African season when I helped Orange Free State to win the Castle Cup – the equivalent of the English County Championship – for the first time in the 100-year history of the club. If my Test match appearances, the pride I derived from being a part of the South African excursion to the 1992 World Cup in Australia, being a member of the team to visit the West Indies, making my first appearance for South Africa against Kim Hughes' rebel Australians in 1987 and my official Test debut against India in 1993 might be considered by others to be greater achievements, then I can tell you that nothing gave me greater pleasure than that one game. Why should such an event stand out so clearly? Simply because the Orange Free State was the epitome of Afrikaans South Africa, almost the birthplace of the misbegotten creed of apartheid. If you are dealing in impossible dreams, then that single event must represent the most impossible dream of all, at least, just a handful of years before, it would have seemed so. Here I was, in the Afrikaner heartland, one of the vital cogs in that cricketing machine, scoring runs and taking wickets in the deciding game against my old team, Western Province. Let me underline that by emphasising that my Free State colleagues only ever saw me as a fellow member of their team. Nothing else counted: not the colour of my skin, not my background, not from whence I came, not my religion. I was, to them, a cricketer of worth, a man of worth, a human being who, like them, wanted success and would bust a gut to ensure that corporately we would enjoy success. Yet there were others who still, even in that historic moment of triumph, saw something else, whose attitude was itself coloured by the colour of my skin and by my religion. And in that moment of victory and during the euphoria which followed, I felt I had, once and for all, proved that these other elements were unimportant, that they had nothing to do with how or why we had achieved that victory. It was an especially sweet moment, too, because I had performed so well: I had scored a century and, in the crucial second innings, taken 5 wickets.

The destination of the Cup remained undetermined when the last round of games began on January 9th, 1993. Natal were playing Transvaal in Johannesburg. A win would secure the Championship for Transvaal, whilst we were entertaining my former team, Western Province, whom Free State had never beaten, at Springbok Park,

Bloemfontein. We were also in the hunt, although in all honesty, we rather expected Transvaal to edge home, particularly as we started our game so badly. Meyrick Pringle struck in the first over of the game to remove Mickey Arthur and Gerhardus Liebenberg followed him back to the pavilion shortly afterwards to have us reeling on 3 for 2. There was something of a recovery through a resolute innings from Hansie Cronje and some flashing strokes from Louis Wilkinson but when I went to the wicket, batting at number 8, we had crumbled to 110 for 6 and worse was to come when we lost another wicket: 113 for 7. Bradley Player and I then really bedded in and added 52 in the next hour but when Brad was picked up off Craig Matthews for 24 that left me and just numbers 10 and 11 to pick up the pieces. The crucial stand followed between myself and Philip Radley. I managed to farm the bowling pretty successfully by taking some very quick singles and together we took the score from 165 to 246 before we went for one run too many and Philip, after resisting for 94 balls, was run out. Allan Donald and I added another 20 to give us a respectable total of 266 and I managed to reach three figures in an innings of which I was particularly proud: 104 not out.

Province made a solid start, putting on 49 for the first wicket, but then we began to nibble away at them, everyone chipping in with wickets to leave them struggling. Eric Simons showed some resistance but when he had reached 40 I had him caught by Hansie Cronje and they were all out for 165, giving us a more than useful lead. Then Hansie took hold of the game by the scruff of the neck with a magnificent innings. He went in first and he and Mickey Arthur put on 166 before Mickey was out for a fine 71. Rudolf Steyn then joined the skipper and flayed the Province attack unmercifully as they added 137 in just 102 minutes before Hansie declared at 303 for 1 with his own score on 161, setting them an unlikely 405 to win. I must say they had a real go at it, Gary Kirsten leading the way with a superb ton. The icing on the cake for me personally was my haul of 5 wickets. I bowled 33 overs to finish with 5 for 68 as we claimed a quite stunning victory.

Meanwhile, in Johannesburg, Natal, in spite of being bowled out for 71 in their second innings, had pulled off a stirring victory by 49 runs. We had, incredibly, won the Cup. It was the culmination of my best-ever season in the Castle Cup, averaging 53.83 with the bat and picking up 27 wickets at 23.88 apiece, having bowled more overs than anyone else in the side. But the bottom line, I suppose, was that I had that season become one of the leading all-rounders in the game and the fact that I was made one of the Cricketers of the Year by the *Protea Assurance Cricket Annual of South Africa* – our equivalent of *Wisden* – was perhaps an acknowledgement of this. At any rate, it is something of which I feel immensely proud. And I had achieved that level of performance in the most unlikely environment of all. As a coloured guy, when you go into the heart of Afrikaner territory, you have a sense that you are bearding the lion in his own den. That may seem sceptical, but I suppose such feelings are an inevitable consequence of a lifetime of having to battle against an unfair system.

Don't get me wrong, I made a lot of very good friends in Free State. My team-mates always accepted me as one of them. The atmosphere in the dressing room was always happy and we were all really good mates. Allan Donald, who is a really great world-class bowler, and I became great pals. But there was dissension. I suppose I have inevitably become the kind of person who is not afraid to voice an opinion and fight for what I believe to be right and I certainly found myself at odds on occasions with the Free State coach, a schoolteacher who had never played top-level cricket but, I have to say, a man who has produced a lot of good young cricketers. In short, Johan Volsteedt and I ended up at loggerheads with one another. The turning point came when we were playing Eastern Province in the 1990-91 season. We had to chase on the last day at the rate of 4 an over. Johan and Hansie Cronje asked me how I thought we should approach it and I said that as Province were operating with three spinners (because one of their seamers was injured) on a wicket which was giving them some help, we would have to keep the scoreboard moving, preferably at 3 to 4 an over so that when we came to the last 20 overs, we would not have to try and slog the spinners. Johan, however, expressed the view that as long as we didn't lose wickets, we could really give it a go in the last 20 and that up until then, the run rate was unimportant. It was a difference of opinion and everybody is entitled to their own views on how best to go about things, but in the circumstances I really backed my own judgement, culled, if

I may say so, from considerable experience – remember, at this stage I had a background of 12 seasons of top-level cricket. In the event, we did it his way and when we got to the last 20 overs, needing something in the region of 6 or 7 an over, were way off the pace, lost a handful of wickets and ended up struggling to save the game.

This was just one instance of what at times were profound differences of opinion. Johan is a very good coach in terms of his ability to look at technique and advise on the technical aspects of the game but, in my opinion, he did not have a good grasp of the tactics that sometimes need to be addressed at this level of the game. The flashpoint came when I was dropped for a game, ostensibly because the wicket we were going to play on was a green-top. But the selection policy seemed to me to be inconsistent because I was restored to the team for the very next game, also on a green-top. I felt that Johan's judgement was wrong and furthermore that the decision had been made not on the basis of my performances, but on the grounds of personality, perhaps even on the grounds of race. In fact I was later told that the President, John Blair, had voiced the opinion that I wasn't really good enough anyway. With due modesty, a glance at my record with Free State is surely enough to scotch that suggestion. In Castle or Currie Cup cricket, I had taken 25 wickets in my first season and averaged 26 with the bat. In my second season I had 17 wickets and a batting average of 41 and in what I regarded as my best-ever season, 1992-93, a return of 27 wickets – 9 ahead of my nearest rival – and with the bat, an average of nearly 54. Those figures, I think, speak for themselves.

But those incidents apart, the triumph that day in Bloemfontein transcended any problems which might or might not have had a racial basis. Every single player could regard the winning of the Championship as a personal triumph. It was a great day for the young captain, Hansie Cronje, who of course went on to take over the reins as South Africa's captain in Australia when Kepler Wessels returned home with injuries; a great day for Franklyn Stephenson, who played such an important part in the season's success at every level, and who had also overcome the barrier of race; a great day for Corrie van Zyl, who had played for Free State for so long. And for Omar Henry, it was the pinnacle in many ways. My career in cricket has not been merely a matter of bat against ball or ball against bat; it has had much more to do with strength of mind – and physical fitness of course – because cricket is so much a game of the mind. For me personally it also represented the culmination of a lifetime's struggle to confirm a belief within me that my determination to succeed and my love for the game had at last been properly rewarded.

That love for the game, has, from the day I first held a bat in my hands, dominated my life, but, right from the start, it also got me into plenty of trouble, at home and at school as a youngster, and later, with the administrators of the game and even with my own community. There have, you see, been many pitfalls, many barriers placed before me as I have made my way through the game. In that sense, the problems have been no different from those faced by aspiring cricketers all over the world. If you want success badly enough, you fight. And you must have that inner strength and self-belief – the stamina to keep going when things seem to be against you. You also have to think clearly, watch, listen and learn, apply yourself with absolute dedication, adapt and always keep yourself in good physical condition. If I could never claim to have been a great player (an expression which I think is too often and too freely bandied about) at least I think I can claim, through constantly working on both my mental and physical strength, to have explored and played to the potential that was born in me. But in South Africa, of course, there have been other hurdles to clear which have nothing to do with ability and talent but everything to do with the issues of race, religion and colour, and not a little to do with opportunity, which has been denied to such a large section of the community. Even with the changes which are sweeping through the country, the democratisation and the theoretical equalisation of all sections of society, it may take a long time for attitudes to change and for true equality of opportunity to emerge. I probably have a reputation for defying authority. That is not to say that I have been guilty of poor discipline. On the contrary, I have had to be very disciplined throughout my life and I can assure you that as a child I was subjected to strict discipline. However, I have always, as the song goes, done it 'my way'.

My innings began in Stellenbosch on January 23rd, 1952. I was born in a tiny house in a leafy street in the beautiful university town at the heart of the wine-making district of South Africa. The setting is magnificent, for Stellenbosch is surrounded by mountains. Perhaps that is why, during my years in Scotland, I always felt at home, comfortable in the Scottish environment with its own lovely mountains. My home was a one-roomed house. My parents and I ate, washed, slept and lived in that one room for the first few years of my life. In time, we moved to a two-bedroomed house and later to a slightly larger house in the same street before eventually, in the late sixties, being forced to move to a township on the edge Stellenbosch because the Group Areas Act re-designated the area in which I had lived as a whites-only part of town. My father fought hard against that enforced move but eventually had to concede.

I was lucky in that both my parents came from very sport-orientated families. My mother had been a good netball and table-tennis player and my father had played rugby and eventually became a single-figure handicap golfer. He played some cricket but it was not really his sport, although I believe he was an exceptionally good fielder. His prowess at golf resulted from the fact that as well as doing a full-time job, working for a bookbinding company which did a lot of work for the university, he also went caddying at the local golf course. He used to come back from caddying and practise with the three clubs he owned on a piece of rough ground so that in time he became a good golfer. I had three brothers and two sisters but in the early years I alone lived with my parents, simply because the house was not big enough to accommodate us all. My brothers and sisters lived with my grandparents until we were able to move to a bigger house and the only time I saw them in those days was at the weekends when we went to visit them. All of us had an aptitude for sport and we all played a variety of them: rugby, soccer – the only game we played at school – table tennis and golf. But all these activities were organised on a totally informal basis, in the case of the outdoor sports, played on whatever areas of rough ground that were available, or in the street.

My father also organised the delivery of newspapers throughout Stellenbosch. He had a team of boys who delivered the papers and inevitably I became one of his team, getting up at six in the morning and delivering a stack of papers before going to school. This way, I was able to earn a little spending money. He was a very likeable man and everyone, it seemed, liked and respected him, not least for the way in which he was always prepared to work hard in order to provide for his family. And, I might say, he earned the respect of many white people, a fact which, in the fullness of time, as I began to make an impact in sport, was to greatly benefit me. Our ancestry almost certainly derived from Indonesia some time in the eighteenth century. In those early days of South Africa, Arab slave-traders brought many people from the East as slaves and that undoubtedly accounts for the large number of Muslims in the country.

In terms of cricketing background, my mother's brother was a fine player, far better than me, apparently. I never actually met him, or if I did I was only a babe in arms, for sadly he died very young. But by all accounts he was a real rising star and had he been given the opportunity, I am told, he would have gone right to the top. Perhaps I inherited some of his talent, I don't know. My own first experiences of cricket came when I was about five years of age. It was then that my father started to take me to Newlands, usually with a family friend, Salaam Raziet, who was himself a superb cricketer and who played for the non-white South African team. I remember watching him when I was a kid. He was relatively well off and ran his own business, and he used to take us to Newlands in his van. The first clear recollection I have is of when I was about nine years old. John Reid, the New Zealand batsman, certainly made quite an impression on me. I think it was the way he punched the ball away with those powerful forearms of his. His power was awesome as he repeatedly pierced the off-side field. That was possibly the first time I had looked at a player and, subconsciously perhaps, begun to analyse his method and technique. At a later stage, when I was about 12, I also remember watching Mike Smith in much the same way, except of course, that he was so different. He didn't so much power the ball away, he just seemed to lean on it. He epitomised the image of the typical English gentleman, almost languid, unhurried and very much, it seemed to me, in command.

But as I have said, it was Trevor Goddard who ultimately became my hero. It must initially have been his left- handedness that drew me towards him yet there was something else, an indefinable quality which

I perhaps did not understand at that stage of my young life. Apart from the natural talents with which Trevor Goddard was imbued, he had another quality which perhaps, in a way, I inherited, and that quality was his determination, allied to great powers of concentration. We all, those of us who aspire to great cricketing heights, need role models from whom we can learn to develop some qualities depending upon our own temperaments. I couldn't have chosen better. Goddard's application, his nagging accuracy as a bowler, was something I copied and have copied all my cricketing life. In terms of bowling, accuracy has been my watchword and without question it is something I gained directly from him. I also think that particular quality was one that especially suited my own personal approach to the game as I developed. So he was an ideal role model for me.

But if Trevor Goddard always remained my first and foremost idol, there were other players to watch who provided me with further building-blocks for my own game, for of one thing you can be sure: once I was hooked on cricket, my concentration on the game and on particular players never wavered. That is when, I suspect, the quality of dedication began to emerge. Not for me the fun and games indulged in by some of my friends, who would periodically become bored with the cricket. And not for me the fun and games in the back of the van as we returned from each day's play. I simply sat in silence, continuing to absorb what I had seen. If I wanted to be like those untouchable heroes and, in my own mind at least, I could fulfil that wish by becoming, in my imagination, Trevor Goddard in our street 'test matches', even then perhaps I was taking the first steps along what was to be a long and winding road towards cricket as a profession. Newlands, as I have said, was the focus, the shrine; Goddard, especially, a veritable god. If, in those waking days, I had little eye for cricketing technique, I did, when the opportunity arose and we were able to watch the players at the nets before the day's play had started, watch and absorb little nuances like the way the bat was held and gripped and also how the bowlers held the ball.

By now the fever had gripped me. Cricket was fast becoming the all-absorbing focus of my life. The street 'test matches' saw me playing with ever greater determination. Such games were, I can tell you, played in earnest and there were frequent arguments about whether a batsman was out, all the usual things which, from time to time, led to fights, just as they do in every street in the world where schoolboy cricket is played. Often these 'tests' would go on for days in the holidays – five-day matches played on the pavements of Stellenbosch, sometimes just between my own circle of friends, sometimes against other boys from adjoining streets. To say these encounters were competitive in the extreme is no exaggeration. Such was my zeal that other things went by the board, including my schoolwork and, all too frequently, my homework – and that spelled trouble! Many's the good hiding I've had for putting cricket first and my studies last. Even worse was one incident when I was delegated by my father to take a message to a friend of his but became so absorbed in a game of cricket that I forgot. Worse still was the crime of deception, for when I was asked whether I had run the errand, I foolishly said that I had. Subsequently, my father learned that I had told a lie and another thrashing resulted. I learned a painful lesson which I never forgot – never again!

Let me make no bones about it: my father never discouraged me from playing cricket but he demanded from me, as he demanded from the rest of the family, honesty and integrity at all times. He was a strict disciplinarian and expected nothing less than honesty but, by the same token, he was also fair and essentially kind. I could not have wanted for anything he was able to provide and he and my mother gave me tremendous support, unwaveringly, through some hard times later in my life. In retrospect, I have no doubt in my mind now that he was convinced that I was going to make a success of cricket. That he had a profound influence upon my development there can be no doubt. But there were many others. There have been many turning points in my life, many people who have influenced me: Trevor Goddard, of course, Eddie Barlow and, very significantly, Basil D'Oliveira.

Our paths first crossed in 1967 when, already established as an England Test cricketer, Basil came back to his native South Africa to coach young cricketers in the coloured community. He was one of a handful of cricketers who, because of the system of apartheid which stifled opportunity for non-whites, chose instead to further his career as a cricketer in England. That he was eminently successful is a matter of history and I doubt if even Basil was aware of the lifeline he created for so many of his coloured compatriots back home. Unconsciously, perhaps, he became a huge folk hero for the black community in South Africa and in time, one of my personal idols. Furthermore, he almost became a surrogate father to me, for having seen me during a coaching session in Stellenbosch, shortly after my 15th birthday, he wanted to take me back to the UK with him in the belief that I had what it took to make it to the top in English cricket. My parents, for very good reasons, declined his offer but the belief he expressed in my capabilities at that time served to inspire me and create real ambition in me. England, and playing cricket in the country which had given birth to the game, became a long-term goal for me.

Many years later, I did indeed follow in Basil's footsteps to play in Lancashire League cricket and then, by accident rather than by design, I ended up playing in Scotland and eventually for Scotland. Some years after making my debut at Newlands, incredibly, I found myself making my way on to the hallowed turf of Lord's, playing for my adopted country. Even more incredibly, I captained the Scots and savoured the excitement of playing against the top-class county teams in the Benson & Hedges and NatWest competitions in a stay of some 13 seasons during which I was a professional in the Scottish leagues. So many people helped me along the way: players and officials, relatives and friends and two people from the white community in Stellenbosch to whom I used to deliver papers, Mrs Schoeman and Dr Anton Rupert. However, the route has been hazardous. Controversy has marched shoulder to shoulder with me along the way and it still does.

When I returned to Stellenbosch in 1992 to put down permanent roots and provide a stable family home for my wife and children, I was eventually appointed to the position of Director of Cricket Development to the Boland Cricket Board, responsible for the development programme and coaching. I sincerely thought that such a job would provide me with the security I wanted and also present me with the kind of challenge to which I have always responded. As it turned out, there were undercurrents and, needless to say, disagreements. Controversy had once again become my shadow. Boland, of course, had hitherto been a 'B' province. In 1993 they were, so to speak, following in the footsteps of Durham in the English counties and becoming, for the first time, a first-class 'A' province, a terrific adventure of which I was delighted to be a part. With Bob Woolmer as coach – and they don't come any better qualified than him – and Phil DeFreitas engaged for the 1993-94 season, I really did feel that I would be in a position to plough something back into the game that had given me so much. Cricket became a way of life for me as well as my profession. To put the icing on the cake towards the end of my playing career, here I was, back in my native Stellenbosch, setting up a cricketing academy which, if properly run, could provide today's generation of youngsters with the opportunity to reach their potential – something that was certainly denied to me.

It will already be quite clear, even in this first chapter, that I have a fervent belief in the ethos of providing equal opportunity to people from whatever background, whether privileged or not, whether they are black, white, brown, yellow or sky blue pink and, needless to say, irrespective of their religion. That was therefore one of the main templates by which I hoped to fashion the academy. In short, if a kid has talent, whether he comes from the wealthy section of the community or from a squatter camp, I want to see that kid given every opportunity. Perhaps I was asking too much, expecting too much, but that hope was the central reason for me accepting the job in the first place.

It wasn't long before I found myself at odds with people on the Boland Cricket Board. One clear reason for disagreement emerged when I tried to help the young student cricketers at the University of the Western Cape, a university where the vast majority of students are coloured. There, resources are somewhat thin on the ground and I felt that I could help these young guys to become better cricketers, help nurture cricket at the university and, to put it bluntly, help my own kind. But because the university is situated in Western Province territory and not in Boland, my Boland employers objected. I can be stubborn, especially if I feel I have right on my side, but on this occasion I pulled back. However, my relationship with members of the board and some senior staff members continued to go downhill and in the end we parted company with the Boland Cricket Board asserting that my administrative duties were not being properly fulfilled.

Naturally enough, the whole affair left a bad taste in my mouth. I believe that their decision was, once again, not made on the basis of sound judgement but on very personal grounds. It is another example of how controversy seems to have stalked me throughout my life. Because I have had to fight so hard for everything I have achieved, it may be that once I have made up my mind about something, I am hard to shift. It may also be the case that I am not mealy-mouthed. I do tend to be somewhat blunt in my approach sometimes and if I think I am right on an issue, I will stick to my guns. However, I also believe that I have, as I have matured, learned something about diplomacy. Nevertheless, some people believe I am abrasive at times. They may have a point, but I have had to be to get where I have. The experience I have gained playing and coaching cricket right across the world, the demands I have placed upon myself to succeed, and the achievements I can claim have not been won easily. I have had to fight all the way. That has demanded considerable mental as well as physical strength; it has demanded dedication on my part and indeed, dedication on the part of my family, my mother and father and of course, my wife. They have had to make many sacrifices. Perhaps such a background inevitably leads to an inner strength which some people might regard as cussedness. I don't believe that is true of me, although I have always fought my corner. Whatever the future holds for me, I will always want to make a positive contribution to life and in particular to the game which has given me so much, and the game I love so dearly.

● ● ● ● ● ● ● ● ● ● ● ● ● ● ● ● ●

KEN McEWAN
Former South Africa and Essex batsman.

'I am delighted to have the opportunity to express my admiration of Omar Henry's achievements and the manner in which he has achieved them.

'I had the honour of playing alongside Omar when he made history in this country by becoming the first "coloured" cricketer to represent the Springboks. It certainly was a very touching moment when we walked on to the field and a large crowd rose to cheer the home side, and in particular one Omar Henry. It was definitely an occasion that brought a lump to one's throat.

'Whatever happened in that game is history as far as the statistics are concerned. But while pondering over what happened or could have happened during the game, one thing struck me regarding this land we live in. Here was a case where a man, who through far more hardships and dedication than anyone else on the field, had achieved a goal that most people dream of, to represent their county.

'And this was an historic occasion for South Africa and South African cricket. But it could have all gone sour, as have many progressive steps in this country. For instance the team was staying in a luxury Durban hotel, sharing meals and having a quiet drink together, totally oblivious to the difference in colour or race between Omar and the rest of the team. But imagine what would have happened if we had gone across the road to the beach for a swim. Some young police constable, in the course of his duty, could have asked Omar to swim elsewhere. Fortunately, Omar cannot swim!

'There was another irony in that Omar coached children of all races and religions at that time in the Boland. He was good enough to coach in white schools and accepted there, yet his two lovely daughters were not allowed to attend those schools.

'Despite such injustices, Omar battled through quietly, not making an issue of them, but at the same time demonstrating to his community, to South Africans in general and to everyone around the world, that change could come peacefully.

'Omar has undoubtedly made a large contribution both on and off the field, both in terms of cricket and his contribution to South Africa's future. He has been a fine player and deserves great credit and reward for achieving what he has in the face of such hardships.'

• • • • • • • • • • • • • • • •

CLIVE RICE

Former captain of South Africa, Transvaal, Nottinghamshire and Scotland.

'Omar Henry - part Scot, part Capetonian, but dedicated to both territories.

'Omar started with Western Province as a spinner to partner Denys Hobson. Those were the days when the Newlands pitch was sandy and responded to spin. Eddie Barlow was in the forefront and how often we saw a dramatic win pulled out of the bag by the spin twins. The combination of a left-arm spinner with a right-arm leg break and googly bowler proved devastating. No match was over before the last ball was bowled.

'Omar, quite rightly left for greener pastures, more suited to his type of cricket, and moved "next door", to Boland. Here the wicket turned and the combination of Pine Anker's off-spin and Omar's left-arm spin dominated the results of the "B" section in Stellenbosch.

'The experience of playing for Scotland benefited Omar's bowling tremendously. The slow, wet wickets that have taken spin have caused many counties untold problems. In fact speaking as an ex-county captain, I know that a professional team could end up extremely embarrassed, losing to the ten amateurs and one professional from Scotland. Lancashire and Northants were embarrassed in this way and Worcestershire came very close to falling into the same trap. The professionals are on a hiding to nothing and Omar was at the centre of Scotland's development. All departments of their game have improved, which is closing the gap between them and the counties.

'I remember only too clearly when Transvaal came close to losing to Boland as Boland fielded like men possessed. They caught everything that went in the air. They flung themselves around the field, cutting off boundaries, and thoroughly frustrated our batting line-up, which included the likes of Cook, Fotheringham, Yachad, Pollock, McKenzie, Kourie and myself.

'It was a magnificent display by the Bolanders, Omar no doubt responsible in the background for helping to develop the side and inject that important element of self-belief'.

GUIDING
LIGHTS

If Trevor Goddard was my first and foremost hero – the man who, unknown to him, had a major influence on my life, and a man whose feats in real Test matches I tried to emulate in our street 'test matches' – as I grew into my teenage years, other people began to reshape my life. They did not know it and perhaps, at the time, I didn't either but we are all touched by other people, influenced by them and guided through life by them. A teacher by the name of Les Bergstedt was to have a profound influence on me, and most especially in terms of the development of my cricket. When I started at secondary school, at the Luckhoff High School in Stellenbosch to be precise, I had nothing more than the raw talent I had developed in street matches and, more to the point – apart from my ability to concentrate on and absorb what I saw, for instance, at Newlands in the big games, and thereafter to copy – little or no knowledge of the game of cricket.

What little I understood had come from that and some encouragement by my primary school teacher, Mr Abel. But Les Bergstedt was an absolutely key figure in my life. With the MCC coaching manual ever-present, he began to build for me a deeper understanding of what cricket was really about. He was something of a cricketer himself and, by coincidence, he bowled left-arm spin. He was on the one hand a disciplinarian and in some ways a stickler, yet in other ways he was also something of a visionary. Yes, he wanted me to understand the basics of the game, how important it was to have the feet in the right place; the virtue of a straight bat; the need to understand the rudiments and the correctness of the forward and backward defensive shots, upon which all other strokes are based. But he was also quick to recognise instinctive talent. If it sounds immodest on my part to say that it was with such basic talent that I was equipped – good hand-to-eye co-ordination – then it is only that I believe it is something with which I was blessed, God-given if you like. You either have it or you don't. It was, I suppose, in my genes, that natural talent. And, fortunately for me, Les Bergstedt was swift to recognise that. So he was never guilty of trying to constrain me from playing the shots I had always and have always played by instinct. He guided me towards an ability to choose more carefully when such shots should be played but he never tried to stop me, never tried to restrict my natural flair.

If the coaching manual was his bible, he nevertheless always worked with me in such a way as to harness what talent God had given me rather than doing it by the book. It may seem incredible but there were occasions when just he and I would go down to the school cricket ground. He bowled at me for hours. There were no nets, so every time I hit the ball away into the outfield, he would simply go and fetch it, return and bowl to me again. I like to think that he recognised a natural talent in me and all he wanted to do was to heighten my interest in the game – not very difficult – and to see me develop from the pipsqueak I was when I first started to play at school, with the special pads and bats he had to get for me because I was so small, into the wonder boy I became known as in Stellenbosch.

In my first game, I was hit in the stomach by the ball and laid out cold. Now I've known plenty of kids for whom that was enough and for whom that kind of incident spelled the beginning and the end of an interest in cricket. It was certainly very different from my years of playing with a tennis ball. This ball was hard – and it hurt! Yet I have to be honest and say I never, ever felt frightened. That knock-out blow served only to make me more determined. It also served as part of the learning process. I learned something about myself and I certainly learned how to take care of myself in conditions where most of the youngsters I came up against seemed determined to knock my head off as the ball pinged off the matting wickets. Needless to say, I quickly learned that if I got bat on ball, it was me that was dishing out the punishment – to the bowler. All this, of course, indoctrinated me further. It is not an insult to my religious conviction when I say that cricket was fast becoming my second religion. Hence I progressed from the school second team to the firsts. We sometimes played friendlies against other coloured school teams but our main games were in the local league where, of course, we were up against much older players, adults, in fact. Thus we all learned the hard way.

Let me emphasise again that the conditions in which we played were hardly the best. Usually the grounds we played on had no grass at all in the outfield. Those that did were uncut and it wasn't unusual for 6 runs to go on the board: lost ball, lost in the grass! My visits to Newlands, I suppose, always kept me in touch with the reality of cricket as it should be played: on a smooth and lush green outfield on which fielders could swoop and pick up with one hand, get behind the ball confidently, knowing that it wouldn't suddenly hit a lump or a tuft of grass and fly into your face. But for me such things could and did happen, all the time. And all the time I was learning. With Les Bergstedt's guidance, I developed as something of a swashbuckling batsman, likely to turn a game in a few overs. And if, then, I had not yet begun to understand the wiles of spin bowling, the early lessons I learned from watching Trevor Goddard ensured that I was always striving for accuracy. I was also learning to exploit the matting wickets, not by turning the ball a great deal but just enough. Thus my reputation in Stellenbosch, at least, was beginning to go before me. Wonder boy indeed!

Les Bergstedt also taught me respect for the game; and discipline, self-discipline. And he fed my already fervent love for cricket every time I picked up bat or ball. And of course, meeting Basil D'Oliveira also had a profound effect upon me. Basil was already a real living hero for the coloured community of South Africa. He was, you see, the first coloured cricketer from South Africa to make it to the highest level, even if to achieve that goal he had had to leave his native land and become an 'Englishman'. In 1960 he had gone to England to start an entirely new life as a professional cricketer, first as a league 'pro' in the Lancashire League and later as a fully fledged county professional with

Worcestershire. In 1966 he made his debut for England and the whole coloured community in the Cape shared in that triumph. He was the local hero, the man who against all the odds had made it to the top. In our summer of 1966-67, shortly after making his Test debut, he came out to coach in South Africa. Of course, such activities were very much confined to the coloured areas but to demonstrate what an impact his success had on the community, let me tell you that when he arrived in Cape Town – he sailed out from the UK – a huge crowd was waiting to welcome him at the harbour. And of course, everywhere he went, he was followed by adoring admirers. Stellenbosch, I can tell you, was no exception.

I have clear memories of the day he came to coach us. I had just passed my 15th birthday. The coaching was carried out in the middle of the cricket field. Every word he said was listened to, not only by those of us privileged to be under scrutiny but by adults, mothers, sisters, aunts, uncles – anyone who could get near enough to listen hung on every word, whether they had a direct involvement in what was going on or not. In fact I think a few of the local whites were there too. My upbringing dictated that as a youngster, I should only speak when spoken to but I too hung on every word, absorbing every syllable. It wasn't so much that he re-formated my game – he could not, in so short a space of time, take apart and then rebuild someone's technique, even if he had wanted to. He simply offered straightforward advice and encouragement.

Afterwards, he addressed me directly and told me that if he had seen me before he had picked his team of youngsters to play against a select team captained by him, I definitely would have been in it. And of course, I later discovered that he had, that evening, spoken to my father about taking me back to the UK with him. He was apparently so impressed with me that he was quite convinced I could go all the way. But it was not to be. Quite rightly, I think, my parents graciously declined his offer. Remember that in order to qualify to play for England, I would had to have stayed there for three continuous years. If I was in some ways disappointed that my dreams of becoming a professional cricketer – who knows, in time, even a Test cricketer – were dashed, at least for the time being, this experience served merely to fan the flames of ambition in me even more. But I think that my parents were right.

It wasn't that Basil taught me anything specific. All he said, was 'Well played' when I played a flashing shot or 'Well bowled' if I bowled a good ball. He simply encouraged and thus inspired me more. He certainly instilled in me the basic work ethic of the game, encouraging me to make sure that bowlers had to earn their wickets and batsmen their runs. Having since done a great deal of coaching, I can only think that what impressed him was what I might call my latent natural talent. And of course, the publicity I received – the articles in the newspapers – meant that my reputation was further enhanced. The *Cape Times* of January 25th, 1967 printed an article headed, 'Basil Finds Wonderful Young Prospect in Cape'. D.N. Bansda was the author of the piece and he quoted Basil as saying, 'He is the finest prospect I have seen in my entire coaching tour. With the right guidance and coaching, this boy will go places.' All this, not surprisingly, served to make me something of a target for bowlers and batsmen alike. It increased the pressure on me as a player, but I don't think I understood that at the time.

What that visit by Basil D'Oliveira did for me was to focus my mind even more intently upon cricket, and my schoolwork suffered as a result. It wasn't that I was stupid. In fact, had I allowed myself to concentrate on my work, rather than on cricket, I might have done reasonably well academically. I was quite good at maths, and I enjoyed art and woodwork. But my mind was made up. Although my parents were keen that I should go to college, or even university, I just wanted to leave school as soon as I could and get to England to further a career in cricket. England was the focus. That was where professional cricket had its roots. My new hero had carved out a career for himself there – why not me? And of course, that old family friend, Salaam Raziet, in whose van we had often rumbled off to Newlands, had played with Basil in the non-white South African cricket team against Kenya. In his house, there on the wall, was a picture of him in his green blazer with the Springbok head. How often I looked at it and dreamed. I read every word I could find about the English cricket team. Every time they played a Test, my eyes went straight to Basil's score or analysis, to the exclusion of all others. Then, and only then did I read the other scores.

He became my personal if distant guru. Looking back, I suppose I was already building around me my own very personal team of cricketers, from each of whom I could draw something – technique, approach, determination, flair, whatever. Salaam was another hero, closer at hand. Like Basil, he had made it as a cricketer, at least, as far as he had been able in the curious circumstances that surrounded the divided game in South Africa as it was then. Furthermore, he was local and thus he was at least accessible, still playing when I was just finding my way into the game.

The next hero was Eddie Barlow. He worked for Stellenbosch Farmers' Winery and regularly, after school, we were piled into the back of a backie (a covered pick-up) and taken off to a shed at the winery, where we practised for hours on end. Eddie was already an established cricketer, a flamboyant man who always had that ability to make you feel at ease. He bubbled with enthusiasm and always gave the impression that he so desperately wanted you to succeed. We seemed to click straight away, instantly on the same wavelength. He loved cricket so much and I think he recognised very quickly my own instinctive love for the game. He was and still is a real fighter, a positive man when it comes to cricket, a man I could identify with. We became good friends, yet we also had our moments of disagreement. Years later – in 1980-81 – when he was captaining the Western Province side, we were playing at the Wanderers against Transvaal. We were in dire straits on the Saturday night and I went to the wicket with Province struggling to save the follow-on. Eddie was battling away – I think he scored 100 – and as I made my way to the wicket, he met me halfway. His words were very much to the point. 'Listen, there's only one thing that counts here: guts. Never mind technique. You get yourself in there and stay behind that ball and we are here till the end of this day and we will still be here on Monday!' You don't argue with Eddie Barlow so I simply dropped anchor, and we survived to the end of play.

Sunday in those days was a rest day and I remember getting hold of the Sunday paper and discovering, to my fury, that I had been dropped for the next game. I stayed in my room all day, sulking I suppose, disgusted that I could be dropped even though the match we were currently playing was only halfway through, and when play resumed on

Monday morning, I'm afraid I was out almost straight away. We lost the game and afterwards Eddie gave me an absolute bollocking for what he interpreted as a lack of guts. We had quite a heavy set-to but I was dropped and that was that.

I was now consigned to the Province 'B' team and before we went off to the game – it was against Border 'B', played in East London – he simply said to me: 'Now you go there and show me.' I scored 105 not out and took some wickets. I think it was hunger on my part, hunger to force myself back into the 'A' team. I wanted my place back, and badly. It taught me a lesson all right, and it taught me something about myself. On my return to the senior team he just laughed – I was back in the fold. We've been friends ever since and I like to think that in some way I paid him back for the time he had spent with me as a boy and proved to him that I was, above all, prepared to fight.

Some of the other heroes I've already mentioned. The focus, I suppose quite naturally, was upon left-handers. Graeme Pollock, that superb cricketer whose international career was unfortunately truncated by the isolation of South Africa, always commanded my attention when he strode to the wicket. What grace and power he exuded with every shot he played! When the Springboks went out to Australia in 1963-64 we would listen to the radio commentaries in the wee small hours. I remember so well listening to the crackling airwaves with a sense of wonderment when Eddie Barlow and Graeme Pollock put together that record 3rd wicket stand of 341 at Adelaide. One hero – Barlow – scored 201; the other, Pollock, 175. The following season paired England under Mike Smith with the South Africans led by my first hero, Trevor Goddard.

Now, instead of listening to the match on the radio, I was able to see these great heroes in the flesh. First impressions, they say, are important and my first impressions of Goddard were of a tall, slim man with neatly combed hair. It is funny how sometimes as a youngster you notice little things. I noticed in particular that Goddard's trousers were immaculately pressed. We watched them practise at Newlands and, having been made aware of the nuances of the game by Les Bergstedt, I found myself studying in precise detail how each player gripped the bat and picked it up and exactly how the bowlers gripped the ball – all grist to my little mental mill. That, by the way, was the occasion when I wanted to get Goddard's autograph but I was so dumbstruck that I couldn't even ask him for it and he simply walked by.

South Africa took first use of the Newlands wicket and I remember concentrating as if my life depended upon every ball. Again, perhaps I was discovering something about myself and learning how to concentrate for long periods of time. Every mannerism was absorbed and probably copied. Goddard made an excellent 40 runs but Barlow and Pithey were the heroes of the day, taking South Africa well beyond the 200-mark. Each of them, I think, scored a century. Colin Bland then weighed in with 70-odd the next day and South Africa ran up a total of 501 for 7 before they declared. England replied with 440 for 2 and the game was eventually drawn. But it was so great to see these fantastic players.

The game was played in the school holidays and my father was on leave so we watched the game throughout the five days. By then, I was awakening to the fact that all the players we were watching were white – not a coloured player in sight, of course. It didn't then concern me at all, however. Class and quality was what I had seen. That was all that mattered and I absorbed every waking minute of it. England went on to win the series 1-0 but once again cricket had almost completely filled my life for those five days. It was a case of up at five, off to do the paper round and then on to Newlands for a feast of cricket. Getting up at that time was never a problem, and in the summer, it was never a chore I minded doing. But in the winter – June, July and August – it was pretty cold and furthermore it was quite normal for it to rain for days on end. Believe it or not, on occasions the mountains overlooking Stellenbosch sometimes had a coating of snow. But my father always said that nothing would come if you didn't work for it. Furthermore the paper round, as I have said, brought me into contact with other people who were to have a profound effect upon my life.

My starring role with the school team meant that occasionally my name appeared in the local paper, for instance on one glorious day when I took 7 for 30 against the club with which my family was associated, Excelsior. One person in particular to notice these youthful cricketing feats was Mrs Schoeman, the wife of one of the university professors. She was quite a personality, well educated and very active in the community, chairwoman of this and that, especially of some of the local charities. She also knew my father, of course, but imagine my surprise when she took me one day to the local sports outfitter and kitted me out with boots, shirts, trousers, pads and gloves.

Others too had been privileged to benefit from her generosity but to me that benevolent act on her part acted above all as yet another spur. It showed that she had faith in my ability. It wasn't an act of race-orientated charity on her part. She simply believed that she was giving a helping hand to someone who did not otherwise have the financial means to equip himself – and that certainly was the case in this instance. Race or creed did not even enter the equation. One of the most emotional moments of my life came many years later at my benefit dinner in 1988. Mrs Schoeman, who had bought me all that equipment years before, was present as one of the principal guests.

In the winter of 1965, it was back to the crackling radio and unseen tales of gallantry from England, relayed over 6,000 miles by the wonder of radio. The Pollock brothers were the stars. The excitement generated by South Africa's victory over England at Trent Bridge, with Graeme Pollock scoring 125 and 50 and his brother Peter taking 5 wickets in each innings, was universal. But I was even more excited, especially when I went to the pictures and saw clips from the game on Movietone News. Could I, one day, be a part of such an epic victory? The South African team had so many great players at that time. In the very summer in which my close encounter with Basil D'Oliveira had happened, the Australians, led by Bobby Simpson, were the tourists in South Africa. Bill Lawry – another left-hander, of course – was Simpson's vice-captain, another batsman to study closely, and the attack was spearheaded by Graham 'Garth' McKenzie. But our team was so powerful – unofficial champions of the world, they were dubbed – with the magnificent Barry Richards, just 21 then, unable to force his way into the side and Mike Procter just able to scrape in for two Tests.

Again, when I look back, all these heroes were white players, but that never really concerned me. I just knew that I wanted to be a cricketer and that one day I too would walk on the great stages of Newlands, Lord's, the MCG. My dreams may have been just that, dreams – and yet there was a certainty about it all in spite of the fact that I was, by now, becoming increasingly aware that I definitely didn't come from the right side of the South African tracks. During these teenage years, I was soon to be brought face to face with reality when, under decree by the Nationalist government, my family was moved from the leafy streets of Stellenbosch, from the street arenas in which those tennis-ball 'test matches' had been enacted, to a township on the outskirts of town. The area in which I had been brought up was declared a whites-only area under the Group Areas Act and in spite of vigorous protestations on the part of my father, we were forced to move. It hurt because my father had worked so hard and diligently in order to improve the lot of his family and we had settled in a larger house. His objections cut no ice at all and we had no alternative but to move to the Idas Valley. That was how it was in South Africa during the worst excesses of the apartheid system and the Group Areas Act was, in my opinion, one of the most pernicious pieces of legislation ever introduced by the Nationalist government. And of course, my awareness of the great divide was further heightened in 1968 when the D'Oliveira affair hit the headlines of the world press and the England tour to South Africa was subsequently cancelled – the beginning of South Africa's isolation as a sporting nation.

The whole saga was, it seemed to us, quite farcical. Everyone in the non-white community wanted Basil to be in the England team. Because he had become one of my great hero figures and because I followed his progress so closely, I was aware that he was not in the best of form in the run-up to the selection of the MCC party to tour South Africa in the English summer of 1968. We were not fully aware, of course, of the events that surrounded the whole sorry affair, of the diplomacy, gunboat diplomacy and even chequebook diplomacy which was all part of what eventually turned out to be a rather sordid incident which inevitably left many people somewhat tarnished. We knew that in the British Parliament, as early as in January 1967, statements were made declaring that the tour would be cancelled if the South Africans made any moves to ban D'Oliveira from being a member of the touring party. The response of the South African government was immediate and very much to the point. Arrogantly, it was stated that the South African government would not allow mixed teams to play against South African white teams in South Africa; further that if such a player was chosen he would not be allowed into the country as a member of the team.

Some relaxation of this view followed from the then Prime Minister, Mr John Vorster, when later that year he said that apartheid principles could be relaxed insofar as they affected teams from overseas countries with which South Africa had traditional sporting ties. To add weight to the view that D'Oliveira's inclusion in the England team might not be the obstacle it had seemed, a South African selector had intimated to the player himself that there would not, in fact, be a problem.

Various diplomatic channels were subsequently explored, including a meeting between that great lover of cricket Sir Alec Douglas-Home and Mr Vorster. Sir Alec returned to the UK convinced that should D'Oliveira be selected, there would not be a problem. However, other snippets of attempted diplomacy – including a meeting between Lord Cobham, at one time President of the MCC, and Mr Vorster – seemed to be less optimistic.

And so it dragged on and on. We knew little about what was happening. All we wanted was for Basil to be in the England team. In fact, it is debatable which side those of us from the coloured community would have supported he had been in the team, South Africa or England. All this was of course conditional on D'Oliveira's performances in the 1968 season for England against the Aussies, and I had very good reason, therefore, to follow in the papers, with even greater zeal, the performances of my hero. He started well by taking 87 not out off the Australian attack in the First Test, which England lost. In their wisdom, the England selectors left him out of the final XI in the Second Test, which ended up as a draw although England held the whip hand throughout. Now all sorts of statements were being bandied about. Depending upon whom you believed, Basil would or would not be picked for the impending tour; he had been offered a lucrative contract to quit England and establish a new coaching set-up in South Africa; he might even play for South Africa rather than England. Rumour was rife. However, fate took a hand because, after call-offs, Basil was restored to the England team for the last Test and he scored a magnificent 158 in England's first innings from which base his

adopted country went on to a tremendous win. Who could now doubt
that he would be picked for England for their tour to South Africa, or
what a hero's welcome he would get?

The rest is history, of course. Basil was not picked, but when the
Warwickshire medium-pacer Tom Cartwright pulled out of the tour
due to injury, Basil was called up and all hell was let loose. The South
African Prime Minister declared that the MCC team was the team
of the Anti-Apartheid Movement and the tour was cancelled. It was
a tremendous disappointment to everyone. For the white cricketers
of South Africa, it was as if a tourniquet had been applied to their
careers; to the coloured community it was a denial of the opportunity
to see one of their own playing in Test matches in his native country,
albeit for England. It was, in short, a very bad day for South African
cricket in general. Politics – the politics of apartheid – had sadly
triumphed over cricket and sport as a whole. For me personally it was
a huge disappointment. The man had become an important cog in my
cricketing life and I was desperate to see him perform in the Test arena.
But what it most certainly did was to underline and strengthen my own
ambitions one day to follow him to England and make a career in
cricket for myself. The whole incident also served to remind me, if I
needed reminding, that the destiny I had chosen would not be
achieved without difficulty. I already knew that but the D'Oliveira
incident served to emphasise that the road I was now determined to
follow would be stony in the extreme.

My own progress in the game continued apace. The way the game
was played in the non-white community legislated for a kind of
approach which has become very much the style of today's 'instant'
one-day form of cricket. I was an aggressive batsman but that was the
tempo of the game. With fast outfields, runs were scored quickly. If you
beat the field, it was 4 runs on those grassless outfields. As for bowling,
accuracy still remained the first discipline. Centuries were scored with
remarkable frequency in that kind of cricket. It was exciting and very
positive.

When I left school in December 1969, instead of joining the
Excelsior club in Stellenbosch, I decided to go to Cape Town. Although
I was expected to join Excelsior, which was mostly made up of Muslim

cricketers but also included some Christians, I felt I needed exposure to better cricketers and better cricket, with the ultimate goal of playing for the Western Province coloured team. I got a job in Cape Town as an apprentice carpenter with a company called Murray and Stuart, earning the grand sum of 11 rand – about £15 – a week. It wasn't very much but they told me that once I had finished my apprenticeship in five years' time I would get a decent wage – the light at the end of what seemed then a very long tunnel. I think I was probably earning as much as that as a paper boy in Stellenbosch. In fact I actually did enjoy working with wood. Nevertheless, the main driving force remained cricket. I had played for Stellenbosch – a kind of select team drawn from all clubs, including schools, in the Stellenbosch area – but now I wanted to broaden my horizons.

I joined a club called Vineyards. A friend of my father's, Taliep Beharadien, was the captain of the Vineyards side and he was eager to have me play for them. It caused a few problems in Stellenbosch and a few heartaches. I was, even then, branded as a rebel for making that decision. Yet it was a good one. Taliep was a phenomenal cricketer, wristy, rather like the Indian and Pakistani professionals I encountered when I eventually went to England. He batted without gloves but could simply flick the ball away – over square leg – with no apparent effort. Remember we were still, in coloured cricketing circles, playing on matting wickets with rough outfields, but the cricket was full of character – and characters. Thus I learned a lot in new company. After a couple of years, I did return to the Excelsior club in Stellenbosch – by now having been picked to play for the Western Province Under-23s, a terrific honour and another stepping-stone on my route towards total commitment to cricket as a career.

Cape Town cricket provided tougher competition and frankly, it was easier to catch the eye. At work I had some problems because my immediate boss was not remotely interested in sport. But I still managed to force my way into the Province non-white side – the 'B' side initially but eventually into the 'A' side. There were three good left-armers around at the time. Provincial games were played at Green Point or the Rosemead ground near Kenilworth. Cec Abrahams and John Holder – the West Indian, now an umpire – were out playing as professionals and they too made their impact upon me. It was here too that I met Howie Bergins, who was eventually to take me to England. There were so many good players: Saaiet Majiet, a young player of terrific talent, almost Bothamesque; Dickie Conrad, who played professional cricket in the Lancashire League and Rushdie Majiet, who played for Todmorden, also in the Lancashire League. There was a guy called 'Tiny' Abed who played with Basil D'Oliveira – a great cricketer. His brother, Dik Abed, played for Enfield in the Lancashire League for years. There was so much talent that it was difficult for me to break into the Province 'A' side. I was so lucky to play with these guys, and I learned much about the game in those years.

Through seasons 1973-4-5 I undoubtedly made my mark in province cricket and in 1975 we won the Dadabhai Trophy, which was the coloured equivalent of the Currie Cup. We had to go to Johannesburg to beat Transvaal to win it. Bear in mind that there was no money. We somehow had to raise the funds to travel to these games. We had to wear the blazer but we had to buy it and stitch the badge on. All you got was a badge, a cap and a tie. It was fun, even if some of the hotels we stayed at were not, by any stretch of the imagination, good. If there is one thing I remember vividly about one stay in Durban, it was the size of the cockroaches in the hotel – they were huge! I also remember the curries that were served up to us by the Indians. By golly, they used to spice them up, all right.

Nevertheless, it was all good fun and we had a terrific team spirit going. Furthermore, the quality of the cricket was excellent. The hardship of having to organise raffles in order to raise the money for travel, especially when we had to fly and find our air fares, although it was always a hassle, didn't detract from the fun we had and the friends we were able to make – guys like Baboo Ebrahim from Natal, Jock Mahoney, Tiffy Barnes and Hussain Aijob from Transvaal – made it all worthwhile. Sometimes, in those early days of representative cricket, I was of course 12th man – the drinks waiter – but there was one game I remember in particular when I felt I really put my name on the map. We were playing against a strong Transvaal team. At 201 for 7, some 110 runs behind on the first innings, we were struggling but I got really stuck in and concentrated well to finish with 62 runs, including four 4s and a 6. I banged the ball about but also managed to keep the strike with some very sharp singles to keep the bowling away from our two last batsmen. We finished up with a creditable 303 all out and I had a nice write-up in the papers.

The other difficulty which kept cropping up was the attitude of my boss at work. As I've said, he wasn't interested in sport and when we played away at places like Durban, Port Elizabeth and Johannesburg, I had to take time off work and thus lost some of my pay. Naturally, this put pressure on my finances and I have to say that my parents were always supportive and helped me whenever they could.

There were moves at about this time to make cricket multi-racial. The then Minister of Sport, Dr Piet Koornhof, was the man behind this and there were several tours beginning to come to South Africa, mainly organised by Derrick Robins. Significantly, he included in his tour parties non-white players like West Indian John Shepherd and Pakistani Younis Ahmed. Richie Benaud also brought out his Wanderers team, captained by Greg Chappell. Back in 1970, South Africa had thrashed Bill Lawry's Australians four victories to nil. South Africa were due to visit Australia in the 1971-72 season. Jack Cheetham, formerly the captain but by then President of the South African Cricket Association, had suggested that two non-white cricketers, Dik Abed and left-arm spinner Owen Williams, should be included in the touring party but SACBOC (the South African Cricket Board of Control – the national body for coloured cricketers) vetoed the proposal on the basis that selection of the national team should be on merit only.

Unfortunately, Mr Cheetham and his association had not consulted SACBOC about their proposal and they in any case regarded the nominal selection of two non-whites as nothing more than a gesture. The tour was off and that was that.

The real irony of the situation was that Dik Abed, the youngest of four cricketing brothers, all of whom played for the South African coloured team against Kenya, went over to the UK to play in Lancashire League cricket, where he found himself playing against Pat Trimbourne, who, as a white player, had represented Natal and South Africa with distinction. It was odd to think that they had to travel 6,000 miles to play against each other. They were simply not allowed, by law, to play against each other in South Africa. Dik, in his first season playing for Enfield, to whom he was recommended by Basil D'Oliveira, scored over 400 runs and took over 100 wickets which at least proved that in spite of the disadvantage of playing on sub-standard grounds at home, the talent was definitely there.

It is perhaps important to understand that by now a power struggle was beginning to ferment in SACBOC. There was a broad-based desire to unite all the cricketing bodies but there were, within SACBOC, two distinct camps, one led by a small Indian gentleman – a real gentleman, by the way – Rashid Varachia, well spoken, reasonably wealthy and very knowledgeable about the game, who wanted to see unification happen. The other group was led by Cape coloured Hassan Howa, quite a fiery man who expressed his views through a phrase which was to become his hallmark: 'No normal sport in an abnormal society.' It is not putting it too strongly to say that this phrase became the rallying call for those who were even then seeking radical change, not only in cricket but in South African society as a whole. Destiny, in time, was to bring me into direct conflict with Hassan Howa.

Meanwhile, strides were being made. Benaud's Wanderers touring team included some really big names in the game such as Dennis Lillee, Gary Gilmour and, of course, the captain from Australia, Greg Chappell, Mike Denness and Derek Underwood from England and again John Shepherd. The agreement was that the South Africans would include some coloured players in their teams and so Tiffy Barnes, my great friend Howie Bergins, Jock Mahoney and Baboo Ebrahim found themselves catapulted into top-level cricket playing for a team captained by Eddie Barlow. Howie did really well, bowling his medium-pacers with his usual vigour and gusto but the star turned out to be Baboo, who with his left-arm spinners stole the show in the big representative game, taking 6 for 66 in the Wanderers' second innings at Durban.

Maybe now, after all, those dreams of mine were not so impossible. Could it be that one day I might, in spite of the odds being stacked against me, find myself playing in this kind of exalted company? Was that dream of playing on my beloved Newlands nearer to being fulfilled? At least these were steps towards integrated cricket and I could be a part of that. However, for me personally, there were some

GUIDING LIGHTS 41

rather large and dark clouds gathering on the horizon which were to change my life completely.

● ● ● ● ● ● ● ● ● ● ● ● ● ● ● ●

BASIL D'OLIVEIRA

The South African who, as a coloured player, was at the centre of controversy when picked for the England team to tour South Africa in 1967.

'I have known Omar from a young boy when I first gave him some coaching. He progressed to be a fine all-rounder both in his native South Africa and in Scotland. He has made many friends and is highly respected by his fellow professionals. His dedication and work rate is an example to all young cricketers who are hoping to be successful in this noble art.

'As I have always said to young pros, there is no short-cut to success. It is sheer bloody hard work. Omar is the personification of that ethos.'

KANGAROO COURT

All dark clouds, so they say, have a silver lining. However, you don't always see that silver lining initially. I was, at this stage of my cricketing life – I could not, at this juncture, describe it as a career – enjoying my cricket and had, in retrospect, gone as far as the system as it stood in South Africa would allow me. I had established myself in the SACBOC version of province cricket, that is within the somewhat confined orbit of the game as it was played within the coloured community. As things were in those days – the mid-70s – there was a ceiling placed above us. That ceiling was the limitations imposed by the administrators which, I remind you, under the doctrines of Hassan Howa, meant no normal sport in an abnormal society. To reach for the sky beyond that ceiling would inevitably mean breaking out from those restrictions, in other words, leaving cricket as it was played under the aegis of SACBOC and taking the plunge into mixed-race cricket, which by now was beginning to emerge.

I hadn't really given much thought to such a move. In some respects I suppose that my own circle of cricketing friends and colleagues was all I had known. For most of us, it seemed to be the natural home, our lot seemingly determined by the laws of the country on the one hand and the rigid 'thou shalt not compromise' dicta of SACBOC as interpreted by Mr Howa. The principles which therefore governed our actions – where we played our cricket – seemed perfectly natural.

However, at the back of my mind there were doubts. I still harboured the ambition of making cricket my profession and in the circumstances in which I found myself that seemed on occasion to be just another unreachable goal.

Furthermore, life was hard on the financial front. I wasn't paid much in the first place in my 'other life' as a joiner and now that I had made my way into the Province team – at least, the SACBOC Province team – the demands on my time meant that I was having to live on even less because each time I went away to play cricket, I forfeited pay. Besides, I was still somewhat preoccupied with the need to constantly upgrade the standards of my own game. Nevertheless, I did have an understanding of what was going on elsewhere, that some cricketers had defected from SACBOC and they seemed to be doing all right. However, whilst these thoughts were at the back of my mind, I continued to follow the natural route through SACBOC cricket. Little did I know that the day was looming when I would find myself standing at a crossroads at which I would have to choose an entirely new route.

The change of direction came in an entirely involuntary way. We were playing a Howa Bowl game in Durban but it rained and because the ground on which we were playing had no covers, the game was abandoned. On our way back to the hotel, our route took us by Kingsmead, where, needless to say, with the provision of covers, the white game going on there had been able to resume. It was tea-time when we passed, there was no one on the gate – they generally let people in free for the last session anyway – so a few of us decided to stop and watch a few overs of the game. It was as simple as that. That is all we did. I don't suppose we were in the ground for more than ten minutes or a quarter of an hour and the only reason we went in was because of our love of cricket. It doesn't matter where I am in the world, if I see that there is a cricket match being played, I am naturally drawn to it. That still applies and it was certainly the case in 1976 when I was just a young man of 24.

That single act, the 'crime', as it was later described, of entering a cricket ground and watching a few brief overs of a game which, as it happened, was being played between two white teams, was to transform my life, although I had absolutely no notion of that at the time.

However, we had been spotted. By whom, I really don't know – nor do I care. Seven of us had stopped off for those fleeting moments and we thought nothing more of it until we arrived back in Cape Town, where we were informed that because we had been seen at Kingsmead, we were all to attend a disciplinary hearing at the Vinito Hotel in my home town of Stellenbosch. I still didn't attach much importance to the incident. It seemed such a trivial issue so how could I take a disciplinary hearing seriously? How wrong can you be?

I duly attended the hearing, which I assumed would be before members of the SACBOC committee, only to find that the room was packed with about 150 people who, the moment I appeared, began shouting, spitting and swearing. The cry 'Traitor!' was to be heard repeatedly. Some shouted that we should be put up against a wall and shot! I was completely taken aback. Many of these people were, after all, from my own community, some of them I had grown up with, played cricket with. There were, as I discovered, others there who had no connection with the game of cricket. The only reason for their presence was clearly political.

It was immediately apparent to me that Hassan Howa had very carefully set us up. He was obviously wanting to make a big issue of the affair, a kind of showcase to emphasise that he meant business. In other words, the whole thing had been carefully planned and orchestrated by him, and furthermore, he was to be the conductor of the orchestra. We were accused by him of being absolute traitors to our own people, of being in the pockets of the whites and furthermore of having been indoctrinated by Rashid Varachia, Hassan Howa's arch-enemy within the SACBOC set-up, and a much more liberal-minded man. Mr Howa even suggested that we had been egged on to go to Kingsmead by Mr Varachia – an absurd suggestion. At that time, the two men were very much at odds with Mr Varachia in essence wanting to see more integration of cricket, more mixed-race cricket, and Mr Howa maintaining his well-known stance, 'No normal sport in an abnormal society.' There was absolutely no doubt that Hassan Howa was using this so-called incident as a vehicle to strengthen his own position and rally support to his own particular point of view and that he saw our apparent crime as a perfect means of whipping up more support.

Clearly the audience had been well chosen from those sections of the community which already felt the same way anyway. The people present were entirely drawn from the sections of the community who held extreme views. He had even arranged for people to travel from Cape Town, people who, of course, shared his views and could be said to hold pretty extreme political opinions. We were accused directly by Mr Howa of transgressing against SACBOC rules and it was immediately clear that besides making a spectacle of us, he would settle for nothing less than an unequivocal apology from each one of us. The case against us was put in strong terms with frequent interruptions from the audience, mostly consisting of obscenities. We were, it seemed to me, being told to grovel, to apologise abjectly and submit ourselves totally to his will. Even worse was the fact that when I tried to speak up for myself, my voice was drowned by a further volley of invective from the audience. Obviously, we were not going to get a hearing of any kind, certainly not a fair hearing. The alternative to apologising was made brutally clear to us: failure to do so would result in a permanent, lifelong ban from cricket, at least cricket played under the aegis of SACBOC.

I was incensed. The suggestion that we had been put up to enter Kingsmead by Rashid Varachia was, of course, utter rubbish. And the idea that we were in any way, by entering the ground, denoting our support for the white game was equally utter nonsense. I really did not think that what we had done was even significant, let alone the heinous crime it was being made out to be. All we had done was watch a few overs of a game of cricket and the fact that we were ourselves cricketers, playing under SACBOC, didn't seem to me to be relevant at all. I suppose we were recognised as a coloured team, or at least as part of the team, but I couldn't understand why that was significant. I had, after all, spent days and days at Newlands over the years watching Test cricket, so why was this particular action so different? It was, in every sense of the word, a kangaroo court, carefully stage-managed by Hassan Howa to gain maximum effect for his views and court support for them. I had been brought up to believe that if you have done something wrong, then you should admit it, be humble and honest enough to confess your sins. But where was the sin in this little adventure? I dug my heels in and point-blank refused to apologise. In my view, I had nothing for which to apologise. I had no feelings of guilt and in fact thought the whole affair was completely farcical. One of the so called 'guilty men' did proffer an apology but I and the rest of the accused resisted and firmly refused to do so.

The result was instant. Life bans were imposed upon every one of us. What followed did no credit to anyone. Now the wonder boy was no longer the local hero. I was ostracised and much worse. Threats were made – against my life, against my parents, against anyone who might befriend me. People I had known all my life cut me dead, refused to speak to me, sometimes crossed to the other side of the road to avoid me. I was suddenly an outcast in the community in which I had grown up. Furthermore, on the face of it, anyway, my cricketing days were numbered. As it happened, this kangaroo court took place at the end of the 1976-77 season, so I had plenty of time to contemplate and brood over the affair and think about how I could continue playing cricket. The game was so important to me that I couldn't possibly contemplate giving it up. I had progressed well within the orbit of SACBOC cricket and I was determined not to be deflected by this apology for justice. If I felt I had done wrong I would undoubtedly have apologised. Yes, I went into the Kingsmead ground, but very definitely not at the behest of Mr Varachia. I went only because of my deep interest in and love for the game of cricket.

What Mr Howa seemed to be doing was a travesty in my view for he was, by staging that so-called hearing and imposing the life ban on me and the others, acting against the interests of the game he was supposed to be serving. It isn't that I failed to understand his opinion that, until society in South Africa had been transformed and equality of opportunity had been created for people from all races and creeds, there should be no meeting of the waters. But I didn't have to agree with him and I didn't have to be forced to agree with him at a kangaroo court. I stood my ground and I think I was absolutely right to do so. Even if I respected Mr Howa's right to hold such views, it was not his right, in my opinion, to try to force such views down my throat, or anyone else's throat, for that matter. I had a whole South African winter to ponder the consequences of my own determination not to surrender my principles and as the 1976-77 season approached, I took positive action.

It was, ironically, Mr Varachia who made contacts for me and indirectly steered me in the right direction. He, I learned later, was quite appalled at Mr Howa's behaviour. There was a real clash of personalities between these two as well as a clash of views. I did a few odd jobs to augment my somewhat meagre income, and one of them was to help clean a cinema in Cape Town. The cinema, the Bioscope, was owned by a Mr Patel. Here I met Mr Boon Wallace, then the Vice-President of the Western Province Cricket Union, later to become President of the South African Cricket Union. Mr Wallace, an absolute gentleman and a man who worked tirelessly over many long years within the game to integrate cricket, had of course heard of my plight. Furthermore, he obviously believed that I had something to offer the game. Mr Patel apparently gave me a glowing reference and eventually, when I met Mr Wallace, he told me that I could, if I wanted, very easily begin a new career in one of the clubs in Cape Town, where the colour of someone's skin did not matter. He had the contacts and, recognising my enthusiasm for the game and my desire to continue playing, he arranged for the Pinelands club to take me on. Mr Wallace was kindness itself and I am privileged still to number him amongst my friends. However, in the end I did not join Pinelands, as through a family connection I was put in touch with Green Point Cricket Club, situated close to the beach and also near the city centre. Remember that others had trodden this road before me, great cricketers like Howie Bergins, Jock Mahoney, Baboo Ebrahim and Willie Hendricks, so I wasn't exactly pioneering.

As things worked out, Mr Howa did me a big favour. I didn't enjoy the experience of facing that kangaroo court in Stellenbosch and I certainly didn't enjoy the vilification I suffered at the hands of members of my own community. It was a harsh lesson and it left me with a very unpleasant taste in my mouth. However, it was a lesson all the same. It taught me something about myself. I was prepared to go out on a limb by sticking to my own beliefs; I was not prepared to be browbeaten and I certainly wasn't prepared to give up cricket. Such episodes serve to illustrate most clearly the kind of cross-current that can flow in a divided community. There is an irony in that in some respects my own community was now practising a kind of apartheid in reverse. I was the unwitting victim. And of course it turned out to be a blessing in disguise for me because it enabled me to chart an entirely new course, a course which was to take me into an entirely different dimension where the ceiling had been lifted and at last, I could not only see the sky but reach out for it too.

The Chairman of the Green Point Cricket Club, Gerald Mallinick, couldn't have been more welcoming. Race, creed and colour just didn't come into the equation as far as he was concerned. All he wanted was to promote the game of cricket, and to assemble at Green Point the best team available, irrespective of anything other than a player's ability on the field.

And what an eye-opener it was for me when I arrived at the ground at the beginning of the season to start practising. It was another world. The facilities were far superior to anything I had previously experienced. My days of playing on matting wickets were over; it was turf from now on, even to practise on! And if I thought I had been an enthusiastic practiser before, then again, I had my eyes opened wide. The excellent facilities were matched by the enthusiasm everyone showed. They didn't just practise, they trained, they worked on their fitness in a way I had never before experienced. I took to it all like a duck to water – in fact I was hardly ever away from the place. Now I really felt I could work on my game, but quite naturally some doubts sprung into my mind. Could I cope with these entirely new surroundings? Could I make my mark in this new dimension of cricket? Was I good enough? When the season began, I had the task of adjusting to this new environment, not least to the fact that our games were played on turf.

But there was help at hand. Howie Bergins, who was to become such a good friend to me and indeed to play no small part in my progress in the years ahead, was tremendously helpful and encouraging. He took me to the ground for practice in his car, and he constantly watched me, providing those little subtle hints about my game which are so important to any developing cricketer, not trying to reshape the way I played but all the time making suggestions which would enable me to utilise my talents to greater effect. For the next few weeks, I felt my way gently into second-team cricket and then, on November 1st, 1976, I found my name listed in the first team for a game against Stellenbosch University – another irony. But this was to be no ordinary Premier League game, for the University side was packed with emerging stars. They batted first and it wasn't long before I was asked to bowl. At the end of the first hour's play, the University score stood on 50 for 4 with Eddie Barlow, Kepler Wessels and Peter Kirsten all back in the pavilion, dismissed by what Peter Kirsten was later to describe as 'the tantalising spin of Omar Henry'. What a start! It was the stuff of which dreams are made but I was awake and there was the evidence in the scorebook.

However, if I had made an impact straight away, I was soon to be reminded that there were still those who felt I had no right to be playing in this kind of cricket. Much to my disgust, the *Cape Herald* raised the topic of my defection from SACBOC in a somewhat vitriolic article which reiterated the nonsense that had been stated before. They called me a traitor, saying that I had left my own kind for a better life. The *Cape Herald*, I should remind you, is the paper produced for and read by the coloured community. I wonder if they would have bothered if I had come off with 0 for 70 or even failed to make it into the first team at all? The contention that I had gone to Green Point to enjoy a better life was somewhat wide of the mark. I was still very much in my amateur days. It was costing me money – and I didn't have too much of it in the first place – to play my cricket. Others, even more unkindly, suggested that I had become a white man at the weekends when playing cricket, reverting to coloured status for the rest of the week. This was the kind of nonsense talked by a minority of extremists. I have never felt any doubts about who or what I am. Furthermore, I am proud, deeply proud of my heritage and I had good cause to be very proud of my family at that time too. Yes, I was short of money, and my family was absolutely marvellous, helping me financially whenever they could.

I had a moderately satisfying season, never perhaps quite hitting the high spots to quite the same extent as I had against Stellenbosch University, but then it wasn't every week I had the opportunity of bowling at Barlow, Wessels and Kirsten – perhaps that was just as well! The spirit in the team was tremendous. I had probably not given much thought to what it would be like playing alongside white guys, perhaps because I was so focused on my own game. Initially I was slightly apprehensive but that soon vanished – there was not a hint of racism. No one really cared whether you were black, white, brown, yellow or sky blue pink. We were a team and our objective was to go out into the middle and do our very best. Nothing else mattered. And after the game nothing changed; the same attitude ran through every moment of every day we were together. And there was a united feeling of grief when one of our most popular players, Gary Bicknell, was tragically killed whilst returning from a National Service army camp when the train in which he was travelling crashed after the brakes had failed. Gary and I had become good friends. He was only 22 years old and he was regarded as one of the most promising spin bowlers in South Africa at the time.

My own personal life was partly disrupted when I got the sack from work at the end of the 1976-77 season. Things had not been too good for the company and of course my track record of taking time off to play cricket had not done me any favours. I couldn't go on relying on family and friends for money so I was in something of a dilemma. The loss of the job itself didn't concern me – after all, by my own admission, cricket was of far more importance anyway. But you have to live. Then Howie Bergins, who was by now well established as a summer professional with a club in the Lancashire area of England, suggested that it would be great experience for me to go over to the UK with him and play for his club. It sounded great – just what I had always planned to do, go and play in England and take another hopeful step towards a real career in the game. But how on earth could I finance the trip? I was unemployed with no real prospect of a job, no money and, it seemed, no hope of taking Howie up on his offer. But miracles do sometimes happen. A month or so later, after our season had finished, I received a letter from Howie telling me that if I could raise the money for the air fare to the UK, he had arranged for me to be employed by his club, Micklehurst, as a kind of handyman. I couldn't believe my luck, but still the dream seemed as improbable as ever. I still needed to find the money for an air ticket.

Help was at hand. Rashid Varachia and Frank Brache, both of whom had been following my career with keen interest, raised some money. Frank was to become a lifelong friend. He is the brother-in-law of Basil

D'Oliveira and was at the time very active in getting multi-racial cricket off the ground, being one of the driving forces behind the creation of the Cavaliers Cricket Club. The club helped with fund-raising; there were raffles and a whole host of other donations which in the end meant that I had enough to buy the ticket. I have often since wondered if I have justified the faith they showed in me at that time. So I was off on the greatest adventure of my life to date, aware that playing in England would add another important dimension to my game and also conscious that having established myself in the Green Point team, my next goal in South Africa had to be progress towards the Province 'B' team.

I was equally conscious that I would be returning after my half-season in England with little prospect of a job. Some people might well say, and with some justification, that instead of chancing my arm and flying out to the UK just to play cricket, I should have been trying to get myself a job, that such an adventure was a luxury I could not afford. Needless to say, that wasn't the way I looked at things. I was 25 years old and if I was to go any way towards fulfilling my ambition of making a living from cricket, I had to do it, had to take that gamble. It was now or never. Most young players of 25 have already made it but thanks to the system into which I was born, the lack of proper coaching when I was young and the subsequent lack of opportunity, I was only just setting out on that path and I had, I felt, a lot of catching up to do. If I hadn't taken that chance to broaden my cricketing experience, it seemed doubtful whether I would ever be presented with another opportunity.

So with the help of many kind people, the world was now my oyster. When I look back on those tempestuous and sometimes very stressful and unpleasant days following the infamous kangaroo court in Stellenbosch, I become increasingly convinced that fate certainly took a hand. If I had not stopped off that day at Kingsmead, if I had not stood firm in the face of what was a highly charged meeting in Stellenbosch, if I had instead apologised and continued my cricketing life within the isolated community of SACBOC, would I, could I, ever have reached for the sky, played professional cricket, played for my country and travelled the world in pursuit of cricketing fame?

So Hassan Howa, fate and, thankfully, that stubborn streak and determination I inherited through my genes, together with all those people who supported rather than castigated me, all combined to thrust me into a higher orbit, a new dimension. I might still have been sitting somewhere in South Africa wondering what might have been if I hadn't stood my ground. It was my love for cricket that triumphed in the end and the kangaroo court of Stellenbosch most certainly and irrevocably changed my destiny. If it not been so perhaps this book would have been about joinery rather than cricket!

So the hardships and unpleasantness that followed in the wake of that dreadful evening in Stellenbosch were worth it. Perhaps above all, that particular episode in the history of South African cricket serve to illustrate, now that our society is heading for a more 'normal' future, that there are many ways of achieving aims, that a wide-angle lense should sometimes be focused upon our problems and that a narrow-minded approach is not necessarily the right one.

As for me, it certainly changed my life and opened doors for me that otherwise would have been locked, bolted and barred. It provided me with a new, much longer ladder to climb. But was I up to making that climb?

● ● ● ● ● ● ● ● ● ● ● ● ● ● ● ●

FRANK BRACHE

Frank Brache has been associated with Omar since the early 1970s. He is member of the United Cricket Board and was formerly a member of the South African Cricket Union. He was Secretary of the Western Province Cricket Board in the days of SACBOC, which body he also served. He is also the brother-in-law of Basil D'Oliveira.

'Omar Henry, in my view, was a tremendous all-round cricketer, an attacking batsman, a first-class spin bowler and an excellent fielder – the complete all-rounder in my opinion. Coming from a background in which there was no coaching available, it was Omar's raw talent that made him the cricketer he is, a man who, had South African cricket been played on what might be called a "normal" footing, and had we therefore remained in the international cricketing community, would certainly have won many Springbok caps.

'The lack of coaching in the coloured community meant that, in much the same way as the West Indians are "natural" cricketers, so too was Omar. He had already established himself in the Western Province Cricket Board team – that is, the Province team drawn from the coloured community under the aegis of SACBOC – when he "went over" to the South African Cricket Union in the 1976-77 season. The union had been formed when all three of the separate boards decided to come together under the leadership of Rashid Varachia. In the Western Province, the decision to join hands, so to speak, was unanimous but later Hassan Howa decided that his SACBOC members should withdraw. He was famous for his phrase, "No normal cricket in an abnormal society."

'Omar, in my opinion, took the right decision when he decided to split with Mr Howa and his colleagues. He reasoned, I believe, that there was a national trend towards unity and that that was what he believed in. He had to withstand a great deal of criticism from his own community. They even preached against him in the mosque he attended, so as you can gather, feelings did run high. But he stuck it out. Now we are all together in our cricket which, in a sense, vindicates Omar's decision. By the time he had been selected for the Springbok team to play against the rebel Australians, he had nevertheless become a hero for coloured children throughout the country. At last they had a role model to look to from their own community.

'He certainly made a conscious decision to fight the cause from within rather than from the outside. There was a lot of pressure on him and a lesser mortal might have thrown in the towel but Omar stuck it out. There is an old saying that a situation can change people. He decided to try to get inside and change the situation. And now he has all these achievements behind him, which vindicates the difficult route he chose to follow. Now, in a sense, the fairy tale is over. Cricket in South Africa is open to all and Omar undoubtedly has a vital role to play in the future as a coach and adviser.

'His involvement with the University of the Western Cape illustrates the sea-change that has taken place in the hearts of most people in South Africa. Only a few short years ago, because of what they called his "defection" to mixed-race cricket, the people there would not even have looked at him, never mind considered employing him to help them to develop cricket at the university which is, of course, the university to which most of the coloured youngsters go.

'The very fact that he went and played cricket overseas and was successful further demonstrated that Omar's cricketing credentials are based entirely on his ability and have nothing to do with the colour of his skin. But of course, besides representing Scotland he also eventually won his place in the squad that went to the World Cup and was subsequently capped in three official Test matches against India. Most importantly, he has a wife, Conita, who has supported him throughout and shared with him the good and bad times, a very important factor. He is a man of principal and in my opinion, the accusation that he "sold out" in those early days when we were attempting to normalise the sport was entirely misplaced. He has had to fight for everything he has achieved. Eddie Barlow, I think, helped him enormously but he had to have the natural ability in the first place to reach the heights he has.

'Now his main role, I think, will be as an important role model for youngsters coming into the game. The impact he made with Orange Free State was quite amazing, for Bloemfontein is traditionally very much a white-dominated part of the country. Yet Omar, because of his personality and because of his ability on the field, his disposition, transcended that tradition. He was much admired and respected and no one seemed to be concerned about the colour of his skin, which in itself is a tribute to the man.

'Omar, I believe, also opened the door for many others to come to South Africa, like his team-mate at Free State, the West Indian Franklyn Stephenson. What Omar is, of course, is a true professional, and I am certain he will put a huge amount back into the game in the years to come. Quite a man and quite a cricketer!'

ENGLAND, HERE I COME

The dream of going to England to play cricket was first awakened when Basil D'Oliveira wanted to take me back there with him. If my hopes, at the tender age of 15, had initially been dashed when my parents declined Basil's offer, the belief that one day I would follow in his footsteps had always burned within me. Ten years later – thanks to the generosity of people like Frank Brache, Chairman of the Cavaliers club who sponsored me – when I found myself packing my bags and going to Cape Town's D. F. Malan Airport, saying my fond farewells to family and friends and then boarding the plane for the first leg of my journey, to Johannesburg, another dream was on its way to fulfilment. Cricket case carefully packed and passport clutched in hand, I was on my way.

The flight itself was a tremendous experience but the longer the journey took, the more I began to think that I was going to another planet. It is worth remembering that my first language was, and always has been, Afrikaans. I could speak English – just – but I certainly wasn't comfortable with the language. And here I was going to a part of England where not only did they speak English but English with an unfamiliar accent. Only my good friend Howie could converse with me in Afrikaans.

Predictably, I suppose, I arrived in rain. In fact it seemed that in June 1977 it rained non-stop! I was picked up at Manchester Airport by the club President, John Pass, and to be quite honest about it, I simply couldn't understand him. He had what I now know to be a strong north of England accent, and I couldn't comprehend a word he said. I took the easy way out and simply said yes to every question he asked. For instance, although at that time I had no regular girlfriend, let alone a wife, I apparently conveyed to him that I had someone. What the question was I really don't know – probably something like 'Have you got a girl?', to which I replied, 'Yes'.

Soon I was introduced to my hosts, club member Geoff Lawrence and his delightful wife Susan. They were to put me up for the rest of the season and they were so generous and understanding – really kind people – that I immediately felt at home.

Micklehurst is set in the Pennines – the hills which form the spine of England – and is one of many mill towns which surround Manchester, a legacy of the industrial age when cotton was king. The ground, small, compact and very picturesque, was at the top of a steep hill, a little plateau, with the village down below in the valley. It was surrounded by farmland. The conditions were very different. And so, cricket-wise, I found myself struggling. It was a wetter than usual summer – even by Manchester standards – and the wickets were so soft. This was a totally new ball game. And of course, coming from the warmth of the Cape, it seemed so cold almost all the time.

One thing I discovered very quickly was that in Lancashire, they take their cricket very seriously indeed. Howie had given me good credentials, all right – too good! So perhaps more was expected of me than I could deliver in what were, after all, alien conditions. The excitement that was generated within me was soon to be tempered. The wet weather meant that the wickets were even slower than usual. My first game was, for me, a nightmare. If I got 2 wickets, I got no runs and furthermore found the slowness of the wicket very difficult to cope with. In my first few innings I hardly scored a run and kept getting out holing out at cover or gully, playing about half an hour too early. My reputation, built up by Howie, was soon in tatters. It seemed to be 'mission impossible'. There were some tremendous pros about. Roy Gilchrist, the famous, perhaps infamous, West Indian quickie; Sonny Ramadhin, the equally famous West Indian spinner; a number of other West Indians who had been around for some years and had acclimatised themselves to the conditions and a few young Australians. But I didn't perform for Micklehurst. I simply didn't manage to acclimatise. Yet the guys at the club were tremendous.

Fortunately, there was a Pakistani food shop close by and so I could get hold of the kind of food my religion demanded I should eat, halal. I also fell in love with fish and chips. I particularly like the fact that in Britain the fish is filleted because I've always hated fish on the bone. This fish you could eat like ice-cream and I loved it. I also took a great liking to the local bread and because I ate so much of it, I became known as 'Jam Buttie'. I had never seen so much salad in my life. It was the staple diet at tea-time but my reputation for liking jam butties went before me and people were kind, ensuring that there were always plenty of butties for me at tea, even when we played away. And when I had to observe the fasting times decreed by my religion, they were kind enough again to keep my tea until the game was over and the sun had gone down, which is when we can resume eating.

After each game the lads had their ration of beers of course but they respected the fact that I did not drink alcohol. I think they realised that the transition from the conditions in South Africa was difficult but I remember one rather elderly member of the club saying to me that I had plenty of natural talent but unless I adapted my game to English conditions, I might just as well go back home. My inability to adjust began to erode my self-confidence. Was I good enough to make this transition? It was above all a mental battle, within myself.

Then one Sunday I played in a benefit game and everything fell into place. I scored a faultless 50, which, by the way, I still rate to this day as one of my best innings, and made a couple of screaming catches in the gully with 4 wickets as a bonus. Suddenly, I was once again comfortable at the crease and my self-esteem began to reappear.

The people were so warm and members of the club used to take me out. I went to Old Trafford on occasions to watch Lancashire and to the other Old Trafford to watch the Red Devils – Manchester United, whom I had supported since my boyhood. However, when the season came to an end, I certainly did not feel that I had much to look back on with pride. In some respects it was a harrowing experience. However, my natural resilience again stood me in good stead. That one performance at least gave me something to cling on to. On one occasion, if only that once, I had shown that I could master the conditions, difficult though they were, and still emerge as a player of worth. There were other occasions when I felt I had done reasonably well, when we played against Sonny Ramadhin, for example, and he skittled us out for 66 of which I made 44, but in general I knew I had not played to my potential.

In spite of the jam butties, I had kept myself in really good physical condition and now I had the South African season to look forward to. My first season at Green Point had been productive. I had established myself in the club's first team and knew that with that extra little push I might make it to the Western Province 'B' team. But I still had no regular employment and had to rely on what I earned from doing a variety of odd jobs to keep my head above water, with, from time to time, help from my parents. Luxuries were out of the question and I lived a fairly frugal life. So on my return, I practised with even more enthusiasm than ever, kept working on my fitness and in particular really worked hard on my bowling.

In that first season, I had established myself as one of the few spinners to take wickets regularly, and that gave me the incentive to do even better. I put that devastating season in the UK behind me and resolved to really give it my best shot in my efforts to force my way into the Province 'B' team. I was coming up to 26 years of age and I still hadn't made it to the top level. Opportunity is all-important and some players do mature later, but given the right opportunities – denied to me by the political system as well as by the way cricket was played on a racial basis in South Africa – I would perhaps have made the breakthrough much earlier.

I did not have to wait long, for I was selected for the Western Province 'B' team against Northern Transvaal in Pretoria. It was a proud moment: to be picked on merit, a rich reward for all the hard work, the heartbreak and a moment for my family and friends to savour. Mrs Schoeman, who had been so helpful in buying cricket gear for me, was particularly pleased.

Northern Transvaal were on the verge of becoming an 'A' province and a Currie Cup side, so they had a very strong team. I cannot in all honesty say that I made much of a contribution, but again, it was very much a learning process for me. The batsmen played so straight and were certainly not going to give their wickets away. Every time you go up a grade, it becomes progressively harder and never was that salutary fact of life better illustrated to me.

Government regulations meant that permits had to be obtained for me to stay in what was deemed to be a white hotel in Pretoria and there was one unfortunate incident when the whole team went out to a nightclub. Almost inevitably, I was refused entry and the entire team just walked out. Obviously it angered me but I had learned to try to shrug off such incidents. After all, cricket was above that kind of thing, and, as far as I was concerned, much more important.

Back on the cricket field I made what I regarded as an important step forward against Griqualand West at Kimberley. On a wicket that had a good deal of bounce in it, I produced the figures of 32 overs and 5 balls, 20 maidens, conceded just 31 runs and had a haul of 6 wickets. The last two victims were caught and bowled and I really was pleased with my day's work. The *Cape Times* sports pages headlines that day read : 'A day of great cricket deeds: Barry Richards 207... Denys Hobson 6-49... Omar Henry 6-31.' You can imagine how I felt sharing a headline with such great cricketers as Barry Richards and Denys Hobson. The report on the day's play was headed: 'Great bowling by Omar Henry', and in his report Howard Salkow led with the words: 'Omar Henry, the coloured left-arm spinner from the Green Point Cricket Club in Cape Town, stole the show on the first day of this Castle Bowl cricket match between Western Province "B" and Griqualand West when he took 6 wickets in Griqua's first-innings total of 153. Immediately after the Province captain Mike Bowditch brought on Henry it spelled danger. Bowling his orthodox left-arm spinners to great effect, he finished the day with 6 for 31 in 32.5 overs, which included 20 maidens. Henry was not scared to flight the ball and even though he did not get much assistance from the wicket, he did get the odd ball to turn a bit and this is where he made his claims.'

I had a couple of wickets in the second innings and we won by 9 wickets. It was a real boost to my confidence but I was realistic enough to know that I had a long way to go, that at this level, I had very limited experience and a shortfall in basic knowledge of the game. But I was surrounded by excellent players. Again, Eddie Barlow was there and, as always, gave me tremendous encouragement, as did people like Mike Bowditch and Rob Thompson. I had become very friendly with Stephen Jones and in fact struck up a long-lasting relationship with him. In those days, Stephen and I used to sit and talk about the game for hours on end and he was full of encouragement during that marathon spell of bowling at Kimberley after which, I can tell you, I had very sore feet!

I really enjoyed that 1977-78 season and felt that I had made significant progress. The icing on the cake came in February, when I received a telegram from Micklehurst inviting me back to play for them in the 1978 season. What was more, they were offering me the air fare and a job! Howie had decided to give English cricket a miss in order to go back to university. Micklehurst's captain, Bob Wrigley, apparently believed I had potential, even if my performances during that half-season in 1977 had been moderate at best. The invitation came as something of a surprise and I knew full well that I would have to really perform. It was, as I saw it, my last chance – do or die! The successes I had experienced with the Province 'B' team had given me more self-belief and confidence so when I set out once more for England, I was imbued with a spirit of optimism. This time, I told myself, I was going to make a real impact.

It was great to be back in that happy atmosphere at Micklehurst, great to renew friendships, even if I had once again to acclimatise myself to the weather. As it happened, our first League fixture was against Greenfield, who had Roy Gilchrist as their pro. Gilchrist's reputation had gone before him, of course. On the field he was a volatile man, well known for bowling bouncers and even beamers and had been sent home by the West Indians from a tour to India, thus missing out on the Pakistan leg of the tour. On one occasion, when playing for Middleton in the Central Lancashire League, he had been the centre of controversy when, after Middleton had batted first, he removed Oldham's opening bat – literally – with a beamer. The Oldham captain, Bill Lawton, husband of the famous actress Dora Bryan, had instantly declared thus forfeiting the game. Ironically, the

League fined Oldham for their part in the proceedings. The incident serves to illustrate that Gilly was always in the thick of things – a real controversial character.

My first scoring shot was a 6 and I went on to register a ton to win the game. In fact, Gilly and I became good friends and I played with him on numerous occasions in benefit games and for invitation XIs. I knew of his reputation for having been one of the world's quickest bowlers, partner of Wes Hall before Charlie Griffiths burst on the scene. He still had pace – considerable pace when he wanted to really let go – but he had also learned in a long career in Lancashire League cricket to exploit the conditions. He could cut the ball both ways and he was impossible to read. During that innings, I don't know how many times he ripped the ball back into my thighs and left me rubbing the bruises. I actually got on very well with him after taking that 100 off him. I think I earned his respect. He gave me a few bouncers but never a beamer, perhaps because I stayed firmly rooted in my crease! On one occasion, however, when we were playing together for the League, he really let himself go. He had been no-balled four times and when he was called again he wheeled round, ripped one of the stumps out of the ground and threatened to use it on the umpire. He wasn't no-balled again!

Gilly used to talk a lot about his experiences in the leagues, about Basil, for whom he had tremendous respect and, on occasion, about the incident which saw him sent back home from the West Indian tour of the Indian sub-continent. He blamed Sonny Ramadhin for what happened. As luck would have it, they both played in the Saddleworth League, Roy for Greenfield and Sonny for Delph. One thing you could be sure of was that when Delph were playing Greenfield, if they were 9 wickets down, they were as good as being all out. Ramadhin would not face Gilly! But Gilly, one of the most fearsome bowlers of his time at the highest level, was a great guy to play with.

I had a really good season, became, perhaps, the linchpin of the team, and, much to my own satisfaction, managed to conquer the conditions. And I was back at Micklehurst for a third time in 1979, when I had an absolutely fantastic season. Also in 1979, I had the great joy of playing for a multi-racial South African team which toured England, sponsored by Barclays Bank. So, while they were in the country, I was travelling to play for them in midweek and then returning to Micklehurst for the weekend. In that touring squad were the current South African wicket-keeper, Dave Richardson, Lee Barnard, who played for Transvaal and went on to captain Northern Transvaal, Mike 'Fires' Van Vuuren from Eastern Province – all of them white; Owen Finnan from Cape Town, Trevor Roberts, Patel from Jo'burg, Danny Dada from Northern Transvaal – all coloured – and two black guys.

The touring team played against county second teams and combined league teams. (for instance we played a combined Yorkshire League team). Fascinating for me was to play on some of the really famous grounds, notably Canterbury and Arundel, where we played against the Duchess of Norfolk's team. Canterbury was the first first-class English ground I had played on. I found it slightly incongruous with the famous tree, but a lovely ground. And I also had the chance to play against some first-class cricketers like the Cowdrey brothers and, as I remember particularly well because he took a century off us, Mike Gatting, playing on that occasion for Middlesex second team.

Our manager was Colin Milburn. What a great guy he was. He'd had that dreadful accident which curtailed his own career. I had the good fortune to spend a lot of time with him during the tour and I must say I learned an awful lot from him. He was also, of course, something of a wag. I remember on one occasion, he was ordering a drink (not untypically) and the waitress was a bit off-hand. So Colin just dropped his glass eye into a glass. The waitress was never seen again! He was a very strong character, tough but always fair. His reputation was such that we all had a tremendous respect for him. We knew that he had been a player of great heart and he certainly showed that in spite of the horrific accident which robbed him of what surely would have been a hugely successful career in test cricket. He was still quite irrepressible.

I had a good season in 1978 and Micklehurst, for the first time in 20 years, won the League. The following season was even better and we virtually swept the board. One weekend in particular stood out and will live long in my memory. On the Saturday, in a League game against East Lancashire Paper Mill, I made an unbeaten 167 but even that paled into insignificance compared with what happened on the Sunday. We were playing a cup semi-final against a Manchester team called Newton

Heath and, going in at number 3, in fewer than 45 overs I hit 243, an innings which included 23 6s – a world record, I am told. It was one of those days when I got in and simply stroked the ball around from the word go. Even if the ground was not exactly the dimensions of, for instance, the Wanderers ground in Johannesburg, I was timing the ball so well that many of the 6s would have counted on much bigger grounds. Several of the spectators decamped to the car park in an effort to protect their cars from my onslaught! Not surprisingly, that score broke all records.

I thought I was fit but I can tell you that when I passed the 200-mark, my legs had gone and my shoulders were aching. The lads just kept on encouraging me. The local paper quoted one of my playing colleagues, Geoff Storie, who said: 'When Omar was eventually out, we had to hold his drink for him and take his pads off, he was so tired. The funny thing was that before he had even got off the mark, the ball had flicked his off stump but the bails stayed put.' I remember it well, and even remember turning to examine the wicket and then just smiling at the opposition wicket-keeper. The papers also made some capital out of the fact that when I played for Western Province, I was in for my bowling and batted at number 10!

I think what pleased me most about that season was my ability to adapt to the conditions. In my first season, I had been completely unable to adjust to the slow wickets. I hadn't thought things through and was out time after time playing too early. This time, in 1978, and again in 1979, I had worked things out and waited for the ball to come on to me, playing much later. That fabulous weekend in which I scored 410 runs, and took a few wickets to boot, left me on the one hand elated and on the other, exhausted. It took me a week to recover. Instead of trying to hit the ball straight, I waited and picked my spot. I had learned. It was a process of maturation.

During the two and a half seasons I spent with Micklehurst, I also got involved in coaching, especially when it came to the youngsters, and I found that to be a really rewarding experience. In those Lancashire leagues, they take their cricket seriously. The players are not by any means all orthodox in their approach to the game. The pride of each village is at stake every time you go on to the field. It is a real family atmosphere and everything seems to revolve round the local cricket club. That was something new to me. Whole families turned up to support the players, their wives, children, parents, uncles, aunts and even grannies!

Phil Broadhurst, the captain and opening bat, was a terrific guy; Geoff Storie, a schoolteacher, I have already mentioned and I used to love listening to the chats they used to have in the bar about the old days and the stories of Lancashire County, too. Stories of Jacky Bond, obviously a great and charismatic character, and of course of the great Clive Lloyd when he got going with that famous heavy bat of his. Lancashire were the kings of one-day cricket. I watched them at Old Trafford on many occasions and became friendly with the great West Indian bowler Colin Croft and then later with Clive Lloyd.

Old Trafford is, of course, a superb cricket ground, I think one of the best in the world, and when, later, I played there for Scotland, it also seemed to be quite a lucky ground for me. I also remember meeting Colin Cowdrey there on one occasion. He had been involved in the multi-racial tour sponsored by Barclays, so I had already been introduced to him. And it was at Old Trafford too that I was introduced to Mr Edwards, the Chairman of Manchester United and, wonder of wonders, the late Sir Matt Busby himself. What a thrill that was because, as I've already said, United had always been my team. I had followed them in the papers from early childhood. Even more memorable was the invitation to be a guest in the directors' box and watch a game in such company. That was one of the biggest thrills of my life. I was taken into the dressing room and met players like Joe Jordan and Jimmy Nicholl and all those other great names – for that was all they had been to me before. Now I was actually meeting them face to face. The irrepressible Tommy Docherty, who had until a year or so beforehand been the manager, lived close to where I was living. What a character! He was always bubbling, always humorous. But the atmosphere at that famous ground was tremendous. I think that had a terrific impact on me, even more than the football itself.

I also played in a single-wicket competition on one occasion at Royton and found myself drawn against of all people, Colin Croft. We had to bowl 3 overs at each other and needless to say, I received 18 balls, none of which seemed to pitch in my half of the wicket, whereas my own spinners kept disappearing. There could only be one winner, the man with the missiles!

Cricket is a way of life in Lancashire – they never stop talking about it. There were some quaint moments, too. At Upmoor the wicket was towards the edge of the square and there was a river running along that side of the ground. It was little more than a chip – a 9-iron – to the big splash and when we played there they had a team of youngsters standing by with fishing nets to retrieve the balls so that the game could go on uninterrupted. I remember one June day when we played at Micklehurst and down came the snow. We all returned to the pavilion but it soon stopped and there was the groundsman, raking the snow off the pitch. I was batting when we resumed and I can remember clearly hammering the ball through the covers for 4 and watching the track the ball made through the snow!

It would be easy to get completely lost in that kind of atmosphere and many overseas players found playing in the Lancashire League not only a tough experience but a rather unnerving one too. You had to adapt to survive. If you didn't, you failed. There was one ground I played on in Yorkshire which had an enormous slope on it, and huge boundaries. You somehow had to cope with such idiosyncrasies – and with some curious umpiring decisions, too. There was one umpire who was notorious for watching the time like a hawk. What he had in his mind, towards the end of the game, was the time of his bus home. So woe betide anyone who got their legs in front or got anywhere near the ball when playing and missing. The finger went up – the bus had to be caught. But all this meant there was always fun, even in that hothouse atmosphere of competitive cricket. I would recommend any ambitious cricketer to have a go at Lancashire League cricket. You learn things about the game you didn't even realise existed.

A tremendously satisfying season, then, with 12 centuries in all cricket, nearly 300 runs accumulated for the South African touring team and 19 wickets. I returned to South Africa with a new spring in my step. Furthermore, the bush telegraph had been working well and my exploits had reached the pages of South African newspapers. My family and my friends were delighted at my success, proud of what I seemed to be achieving. Yet there was much more to achieve here at home. I had made it to the Province 'B' team, now the 'A' team had to be my target – the big time.

It was during that third season with Micklehurst that another opportunity came my way: the chance of joining the professional ranks and setting off on another adventure which was to take me north of the border to Scotland and provide yet another dimension to my cricketing life. I had indicated to my friends at Micklehurst that I wanted to see if I could get a professional's job. They were very good about it and certainly didn't stand in my way; in fact they encouraged me. I had got in touch with an agent, a guy called Derek Parker who had played for Lancashire as a leg-spinner but who had set up an agency to find pros for clubs in the UK. Through his contacts I went up and played a trial game for Kendal in the Northern League. The cricket was really good and the Kendal ground is very impressive. I didn't do too badly but they didn't seem to be that interested and let the matter drift. However, when one door closes, another opens and I found myself travelling to Scotland to play a couple of trial games for Poloc, who play in the Western Union, one of the top leagues in Scotland and one with a long and proud history. I played a couple of games for them and did reasonably well, and the upshot was the offer of a contract for the 1980 season. Strangely enough, they had employed another South African, or more accurately, a Rhodesian, but he had not made an impact at all.

But meanwhile it was back to South Africa and the sun. The 1978-79 season was momentous for me. On October 21st I made my debut for Western Province in the Datsun Shield, a one-day competition, against Orange Free State at Bloemfontein. Leg-spinner Denys Hobson had been injured the previous Sunday, as had Allan Lamb, in a double-wicket competition. In fact Lamby had broken his nose but pronounced himself fit for the game in Bloemfontein and played with a plaster cast on his nose.

It was some team, captained by Hylton Ackerman and including batsmen like Lamby and Peter Kirsten and quite an attack spearheaded by Garth le Roux, with two excellent seamers in Andre Nieuwoudt and Peter Swart, and off-spinner Richard Morris and myself in the spin department. Nevertheless, we lost to Free State but I was retained in the team for a friendly limited-overs match against Northern Transvaal at the Berea Park, Pretoria, the following weekend. I managed to make my mark in that game, taking 3 for 35 in my 12 overs – the best bowling figures in the match. What really pleased me was that my three victims were all in the top order in a side which was full of confidence as current Castle Bowl champions. I had their top scorer Kevin Verdhoorn caught at mid off by Richard Morris and also clean bowled Kenny Burrow in what was described by the press as 'an immaculate display of tight bowling'. Rodney Ontong was my third victim but the crucial wicket was that of Verdhoorn, who tried to hit me over the top and failed.

It was an important breakthrough for me but I still had to wait to make my Currie Cup (now the Castle Cup) debut. That came along in March when I was selected for Western Province to play Rhodesia in Salisbury on the Police Ground on March 3rd, 1979. I can't say that I made a startling impact on proceedings in that first match. Remember that this was the time of the Rhodesian War, so extra insurance had to be taken out on all the players. I was, as they say, 'over the moon' to be in the team – we were going on to play Transvaal at the famous Wanderers ground after the Rhodesia game. The plane journey from Johannesburg to Salisbury was hairy to say the least and one of the commanders of the Rhodesian army, General Walls, had been blown up so security was tight and the atmosphere was quite tense. However, I wasn't worrying too much about that: I was too intent on concentrating on the game ahead.

As it happened, we had an easy win. I scored 6 with the bat but bowled only 4 overs in the match, 3 of them maidens, without taking a wicket for an analysis of 0 for 4. It was Garth le Roux and Stephen Jones who did the damage, each taking 6 wickets in the match, which we won by the handsome margin of 194 runs, pocketing 17 valuable points in the process. The memory I carry from that game is the fact that I was at last wearing the blue cap of Western Province, a very proud day for me indeed.

We did not, however, fare so well against Transvaal's 'mean machine'. They really were the heavyweights of South African cricket and they beat us by 127 runs. Yet the experience of playing at the famous Wanderers ground – the 'Bull Ring', as they call it – was tremendous.

It is a place of such cricketing tradition. I batted at number 11, scored 14 not out and took my first wicket when Robbie Drummond snapped up Alan Kourie behind the wicket. It was curious that Alan Kourie should become my first Currie Cup victim for we were, several years on, to end up being rivals for the left-arm spin place in the Springbok team.

When I returned for the 1979-80 season, I had a contract signed and sealed in my back pocket to enter the professional ranks in Scotland in 1980. I think that alone gave me a great boost, raised the confidence factor. At last, it seemed, I was about to start a fully fledged career in cricket – another ambition fulfilled. As it happened, I didn't rejoin Green Point but instead signed up with Avendale, situated in Athlone, which is a coloured township just north of Cape Town, close to the airport.

I had been approached by two stalwarts of the club, Chairman Bert Erikson and Mike Stakol, to join them. They wanted someone not only to play for them but to coach as well and this was too good a chance to miss. It meant that I did not have the problem of searching for a job. I could, at long last, forget about being something of an odd-job man in order to keep myself in funds and devote myself entirely to cricket. It was a coincidence that at the same time in both South Africa and the UK, cricket was to become central to my entire life – and even better than that, my livelihood.

Bert Erikson had been a fine left-arm quickie in his day, had grown up with Basil in the Signal Hill area and had also represented the non-white South African side, a good cricketing pedigree. Bert was Mr Avendale and Mike Stakol, an Englishman, was a successful Jewish businessman, Managing Director of a large company. He put the finances in place. It was a strange combination really, Bert Erikson, a Gentile, Mike Stakol a Jew, and me, a Muslim!

Mike was a real powerhouse when it came to finance. He had turned up to watch the end of a game against Claremont in Constantia, a beautiful ground with a fantastic backdrop of mountains. Avendale, which had been formed by the merger of two clubs in 1975, were being thrashed by what amounted to a Claremont second team. Mike was intrigued, and having ascertained that Avendale were not only struggling on the field but also in every other way – they had not much of a home ground, no pavilion and no net facilities – he decided to join them. It was a decision which was to be highly significant for the club in due course, because the man proceeded to transform them. Until then only coloured players had played for them but in time that was destined to change, with players of the calibre of Bob Woolmer and Peter Kirsten later joining their ranks. Through his contacts Mike found enough money – some of which, I suspect, came out of his own pocket – to transform the club and its ground. A new table was laid, a clubhouse provided and nets set up.

Now they wanted me to develop the playing side and I was destined to stay with them for six seasons, some of the happiest days of my life. Between us – and my part in this was very small – we built Avendale into one of the top clubs in Cape Town. It was hard work but it was fun even if we had our setbacks. During the Gatting tour, the ANC actually blew up the clubhouse – I'll never know why – but within 48 hours, the members, many of them craftsmen, bricklayers, carpenters and electricians, had the place restored.

Bert Erikson's energy is phenomenal. You might easily find him serving behind the bar one minute and organising something in the club the next, always on the go, an absolutely inspirational figure if ever I saw one. He had been one of the people who had seen no future in Hassan Howa's SACBOC and cricket in isolation, a view which, as you already know, I shared. He simply eradicated all thoughts of race and got on with the business of cricket. Between the two of them, Mike and Bert really got things going. On Fridays they would organise lunches or cocktail parties for prominent businessmen to raise extra money for equipment, especially for youngsters, and to improve facilities at the club. The proof of the pudding was seen in the regular Friday-night sessions with young players, anything up to 150 of them, being coached. It is from such grass-roots development that cricket in Western Province and Cape Town will flourish in the future. I was just so proud to be a part of it in those formative years.

From a cricketing point of view, the move also benefited me. I could bat in the top order and on occasion, when the situation demanded it, even open the batting. They also asked me to captain the side. I had absolutely no experience of captaincy but I must admit that whatever trepidation had filled me when I first took on that responsibility soon vanished because I found I was able to use the experience I had gained both in playing at Green Point and of course in province cricket and in Lancashire. The experience of coaching was wonderful. My name was well known and frequently appeared in the newspapers and it was a strange experience, filling me with humility, to have these youngsters coming along and looking up to me in awe. But you have to learn to relate to the child, forget yourself and get the best out of him you can. After all, it often occurred to me that each one who came along could end up being a better player than me. And joy of joys, thanks to the tremendous efforts of Mike, who had eventually to return to England, we had such good facilities, many a mile away from the matting wickets and dustbowls on which Bert and I had learned our cricket.

If I had thought that this particular season was going to be the breakthrough one for me I was wrong. I played only once for the Province 'A' team, the rest of the season being spent in the 'B' XI. Off-spinner Richard Morris and leg-spinner Denys Hobson seemed to have the spin places in the 'A' team well tied up. Denys was a superb leg-spinner although he was much more effective at Newlands. His form away from home was never as impressive. Of course, Newlands always has been more of a spinner's wicket but he didn't somehow seem to be able to adapt to the flatter wickets found elsewhere. My best performance for the 'B' team probably came at Kimberley against Griqualand West when, after taking 3 wickets in the first innings, I bowled a really niggardly spell second time around finishing up with the remarkable analysis of 8 overs, 6 maidens, 2 runs, 3 wickets!

Even if I had failed to make my mark in the 'A' team, I was nevertheless satisfied with my progress. I was now a club pro with Avendale, I had just enough money from that job to buy myself a little car, which certainly made life much easier, I was devoting much of my time to coaching and, of course, I had that contract with Poloc Cricket Club in Scotland in my pocket. Cricket for 12 months of the year, what more could I ask for? I had the feeling that ahead lay a whole host of challenges and I felt I was riding the crest of a wave. But I was only too well aware that if there was cause for optimism, there was also cause to step up my work rate, continue to work on both my game and my fitness. I have always been careful with my diet. I didn't eat red meat but I always made sure that I had a well-balanced diet and I always remembered the disciplines Les Bergstedt had drummed into me. Fitness of the body, running to strengthen the legs, meaningful practice to ensure that I was always tightening up my game, not just flaying the ball or hurling it down.

Inwardly I kept telling myself that I would break through to 'A' team cricket and I had built up enough self-confidence to persuade myself that although Western Province, with its in-depth playing resources, was a difficult nut to crack, I would probably have made it to other province 'A' sides. There was a temptation to move at that juncture but I had my pro's job at Avendale, I was still able to live at home and there were no other contracts in the offing. So I knew I would have to exercise patience and strengthen my resolve to keep battling away. One day, I kept telling myself, I will really make that breakthrough and the adventure which lay ahead of me, going to Scotland as a fully fledged professional cricketer, could only help to make me a better player and add to my expanding bank of experience.

I was certain what was in store was going to help me climb the cricketing ladder. Look out, I secretly said to myself, 'McHenry' is on his way!

• • • • • • • • • • • • • • • • •

HOWIE BERGINS

Howie Bergins was an outstandingly talented player who was to have a profound influence on Omar Henry's cricket career. In those difficult days when Omar had left the SACBOC scene and was just beginning to find his way in mixed-race cricket with the Green Point club, it was Howie who not only befriended him but also helped him in many ways to come to terms with this new dimension of cricket. Howie was a vigorous and very talented medium-paced bowler who himself played in representative cricket when the barriers first started to come down in South Africa. He also became a professional cricketer in England, and it was Howie who first took Omar out to England to enable him to begin a new phase in his career.

'I first met Omar as a junior cricketer and we frequently found ourselves on opposite sides during those early days. And then, of course, we played together for a number of years in Western Province SACBOC teams, and in fact he followed me eventually in leaving SACBOC cricket.

'I knew he had a very special talent. He was so typical of so many coloured cricketers with plenty of basic talent but he had that extra ingredient of aggression and never-say-die attitude. There was an occasion when we were playing against each other – and we were friends even then – when he was fielding at short leg and dived to catch me in spite of the fact that I protested I had not played the ball. He told me in no uncertain terms where to go.

'When we crossed the tracks, so to speak, and played mixed-race cricket, Omar, I think, had a much more difficult time of it than I did, perhaps because of the kind of community in which he lived in Stellenbosch. He had a rough time of it. Both of us, when we made that decision to play in mixed-race cricket, did so because we wanted to progress, wanted to play in better surroundings and furthermore, wanted to make progress on the basis of our talent rather than of the colour of our skins.

'When I first went to Micklehurst I found it difficult to adjust, but after a month, I began to acclimatise. Because I was brought up on quicker wickets, I suppose I was able to get in position quickly. Once you adjusted to the slowness of the wickets, it became progressively easier. As a professional, I was quickly imbued with the need to take responsibility and although initially Omar struggled there, he too eventually had that responsibility to take on board. But by then he had shown that he had the talent to make the necessary adjustments to his game and in his second season in the UK he blossomed. That willingness to shoulder responsibility was soon to be reflected in his dedication, his insistence on reaching a high level of physical fitness and his insistence on practising assiduously.

'For me, he really came of age in his early days with Western Province when he took 79 off the Transvaal attack in a Benson & Hedges night game played at Green Point because there were then no lights at Newlands. He simply took them apart, Clive Rice and all.

'He was always learning and you would find him always seeking out the more experienced players, talking to them, learning all the time. There was another instance when he took 7 wickets and won the game almost single-handed. Omar was always willing to work on his game and if initially he was prone to give the ball too much air, he soon adjusted to bowl a flatter delivery, especially in one-day cricket. He also developed a real element of guile in his bowling.

'I was absolutely delighted when he won a Springbok cap. When his selection was announced, we made him lead the team out and the reception he got was absolutely tremendous. But the real thing came when he was picked against the Indians. While the rebel tours kept the game alive here they seemed to set the rest of the world more firmly against us. Then, at last, we made it out of the wilderness, made it through the ignominy of the Gatting tour, which I thought was the 'wrong tune played at the wrong party', and no one deserved that first official Test cap more than Omar.

'I am certainly of the opinion that Omar is perfectly poised to plough a lot back into the game and give back to the young cricketers what cricket has given him. He is an inspirational player and I believe he is still capable of turning in match-winning performances, but most importantly, he is the right man to encourage the next generation of cricketers. The youngsters worship him and he has shown what can be achieved in spite of all the difficulties. What a tremendous example to all those aspiring kids!'

McHENRY,
THE PRO

At the end of the 1979-80 season at home in South Africa, I prepared myself for another test. My job at Avendale had given me good preparation for my next undertaking, which was to return to the UK as a club professional with all the responsibilities that go with that job.

Not only was I beginning a new phase of my cricketing career, I was going to Scotland rather than England and hence into the unknown. Apart from two trial games played for Poloc at the end of the 1979 season, I really knew nothing about the standards of cricket in Scotland. When I joined Howie Bergins at Micklehurst, at least I had him as a reference point, someone to give me advice about the wickets, how to adjust my game, what kind of players we were coming up against. At Poloc, indeed in Scotland, I had no such reference points. However, I was not the only South African to be playing in the Western Union competition, a league with a long tradition and a fine history. Craig Stirk, a white South African, was playing at nearby West of Scotland.

Poloc Cricket Club has a delightful setting. The ground stands in the wooded park of what was once a country estate on the very edge of the city of Glasgow. The parkland, now publicly owned and made into a country park, is really lovely on a warm summer's day, with Highland cattle grazing in the fields adjoining the cricket field and a river running close to the ground itself. In many respects it is all that you might expect of an English country estate ground – except that, incredibly, it is close to Glasgow's city centre and very much in Scotland.

The experience of playing those two trial games at the end of the previous season had been enough to demonstrate that this was also a very friendly club. I could not have been more warmly welcomed, believe me. However, the club had not been too successful in its recent history. I was following some fairly famous names, including none other than Hanif Mohammad, and I saw it as my job to perform well for them and provide the encouragement and backing to the amateur members of the club and especially to the crop of youngsters I soon found to be so full of promise; and beyond that, of course, to help them to success in the various competitions in which they played. The Western Union is a highly competitive league which was established in 1893, so there was plenty of cricketing history to dwell on. Poloc had first won the title in 1928 but had had to wait until 1956 to win it again. They shared the title in the two following seasons and triumphed again in 1964 but since then had had a barren time of it.

The ten clubs which play in the Western Union are all from west central Scotland, most of them in or near Glasgow. Clydesdale is one of the oldest established clubs in Scotland, having been founded in 1848. Their Titwood ground is magnificent and would, in my opinion, grace the English county game. Titwood is no more than a mile or two away from Poloc's Shawholm ground. On the north side of the River Clyde is Hamilton Crescent, the home of West of Scotland. Although smaller, this too is a magnificent ground and with Titwood frequently plays host to Scotland's international opponents. As a matter of fact, Hamilton Crescent hosted the very first international football match between Scotland and England way back in the 1870s. Uddingston's ground, like Poloc's, is set in an estate, in their case, of Bothwell Castle on the southern fringe of Glasgow near Hamilton. Their closest rivals are Drumpellier from Coatbridge, who play at another quite rural ground, Langloan. Both clubs have long and illustrious histories.

Just to the West of Glasgow lies the old textile town of Paisley which has two teams, Kelburne, who play at Whitehaugh, and Ferguslie, based at Meikleriggs, whilst further west, once at the heart of the Clyde shipping industry, Greenock too has a club of tremendous history and tradition and a delightful, compact ground called Glenpark. The two

Ayrshire clubs, Ayr, who play at Cambusdoon just on the southern fringe of the town – another delightfully picturesque ground – and Kilmarnock, who play at Kirkstyle, also have longstanding traditions.

There have been some pretty famous names in the Western Union. In quite recent times, apart from Hanif, his younger brother Sadiq, who also opened the batting for Pakistan, played for Drumpellier. Another Pakistani, Salah-ud-Din, played for both West of Scotland and Ayr, succeeding that great cricketer Intikhab Alam at Hamilton Crescent when the leg-spinner and latterly Pakistani international team manager departed to play for Surrey. The Australian Bob Massie, who will never be forgotten for his remarkable bowling return against England at Lord's, had several successful seasons with Kilmarnock; Ashley Mallett played for Ayr, who of course produced none other than Mike Denness, who went on to captain England. Many other Test players and overseas stars as well as former professionals from England have graced the cricket grounds of western Scotland, so I had something to live up to, a rookie pro trying to carve out a career for myself in this foreign land.

The fact that I remained for no fewer than 13 seasons in Scotland in itself pays tribute to the friendliness of the people in that cricketing outpost. There is some very good cricket played up there, too. Of one thing you can be sure, they play the game very seriously and very competitively. Needless to say, I found that suited my temperament and my approach to the game. However, I soon found that one of my tasks was to get my new playing colleagues fit, both physically and mentally. I was subsequently to play in the two other main league competitions in Scotland, the East League, based around Edinburgh and Fife, and the Scottish Counties, and everywhere I went, I found the Scottish folk wonderfully friendly and the players themselves eager, to say the least. I really fell in love with Shawholm; its setting, I think, was an inspiration to me. The other inspiration came when I started to look at the young players around the club. There was some real raw talent there, on which I felt confident I could work. What they seemed, above all, to need was motivation and guidance.

My decision to move to Scotland had been difficult. The guys at Micklehurst had indicated that they would like me to become their professional. I was flattered but really felt that I had gone as far as I could in that environment. I had become, in all modesty, one of the leading players in the Saddleworth League. What I needed now was a new challenge, a challenge which would pit me against better players. The Micklehurst players were astonished that I opted for Scotland. Like so many people in England, they were ignorant about cricket north of the border. It was Don Haines, the President of the club, who signed me for Poloc. Later we were to work very closely together in the Scotland set-up because he became Chairman of the Scottish selectors. In addition to my club commitments, I was able to coach at a private school and within no time at all, we had literally hundreds of kids coming to the club which in itself provided an insurance for the club's future prospects. The captain when I first went there was Ron Hogan, who had played for Scotland as a quick bowler. He was an aggressive man and was well aware that changes would have to be made to achieve success. I had enjoyed two great seasons in Lancashire and had become hungry for success. So it was a good combination and we worked really well together.

The cricket in the west of Scotland was very competitive, as I said. There were some really good grounds but again I had to adapt my game to some very slow wickets. It was a problem I had faced during that first expedition to Micklehurst but now, I felt, I was much better equipped to handle it and make the necessary adjustments. But the game had just as much edge in Scotland although one of the advantages they had lay in the structure of the game there, which gave good players the opportunity to climb the ladder. Apart from league cricket, they also had a further senior level in district cricket – select teams from the four District Associations – and then of course those who had aspirations to play at international level had the ultimate goal of playing for Scotland in front of them. In other words, there was a natural progression as, I suppose, there was and is in South Africa.

It is worth remembering that England is very different. The professionalism of the game in England really means that unless a club player shows outstanding talent, outstanding enough to become a professional with a county, the same natural progression from club cricket standard upwards is not available. In Scotland there was a ladder which led to that highest pinnacle of playing for your country, just as there is, in a sense, for club cricketers in, say, South Africa. If you do well enough, you can progress through the Province 'B' XI on to the full Province side. So I quickly recognised that in Scotland there was a natural process of advancement, albeit entirely on an amateur basis.

This meant that there were goals for kids to aim at. You could encourage them because it was easy to identify just how these kids could fulfil ambitions. Of those I initially had contact with there was, for instance, Gareth Kirkwood, a left-handed batsman and useful seam bowler, who, in time, played for Scotland; Donald Orr, a really promising young wicket-keeper-batsman who went on to make the place behind the stumps in the Scotland team his own, and Ronnie McGregor, a left-arm seamer who eventually made it into the Scottish 'B' team. Potentially all of them were good players who, given the opportunity, might have made it to English county cricket.

Needless to say, I found the Scottish dialect initially hard to handle but I soon began to unravel it. I found myself striking comparisons between the warmth of the welcome I had received in Lancashire and the equally warm reception I'd had in Scotland. There is a natural affinity between the north of England and Scotland and it was as easy for me to fit in at Poloc as it had been at Micklehurst. I felt wanted; they made me feel at home and part of them and that encouraged me to put everything I could into this exciting new challenge. It was important to have that kind of background against which you could put in place the kind of structure that would stand the club in good stead in the future and so we practised hard. That in itself was a change. The practice facilities were not so good and very quickly we got the club to invest time in making the net wickets much better and more reliable and I had every co-operation from the club and, of course, from Ron Hogan himself.

It was an exciting time for me. I was a part of a resurgence at the club. The membership began to grow and, above all, parents were sending their kids to the club. The players themselves needed little encouragement to increase their efforts. Perhaps I became the catalyst. Within a matter of weeks, there was a new spirit abroad at Shawholm and if I take some credit for that, then a lot of other people share in it.

By absolute coincidence, the club had found a flat for me in a district called Newlands, so I could not help but feel at home. It was quite close to the ground and I could stroll over there in the morning. In fact, in my second season at Poloc – I had a three-year contract – I also took some responsibility for preparing the ground for games. I got into a routine of going there each morning and helping to prepare the wicket for Saturday's match. If, on one of those rare occasions, we had a dry spell in Glasgow, we would water the wicket, but that was not normally necessary, I can tell you. In the afternoon I would go off to Kelvinside Academy and coach the pupils, some of whom came to Poloc, although many were members at West of Scotland.

Kelvinside was and still is a progressive school and eventually we got an indoor cricket centre there and in time, a bowling machine and a video camera. There were some really good players there. Donald Orr was one of the kids I coached there as well as at Poloc. He was quick to make a breakthrough, appearing for Poloc's first team when he was 14 years of age, a lad with really good hands and a very good sportsman. He once took me on to the golf course and after just one hole, I had been put well in my place. One of the other talented youngsters was Jon Williams, who went on to captain West of Scotland and play for Scotland's 'B' team, and a young Indian lad called Agrawalla, a terrific enthusiast for the game who was eventually signed up by Derbyshire for the 1993 season although unfortunately, through injury, he couldn't play for them. He was an exuberant, bubbly little chap, a good batsman and a very promising leg-spinner.

After my session at the academy, I would return to the club to organise junior practice or get involved in senior practice. It didn't take long to add a fielding practice on Friday nights to the senior nets on Tuesdays and Thursdays.

On the field, things went really well. Ron Hogan really welded Poloc into a good side who played hard and to win. There was always a pride in their performances which ran right through the team. It was a real good-quality side. We had a Kenyan called Muti Kapoor, a leg-spinner who seldom bowled a leggy – it was either a googly or a top-spinner – and another boy of Indian descent, Chris Mukerjee, a really wristy batsman, plus Chris Lafferty... there were so many promising young players but there was a nice balance with experienced players like Tommy Robertson, Hogan himself and Hugh Wyllie. It took time to get everything together and in that first season, if we failed to win anything, at least we made a lot of progress. Derek Underwood's brother Keith captained the second team and he really began to bring on youngsters. We would discuss these youngsters regularly and monitor their progress.

There were some really good professionals around such as Steve Ward, an Australian who played for Greenock and who was picked eventually as Scotland's overseas professional, and Budi Kunderan, who had played as a wicket-keeper-batsman for India. He played for Drumpellier and even when he had finished as a pro, having settled permanently in the Glasgow area, he continued to play for them as an amateur. Brendan Bracewell, the New Zealander who became his country's leading off-spinner, played at Ayr while Clydesdale, one of the strongest teams – in fact they won the League in my first year – had the former Sussex opening batsman Terry Racionzer, a player of real experience, who, after a spell as a county professional, had rejoined the amateur ranks.

The only real weakness I could identify was fitness, which I soon began to work on. The players, I must say, responded magnificently and with terrific enthusiasm. That extra dimension of fitness, plus the skill we had in the team, was, I was sure, bound to pay off.

It wasn't a spectacularly successful season for them and only moderately successful for me personally, but I was certain that having coped with my first season, I could go on to greater things and furthermore that the team could win something. Talent is one thing but motivation is quite another, and during that first season, the fact that we had created competition for places in the first team was motivation enough for the crop of youngsters coming through. I was convinced that in my second season success would follow. And I have to pay tribute to the older members and the committee members who were always so helpful and encouraging.

What was more, I learned a great deal myself. The experience broadened my whole spectrum. Later, when I got married and took my wife with me to Scotland, the welcome for her was just as warm as it had been for me. Even more significant was the upbringing my children had in those circumstances. It was so different from my own background. My kids could grow up in a free society, free to do what they wanted to do, to go where they wanted, when they wanted – so different from the South African upbringing under the law of apartheid which always insisted on divisions and controls. If things are now changing in South Africa, I believe that my children, having spent a good deal of their time in Scotland, had a considerable advantage, not being subject to the same constraints and being treated as equals by both adults and of course their peers.

When I returned to Poloc for a second season in 1981, we really benefited from the build-up we had put into effect the previous season. The more I demanded of the players, the more they seemed to respond. And that was reflected in results because we managed to win the League title. I had also seen a new challenge for me personally. I knew that the Scottish cricket selectors would look seriously at a player who had had two years in the Scottish game and suddenly there opened up before me the possibility that I might play for Scotland. It wasn't that I had lost the belief that I would, one day, play for my native South Africa: this was simply another challenge which presented a whole different range of opportunities.

It should be remembered, however, that whilst I was playing in Scotland during the South African close season, when I returned I was looking to advance my career at home. Currie Cup cricket, in spite of South Africa's isolation in terms of the international game, was still very tough. Perhaps it was even tougher as a result of the absence of Test matches because it represented the ceiling of achievement for our players. And for that kind of cricket, you needed to be physically and mentally fit, prepared. Thus the possibility of playing for Scotland was, I thought, a natural progression for me. It could expose me to higher-class cricket and that could do me nothing but good.

Quite incredibly, that was another dream that was to be fulfilled, for my first game for my newly adopted country was, believe it or not, against Kim Hughes' Australians in 1981 at Titwood on a rather damp day. I didn't do too badly, scored a few runs and took a wicket and was reasonably economical. It really represented a trial for me and after the game I was offered a three-year contract to play for Scotland. It seems strange in retrospect that I should first play against the stars of Australia, not in South Africa but in Scotland. I soon had first-hand experience of the way in which Australians always play their cricket: uncompromising and hard. It really was a formidable side and, on a personal basis, playing against them was a quite wonderful experience for me. I believe that was another of those major turning points in my cricketing career: the chance to appear in an international arena against some of the best players in the world.

The Scottish team was captained by Richard Swan, a man for whom I have tremendous respect and a guy who has done wonders for Scottish cricket. He is someone who, I hope, will play a significant role in the future of Scottish cricket now that he has retired from the game at senior level. It must be admitted that when Scotland first went into the two major English competitions, the Benson & Hedges and the NatWest, they were there for the taking. But they had some good players: Richard Swan himself, Terry Racionzer, Sandy Brown, Jack Ker and a man who I felt should surely have played professional cricket, off-spinner George Goddard. He was a really class spinner who I'm sure will also have much to contribute to the game in Scotland. He always showed such discipline and control. Dallas Moir, the tall left-armer, was another who clearly had the talent. In fact he went on to play for Derbyshire and, I'm sure, would have had a glittering career in first-class cricket. In the end, he basically decided that professional cricket was not for him and I believe that to have been a loss to the game as a whole. They were all good players but in all honesty, they simply weren't fit enough to give a really good account of themselves in one-day cricket against the county professionals. So between us, Richard Swan and I began to look to the younger generation for future Benson & Hedges games.

We certainly needed more flair in the field. One-day cricket is very demanding both physically and mentally. What was vital was the establishment of a higher plane of cricket in Scotland. If you look around the world, and indeed at every sport, there is a natural progression from club, through various grades to the international level. So we set about the business of strengthening the ladder by increasing the number of district games which would bring together the best players in the country and introduce young players to the disciplines necessary to succeed at the higher level. Naturally enough, there were criticisms of our strategy. Tradition dies hard and it dies harder in Scotland, it seems.

Meanwhile, I had signed another contract with Poloc and I must say that apart from the success on the field, what gave me the greatest pleasure was the number of youngsters I was able to bring on. That's how you must look at your job as a professional. It isn't just your own performances that count, or the success of the team. I think that the success of a professional should be judged by the number of youngsters he is able to produce. It is what you, as an individual, as a coach, as a motivator, can bring out of the game.

I seemed to take on this responsibility as a natural course of events. I learned so much about myself. I was always putting myself to the test, examining the contribution, in the widest sense, I was making to the game I love. It is a creative job if you do it properly and if you approach it properly. In many respects, you are constantly examining and extending the boundaries of your own potential. It was very demanding and each morning when I woke up, I found myself thinking about the job, trying to work out what I should do next to improve things, in the broadest sense of the word. I really grew into the job naturally. Each new idea that sprang to mind had to be carefully thought out. I soon realised that it was absolutely pointless to rush at new ideas like a bull at a gate. You had to take the establishment along with you. If at times I have been confrontational in my attitudes, I also learned the discipline of approaching things rather more obliquely. It hasn't always been like that, and it still isn't. My only excuse is that whatever changes I may advocate, in Scotland, in South Africa, indeed in the world, they are, I believe, for the good of the game in general.

My progress with Scotland took me into the Scottish side but it also involved me in coaching too. The Scottish Cricket Union already had a National Coach in David Wilson, who concentrated mostly on youth coaching. My responsibilities were thus confined to the international aspect of the game; coach to the international team and to the 'B' team, which I then captained. This was a tremendous opportunity because it allowed me to look very closely at the youngsters with whom I was playing, examining their potential for the full international team, and travelling the country to see good young players. It was hard on my wife because although she came to Scotland with me, she hardly ever saw me. It was much the same at home in South Africa. All the time my commitment was growing by the minute.

The importance of providing that stepping-stone through district cricket is well illustrated by the Freuchie bowler, David Cowan. He played for the famous village team in Fife, a team which had made history by winning the Village Cup at Lord's, an event which I'm sure rocked the establishment. Imagine what the pundits at Lord's must have thought about kilted pipers appearing on the hallowed turf and, most dramatically, the trophy heading north of the border. But that was what they were, a village team.

The minute I saw him, I recognised that here was a raw talent, a strong boy who could really bowl. He was as strong as an ox. He is a good-ball player, and although perhaps he lacked coaching in his growing years, he definitely had the potential, so he was immediately plucked from the environment of village cricket and thrust into the district team. The proof of the pudding is always in the eating and he certainly proved his worth in the years that were to follow by turning in some really sterling performances for Scotland. It doesn't matter at what level you are talking, Test, county or province cricket, or, in the context of the Scottish game, district, 'B' team or full international games, the test is one of mental strength. You either have that strength or you haven't.

Playing for Scotland also added another dimension for me when we played the professional counties in the Benson & Hedges and NatWest competitions, basically nine or ten amateurs against 11 professionals. Again it was a personal measure for me but it was also a measure for the Scottish players. They could assess their progress and many of them were brought up with something of a start. The problem, in essence, was that most of the Scottish players went into these games with an inferiority complex. It wasn't surprising, of course. After all, it isn't every day you find yourself pitted against players of the calibre of Graham Gooch, John Emburey or Clive Rice. They are hard to live with even if you are yourself a first-class player. I certainly saw it as part of my job to change attitudes and again, there were times when it became somewhat confrontational. There were arguments and disagreements but I always contended that if Scotland, as a cricketing entity, was to make progress, there were many hard lessons to be learned.

Some of the players – good cricketers like Terry Racionzer, who had first-class experience – tended to sit on their bats somewhat and forget the scoring rate that was necessary to provide a genuine challenge to the county teams. Against them, you have to keep the score moving, the strike rotating, if you are to compete with them. Otherwise they simply steamroller you. I wanted to instil a real sense of pride in them. The number of caps, as far as I was concerned, was irrelevant. What mattered was how the team performed and how many times they got a result. The simple answer in the second case was of course, at that stage, never!

In that first season in Scotland with Poloc in 1980, I must say that I was very impressed by the standard of cricket, impressed by the technical standards and the enthusiasm. It certainly compared very favourably with the cricket I had seen in Lancashire. But those traditions had to be overcome. There had to be a new approach and eventually we began to coax young players to have sufficient belief in themselves to compete more vigorously, even against the county teams.

There were bitter pills to swallow and I remember games when we were absolutely obliterated by teams like Derbyshire, Nottinghamshire and Lancashire. Imagine the leap that has to be made by young players from league cricket suddenly finding themselves facing someone like Colin Croft at Old Trafford. That was the challenge that confronted Russell Jones from Clydesdale when he came into the side. Batting in the top order, he suddenly found himself with hardly a ball in his half, almost every ball searing past his nose.

For my part, I found it to be a tremendous experience, an exposure to world-class players which I couldn't have enjoyed anywhere else. On a very personal basis, it was another challenge to me and another step in my personal ladder.

The experience of facing Richard Hadlee, when he played for Nottinghamshire, was absolutely invaluable. And of course, there were great batsmen like David Gower at whom to bowl. All this was part of my further cricketing education. Bowling at Clive Lloyd, David Lloyd, batting against the likes of John Lever, all added to the experience I was gaining.

By this time, of course, I was playing Currie Cup cricket in South Africa. My honest assessment was that man for man, Currie Cup cricket was marginally tougher than English county cricket, at least in terms of the home-grown players. The difference perhaps was reflected in the fact that when Scotland, played against the counties, we were always facing two or three world-class cricketers, every time; the Javed Miandads, Gordon Greenidges, Malcolm Marshalls, Courtney Walshes and Robin Smiths of this world. To me it simply opened up my entire cricketing life.

To be honest, I believe that English county cricket is too intensive. I know they have to make money for the game, provide good Test players for England and of course get people to come through the gates. It is big business these days and I'm afraid that the need to make money has become too much of a driving force in the game in the UK. I certainly applaud the new four-day format because I believe it provides a better structure for English cricket. Cricket, like a car, needs servicing from time to time and the servicing takes place at the nets. If you are spending all your time hurtling from one place to another, playing one game on a slow turner, the next on a green-top and the next on a flat, easy-paced wicket, you need to attune yourself. Cricket, more than any other game, is about mental strengths. It is a game of the mind as much as it is a game which demands physical strength and stamina. I firmly believe that you can even go into a Test arena without necessarily being equipped with the best technique in the world and, if you are mentally prepared, succeed. Look at Allan Lamb; he doesn't always play according to the MCC coaching manual of my youth but it is amazing just how often he hits the ball with the middle of the bat and seldom gets an edge.

My days with Poloc were happy days. We won the Western Union twice in my time there and the Scottish Cup once when we beat Greenock in the final. On that memorable occasion, we batted first and frankly didn't make too good a fist of it on a damp wicket, scoring only 127. Greenock, always a good side, started well but gradually got into trouble. Unfortunately, one of our bowlers, Tommy Robertson, was injured and couldn't complete his spell so our captain, Lee Creasey, had to fill in but whilst Greenock seemed to tense up, we bowled tightly and we started to take wickets. They began to panic and we managed to bowl them out. Their off-spinner Charlie Stewart always seemed to be my *bête noir*. He used to get me out regularly and he did it again on this occasion. And they had Jack Clark and Peter Duthie, both of them internationals – a pretty useful attack. But we fielded particularly well and won the Cup with a real team effort. I also think we were a fitter side and that gave us, as much as anything, the edge.

In the following season, 1985, we met Greenock once again in the final but this time the roles were reversed and, without taking anything away from them, it was a matter of us losing the game rather than them winning it. Nevertheless, it was a tremendous fillip for the club to be in the final for two successive years.

It was a tremendous time for me at Poloc. There was a marvellous spirit and a lot of very good players emerged from the junior ranks. I worked hard in those years; so did the players, and they deserved the successes they enjoyed. But after six years, the time had come for me to move on. By now I had been appointed as official player-coach by the SCU and was registered as their overseas player. However, in 1983 I once again found myself at odds with the selectors. Confrontation again...

I wanted to bring in some younger players but there were those who wanted to stick by the old guard. Hamish More, a veteran of the Scotland team in the past, and I were at odds over the selection of the team to play Ireland in the annual three-day game. I wanted the young Aberdeenshire all-rounder Mike Smith in the side but some of the selectors disagreed with me. They suggested that Mike had an attitude problem but I was convinced he had the basic ability and maintained that he could be worked on. He was cocky, all right, and perhaps lacked some respect for the game. But I wanted him in and, as it happened, when someone else withdrew he did make it. However, the incident served to drive a wedge between me and some of the other selectors. The result was that in 1984, the SCU decided to axe me and Desmond Haynes, the West Indian, was engaged as our overseas player.

Desmond is a fine player, one of the best in the world, but he wasn't playing his cricket in Scotland and furthermore, the early qualifying rounds of the Benson & Hedges are of course played at the beginning of the season in April when the wickets, especially in Scotland, are notoriously soft. Unfortunately, he hardly scored a run for them and his selection was therefore something of a disaster.

I was restored to the fold the following season and with Morrison Zuill as Chairman of Selectors, I once again tried to introduce some new ideas. Again, there was resistance. Tradition yet again won the day against real progress. I wanted to set up a new Area Championship, the vital stepping-stone between league cricket and international cricket. I did manage to institute practice camps for players we thought were good enough to be in or on the fringe of the international squad, but I was keen to introduce an Area Championship League to run throughout the season, played as a longer game in order to give the players better experience. I was delighted when, almost ten years later, in 1993, a full and proper Area Championship League was eventually set up.

So once again I found myself at odds with the authorities. I just wanted to change things to better equip Scotland at international level; to instil a kind of professional approach and create a ladder whereby young players could progress through the game and become better performers. I just didn't believe that the men in charge had enough courage or vision and in the end they settled for a kind of halfway house. One of the problems in Scotland is that there are not enough people who understand the professional game. Yet they were heading more and more towards first-class cricket with more and more emphasis being placed on the Benson & Hedges and NatWest games.

There was a new generation of cricketers beginning to emerge, many of whom were to eventually play for Scotland. I was keen to have six area teams – 66 players – playing against each other on a regular basis. In other words, the best against the best. This creates a system by which the cream of players can rise to the top. And I must say that Richard Swan, the Scottish captain, backed me all the way. The opposition was based on cost but I always believed that sponsorship could be found and that an integrated system which would give each area its own coach, for juniors as well as seniors, was the right way ahead.

Perhaps I was over-imbued with the spirit of progress and a belief that, given the commitment on the part of the players and the self-belief, Scotland could really compete and give the counties a good run for their money.

There are parallels to be drawn between this situation and the one in which I found myself when I returned to work for the Boland Cricket Board in 1993 with the responsibility of organising development. The problem we face and have faced for so many years in South Africa has been apartheid, and it will take some time for that legacy to disappear. In Scotland, there are also divisions. At school level, for instance, private schools very much dominate the scene, so there is a distinct danger of there being a divide there, too – but on the basis of class rather than colour. In other words, there are too many youngsters in Scotland who do not have the opportunity to play cricket because they do not go to the right schools.

Just to give you a classic example, when I first went to Glasgow, I remember going to a primary school in the east end of the city near Parkhead, home of Glasgow Celtic. The kids knew nothing about cricket at all but a couple of sessions proved to me that there were plenty there who had a real talent for the game, good hand-to-eye co-ordination, good ball sense – but no opportunity to actually play the game, even though some of them got quite excited about cricket. And this in spite of the fact that the kids at first believed that the game was, as they put it, a 'poofter's' game. They soon changed their tune but they had no opportunity to follow it up.

And when I went to Kelvinside Academy, I soon saw that even in the private sector they needed better facilities and the stimulus to improve things. Because they had a number of interested people at the school – the headmaster was the father of Colin Mair, who became captain of the successful West of Scotland team – they did something about it and before long a string of good players was emerging from the school. Those boys were lucky: they had the opportunity.

There is, without question, a natural talent in many Scottish kids which has manifested itself in the great golfers, rugby players and footballers Scotland has produced. If that talent could be harvested and harnessed, Scotland could produce so many good cricketers that they could really make an impact in the international game.

I fear that many of the administrators are not well enough equipped to handle the rate of progress which I think could be achieved in Scotland. There are not enough people who have a professional enough background. Perhaps it is past generations of administrators who should shoulder the blame because I know that cricket has a long and distinguished history in Scotland; that much earlier in the century, it was not unusual for thousands of people to attend cricket matches. There is a picture at Poloc which shows the crowd five or six deep right round the ground. I have no doubt at all that Scotland could, with the right financial backing and with a real effort to spread the game, compete on an international basis. Why can Scotland not follow the route followed by Sri Lanka? It would be a great asset for the ICC because the UK plays cricket when most of the other nations are in their close season. So it would offer the chance for countries in the Southern Hemisphere to stage tours in Scotland as well as in England.

I have never been convinced that the Benson & Hedges and NatWest was necessarily the right route for Scotland to follow. I know they applied for ICC membership in 1993 but they should perhaps have trodden that road much earlier and with much greater enthusiasm. Again, I blame the Scottish administrators for a lack of vision in not aiming to establish an international dimension to the game. Playing against English counties does not represent an international dimension. Scotland is a separate country and it deserves therefore to have the opportunity to play on the international stage, no matter at what level.

I sincerely hope that their application to join the ICC, which was rejected in 1993, succeeds in 1994 and that they will go on to play in the Mini World Cup and thence, it is to be hoped, in the World Cup proper. But there needs to be an integrated set-up in Scotland, a structure which encompasses the clubs, the schools and, vitally, the universities. But to achieve that I suspect there will have to be many changes in the structure of the SCU and furthermore, changes in the kind of people running the game. There are people who could take Scotland through the blueprint stage and make real progress. There is no place for 'nice' people. What is needed are people with vision and dynamism.

Back in 1985 and 1986 however, all these things were well beyond the horizon. I was back in the fold and there was a job to be done. I had, in 1986, moved on from Poloc to Stenhousemuir because I wanted to broaden my experience in other leagues in Scotland. I think I had done as much as I could at Shawholm and I needed a new challenge.

It was of course a momentous year for Scottish cricket because we pulled off a fantastic win over Lancashire at Perth in the Benson & Hedges. They were regarded as one of the best one-day sides in the game with players like Clive Lloyd, Patrick Patterson, Graeme Fowler, John Abrahams, Mike Watkinson and Neil Fairbrother – some great cricketers.

The Perth wicket was typically slow for so early in the season and so I was surprised that they elected to play Patterson and go in without Clive Lloyd. It wasn't a wicket for him at all and of course he could bowl only 11 overs. What was needed on a wicket like that was someone who could bowl good line and length and do a bit with the ball. That, I think, was their first mistake. The second was to underestimate us. We had begun to gain in confidence and we were not quite as fearful, even of Patterson – even less so on that particular wicket. There was a determination on the part of the Scottish guys to underline that Scotland were no longer the pushover they had been in the past.

We batted first and, on that slow track, did reasonably well with everyone chipping in, but we really won it in the field. It is also worth remembering that the Lancashire players were in a different environment. The North Inch in Perth is a very open ground. Needless to say, there are no stands and so it was a strange setting for players used to playing half their cricket at Old Trafford. Our fielding was really tight and every time they got a partnership going, we seemed to get a wicket. Richard handled the bowling really well. Every time we got a wicket, he brought back our best bowlers. Willie Donald bowled especially well that day but so too did Alan Stevenson, the off-spinner, and Peter Duthie. There was real desire, real commitment and it was the Lancashire heads that went down. I played my part and I like to think that I helped to galvanise the players into having the hunger to triumph on that historic day. Perhaps because I had come from a different background, I was able to bring, in some way, a different dimension to the game. What we had begun to threaten had at last been achieved. It was a great win and, in retrospect, it was one of those events in my cricketing life which I shall always remember with pride and affection, not perhaps as memorable as making my debut at Newlands or when I was a part of that Orange Free State team that carried off the Castle Cup, but memorable nonetheless.

It was a just reward for the captain, Richard Swan. Richard was always a gentleman, a man you could trust. He loves the game and his vision is something which I feel it is vital is not lost to Scottish cricket. I don't believe he was given adequate backing and he might perhaps reflect now that in the early years he was perhaps sometimes too much of a gentleman and regret that he was not firmer with the authorities. Richard is a farmer and so he is under tremendous pressure during the summer. Nevertheless he gave a great deal to the game and put in a tremendous amount of effort and time. We didn't always agree, for instance on bowling changes or field settings, but we were always able to discuss things rationally and without rancour. In fact we really did become great friends over the years and I like to think there was a mutual respect between us. I certainly respected him both as a man and for his cricketing judgement.

He was also a fine player because he, more than most Scottish batsmen, was capable of playing off the back foot. Technically he was in essence very correct. As a captain, he did not always have the best of material to work with but there were some fine seam bowlers like Jack Clark from Greenock and Frank Robertson from Aberdeenshire, who had a bit of pace about him, and of course he also had some good spinners, notably Dallas Moir and George Goddard. But we never had any real pace, so the attack was much of a muchness when compared with that of the county professionals. It was particularly evident when we went to play our games in England on firmer, faster wickets on which batsmen could play on the up.

Gradually, as the transition began to roll forward and we brought in younger, fitter players, we began to gain even more confidence. A couple of years later, of course, we had Clive Rice as our overseas professional. He too made an impact, even if he never quite managed to perform at his best for us. But he did bring that extra degree of professionalism which undoubtedly rubbed off on the team. He was a tremendous team man and always commanded 100 per cent respect, which also helped to lift the team. I think some people thought that he under-performed but the impact he made was not just as a player: it was also the contributions he could make with a few quiet words to the other players. He was, above all, always positive and I personally think his presence had a much greater and longer-lasting effect than people outside the dressing room understood.

However, it was to be a year or two before Scotland managed another win against a first-class county, by which time we had a completely rejigged team. In fact, in 1990, we came closer to qualifying for the second round than we have ever come. Although we managed to beat Northamptonshire at Northampton to record only our second Benson & Hedges victory, the crucial game had been played over the preceding two days in Glasgow when we entertained Nottinghamshire at Titwood. The weather ensured that the game would be played over two days rather than one. Notts, of course, were the Cup-holders, a powerful team with Test stars such as Chris Broad, their captain Tim Robinson, Derek Randall and Bruce French. They also had in their side Franklyn Stephenson, with whom I was later to play for Orange Free State, and a man who could turn a game in a matter of minutes.

We did well to reach 208 for 6. We had in our side Gordon Greenidge, the great West Indian opening batsman, who had just retired from the first-class game and was playing as a professional for Greenock. Unfortunately, having scored a magnificent 50 in the first game against Essex, he was caught off Stephenson for just 1 in the Titwood game. Richard Swan gave the innings a really solid middle with a gritty innings of 53 and I had one of my best B&H knocks for Scotland, going in at number 6, with an unbeaten 62. The crucial partnership between the captain and myself, which saw us add 90 for the 5th wicket, gave us a real chance.

Things went well for us at the start on the second day – rain had shortened the first day's play – for we had both Broad and Pollard back in the pavilion with only 20 on the board, the big England left-hander bowled by David Cowan and Pollard removed through a catch by Greenidge off Jeremy Moir. But Tim Robinson really bedded in with support from Paul Johnson to take them to 95 before Johnson was bowled by Clarence Parfitt. Clarrie was absolutely superb that day. His figures alone speak volumes for his bowling performance. In his 11 overs he conceded only 16 runs and took 4 vital wickets, including those of Randall and Stephenson. Originally from Bermuda, Clarence had played in Scotland for several years during which time he had become the scourge of Scottish batsmen with his unique variety of left-arm spin, delivered at almost medium pace. It was a wicket that suited him but he really did bowl magnificently. Any Test player would have been proud of those figures.

Yet the luck just didn't run our way. I picked up a side injury which was so painful that I had to be taken to hospital. Consequently I bowled only one over and Richard had to use Mike Smith, in as an all-rounder and expected to be used only as a back-up bowler if at all. In the event he had to bowl the rest of my overs, 10 of them in all, and Notts ran out winners with 6 wickets down and only 4 balls to spare.

It was a game of ifs. If a catch the Scottish players were convinced Bruce French had offered behind had been given out; if I had not been injured. So near, yet so far.

I wasn't able to play the following day against Northants, nor was my mate Allan Lamb able to play for the opposition. Again Scotland found themselves batting first and Gordon Greenidge and Iain Philip, with whom I had played at Stenhousemuir, put on 54 for the 1st wicket in spite of the bowling presence of Curtly Ambrose. Swannie had another good innings, this time showing plenty of aggression, and a total of 231 for 8 was a commendable effort. Wayne Larkins looked as if he was going to win the game single-handed but him apart the Northants early order was whittled away by some fine bowling from Moir, Cowan and Dougie Brown, who had learned his cricket with Clackmannan County but by then was on Warwickshire's staff. It was really tense towards the end with Brown brilliantly running out fellow Scot Jim Govan, who had a typically battling knock of 30 late in the innings, with a superb throw, but in the end the Scots scraped home by 2 runs for a really tremendous victory. How I wished I could have been out there with the boys and how sad it was that we had just failed against Notts.

I was fit enough to play against Leicestershire later in the week in the final match but although we did reasonably well to reach 215 for 8 with me top-scoring with 48, it was never quite enough on a wicket which I must say rolled out for the Leicester batsmen. Nigel Briers had a fine 93 not out as they cruised to victory with 3.5 overs in hand. On that occasion, our seamers couldn't get it quite right and although Clarence and I, with our contrasting styles, bowled tightly (0 for 39 and 0 for 29 respectively), there were never quite enough runs in the bank.

It was unquestionably our most successful campaign in the Benson & Hedges. It is sad that the qualifying rounds have now gone, denying Scotland the kind of adventures in which we were involved during that memorable week against Notts and Northants. What was so frustrating for me was that I have hardly ever been injured badly enough to miss a game in my whole life. But I can tell you the pain I felt was extreme, to say the least. At one time I thought it was my heart because the pain was right across my chest. It seemed to be a pulled muscle or a muscular spasm and it couldn't have come at a worse time.

I was proud of the way the Scottish team took on and beat a powerful Northants side and Iain Philip certainly well deserved his Man of the Match award for a superb knock of 95 in which he produced some of the best square-cutting I've seen from any batsman. It proved something to the players and if, since then, they have not quite scaled the same heights, they have given a few teams a scare or two: Sussex at Hove in 1991, when they lost by only 4 runs on the last ball and Hampshire who, I believe, were saved by the rain at Hamilton Crescent when staggering on 19 for 3 chasing 150 with their captain Mark Nicholas out of action with a broken bone sustained when fielding. So Scotland certainly have had their moments. What a pity their involvement in the Benson & Hedges is now down to one game. I can't think that is good for the game of cricket in the more outlying parts of the UK.

I'll return to that 1990 season in due course but it is worth dwelling for a minute or two on Gordon Greenidge that season. He, like Clive Rice, had a presence: a few quiet words here and there; his demeanour at the wicket; the way he scored his runs – even if he only had one 50 – you could feel the confidence flowing from him throughout the team. If we could see more professionals like Gordon going to Scotland, the game there would be richer. Whether a professional is a Test player

or not, what counts is what he can re-invest in the game. It is no use a
pro just going to the nets, practising and then going out on a Saturday
and playing merely for performances and figures. He must be prepared
to put back into the game what he has got out of it, and that is what
Gordon Greenidge did.

As a club pro, you have to live with your team; you have to be
absolutely honest with your club and with yourself. That was how
Gordon Greenidge went about his job and it came as something of a
surprise to me when he wasn't re-engaged by Scotland as their overseas
pro when he returned to Greenock in 1992. I always believed it
reflected badly on the administrators and also illustrated the divide
that exists between east and west – Edinburgh and Glasgow – which is
in itself so counter-productive but, unhappily, very much part and
parcel of how Scottish cricket seems to be run.

Cricket in the west of Scotland is tough. They play aggressively; they
are cocky and they have a belief in the quality of the game there.
However, they sometimes take their parochialism too far and it took
them some time to begin to build for the future. Now, however, they
seem to be on course with some excellent youth coaching schemes. By
contrast, the players from the east of Scotland never seem to want to
play against teams from the west. The East League was not quite as
competitive, perhaps reflecting the gentility of the capital city. There
are perhaps too many preconceived notions about what it takes to be
a good cricketer; too much emphasis perhaps on correct technique,
slight detachment from the reality of competitive cricket. And the
County Championship was a kind of mixture of the two. Aberdeenshire,
for instance, were a tremendous team when I first went into the
counties with Arbroath. They had plenty of good youngsters too.

I have sometimes thought that too often the quality of aggression
which is so important if you want to be a winner is forgotten. In my
limited experience of watching cricket in the Borders, where there is
such a strong tradition of rugby and ball-playing skills, there is plenty
of aggression in their cricket but seldom is it properly harnessed.

There has been much debate about a National League in Scotland.
I have very mixed feelings about such an idea. It is my belief that the
Area Championship is a much more important competition to concentrate

on, especially as it has now been extended with sponsorship help from the Royal Bank of Scotland. Because this competition palpably brings together the best players in the country on a regular basis, I believe it provides the basis for the future. It is the testing ground for potential international players.

● ● ● ● ● ● ● ● ● ● ● ● ● ● ● ● ●

RONNIE McGREGOR

Ronnie McGregor was one of the crop of youngsters who benefited from the arrival of Omar Henry in Scotland. He was a junior member at Poloc when Omar arrived at the club in 1980, broke through into the Poloc first team and then later moved to Ferguslie, where he became one of the leading medium-pace bowlers in the west of Scotland. Now playing for Clydesdale, he made his way into the Scotland 'B' team and also toured Pakistan some years ago with a Scottish select side, turning in impressive figures on the unhelpful wickets in Pakistan. He remains one of the most effective seamers in the game in Scotland.

'I first met Omar in 1979 when he played two trial games for Poloc in the Western Union. His successes in these games led to the club employing him for the next six seasons, a spell which brought great success to a club that had spent too many years in the doldrums. Records show that his many all-round displays led to three League Championships and success in the Scottish Cup. However, to attempt to quantify his contribution during this spell in terms of "gongs", personal performances and statistics would be to belittle the effect that Omar had on the club and its players.

'Many clubs believed that Omar *was* Poloc and that to overcome the team they only had to take care of him. But Omar was able to bring the best out of everyone around him by getting them to realise how big a part they could play and by encouraging them to play in the most positive fashion. This not only brought further success in competitions for which Omar, as a professional, was not eligible, but also his efforts made some average players achieve personal successes of which even they thought they were incapable. He eventually moved on to play with Stenhousemuir, Arbroath and West Lothian and brought success to all these clubs by employing the same philosophy.

'Long before leaving Poloc, he had already become involved in the Scottish national team set-up and it came as no surprise to those of us who had played with him just how much of an effect he had on the development of our national team.

'From the outset of his time in Scotland, Omar actively encouraged any players who wanted to go overseas to develop their cricketing skills and experience, knowing that in the long run this would be beneficial to Scottish cricket. It must please him to see just how much many of these players have improved and also to see how many native players are now being employed as professionals by Scottish clubs.

'He was also at the forefront in trying to put in place a structure to bring the best players to the top of our game. He lobbied long and hard for a meaningful District Championship as a link between club and international cricket and it was somewhat ironic that in the first season in which he was no longer directly involved, 1993, this finally came to fruition with a season-long home-and-away Championship. That the winning district should then go on to beat all comers in the British Championship would indeed have been very sweet music to Omar's ears.

'In 1990, it was my good fortune to play under his management on my debut Scotland "B" trip to Leicestershire and Nottinghamshire. My abiding memory of this trip as a somewhat late arrival on the international scene was the great respect and affection all the other younger players had for Omar as a coach and motivator. He even managed to convince this ageing cynic that, underneath all the irrelevant distractions, the innate abilities of Scottish players are every bit as good as those of their English professional counterparts.

'That he is no longer involved in Scottish cricket is a source of great personal sadness to me as we encounter precious few people of his calibre to help develop our game further. But the mark of Omar Henry remains in the many people he has brought through the system and it falls to them to ensure that his legacy will continue to bear fruit for many years to come.'

• • • • • • • • • • • • • • • • •

GRAHAM GOOCH

Former England captain, who played with Omar Henry
for Western Province.

'I first met Omar when I toured South Africa with the English SAB XI back in 1982, and over the next seasons or so, I was to appreciate his value to the whole Western Province team. He won many an exciting contest for us on those windy nights in the Green Point stadium.

'He has come a long way since those evenings, via Scotland, and eventually he represented his country. And, of course, he also played for Scotland. A more unlikely looking Scot I have never seen! Maybe if he had ginger hair it would be more feasible!

'He turned up a few years back to play for the "Jocks" against Essex at Chelmsford in the Benson & Hedges Cup qualifying rounds. Well, they caught us on a bad day and we totalled over 300 runs in our 55 overs. Omar's flighted left-arm spin was, I'm afraid, carted, slogged and smashed into and sometimes over the nearby River Cam.. Suffice it to say that they came second and could not claim another famous victory over the English.

'It obviously didn't affect him, for he went on to make it to the full South African side. I'm pleased that he achieved this as it is every sportsman's goal to play for his country, an honour he well deserved for his wholehearted efforts for the game of cricket.'

SCOTLAND THE BRAVE

My move from Poloc after six very happy years was prompted, as I have already said, by my desire to gain experience of the other major competitions in Scotland.

Stenhousemuir, who play in the East League, engaged me as a replacement for the magical Pakistani leg-spinner Abdul Qadir – quite an act to follow! At that time he was probably the world's leading leg-spinner and he had certainly made an impact, dominating the League and taking them to the League title. He had spent just one season there but because he was a bit of a character, an individual, one season, apparently, was enough for both him and the club.

This was a side which boasted plenty of experience but frankly, there was little in the way of young talent coming through. They were in danger of coming to something of a dead end once their experienced players had come to the end of their careers. As I have already emphasised, it is vital to bring youngsters through the system and blood them gently. Qadir had done no coaching at all, yet Stenhousemuir is ideally placed to harvest young talent. Several schools are close at hand. For some years, therefore, they had not bought their insurance for the future, not invested, and there was a real job to be done. Here was the challenge, then; just the sort of challenge to which I respond with enthusiasm.

There were some quality players in the side. Douglas Zuill, son of

Morrison, who had been one of the most prolific batsmen in Scottish cricket, was one of the few really talented young players. Not surprisingly, with his pedigree, he was in essence a correct batsman, but I always felt that he tended to play with 'hard hands'. Sometimes touch is so important in batting, especially when playing against spinners, and it was perhaps such touch that was missing. In Graham Gardener, they had a really good all-round cricketer, tall and whippy as a bowler and a really good natural striker of the ball as a batsman. However, I felt that perhaps he had not been made to work hard enough on his game by the senior players.

Their batting was largely built around Iain Philip who, although born locally, had emigrated to Australia as a youngster and really learned his cricket there. In fact he had played club cricket in Western Australia for the same club as Barry Richards, one of South Africa's really great batsmen and a man who, of course, had plundered thousands of runs from the English game during his time with Hampshire. The experience of playing with such a magnificent batsman had undoubtedly rubbed off on Iain.

Iain's single-minded approach to the game reflected that association. He simply will not allow bowlers to get on top of him and always scores his runs in good time. He is run-hungry and furthermore he is a man who hates losing: vital qualities for a batsman who was, in the years ahead, to make a considerable mark playing for Scotland. He took on the English county bowlers as to the manner born. When we played together at Stenhousemuir, he always wanted to dominate the strike but then, of course, I wanted to do precisely the same once I had got in and that led to some conflict between us. He many times suggested to me that he was the senior player, in spite of the fact that he was playing as an amateur and I as the pro. It certainly added a little spice to our partnerships. In other words he played his cricket essentially in the mould of a professional, which was what made him so successful against the counties. He did not think himself to be in any way inferior to them. In time, of course, he did become a professional with Poloc, then for Selkirk and later for Stenhousemuir.

He has his own particular style, always looking to move back and across and thus he is able to play well off the back foot, always a priceless asset at that level of cricket. The technique he employed can be very successful but if, as inevitably will happen, the timing of the movement falters, it can spell trouble and on the few occasions that happened, then the two of us would go down to the nets and work on it, trying to get the timing right again. He and I were kindred spirits and if we didn't always see eye to eye, we did get on well and in some respects, became a team within a team (without, I hasten to add, interfering with the welfare of the team as a whole).

Iain always harboured ambitions of captaining Scotland and in time, it became evident that he would have to be considered, along with his very successful opening partner in the Scottish team, Bruce Patterson, who harboured similar ambitions. We gave both of them a try but I always felt that the establishment was a little nervous of them. They are both pretty outspoken and that didn't always go down too well in the committee circles. My own eventual accession to the captaincy of Scotland came when Richard Swan decided to step down. At that time, there was really no one else to do the job and as, in effect, I had been his second in command, I was perhaps the natural successor.

Stenhousemuir is a fairly clannish club. I didn't feel there was enough enthusiasm and backing for me in my efforts to bring on young players, so after helping them to a second successive title in 1986, after which we drifted out of the picture as Grange won the League the following year, I once again felt it was time to move on. The Stenhousemuir ground, called the Tryst because this is where the old cattle markets – the Falkirk Tryst – were held in days gone by, can be a lovely place to play on a summer's day with the larks rising and singing from the golf course nearby, but when it is grey and dull, because of its exposed nature, no matter where the wind blows from it can be bleak!

My next port of call was Arbroath, who had just gained entry to the Scottish County Championship from the Strathmore Union. Arbroath provided quite a contrast. Whereas the old heads and older players dominated the scene at Stenhousemuir, Arbroath was absolutely full of young players and they had the enthusiasm to match. Arbroath is situated on the east coast of Scotland, between Aberdeen and Dundee, and is famous for its 'smokies' – smoked herrings. Because it is on the eastern side of the country, it is drier than either Poloc or Stenhousemuir.

However, if it did rain, there were no covers at Lochlands Park, which is a neat and enclosed ground.

If anything, the people at Arbroath were even more friendly and there was a really happy atmosphere at the club. Clarence Parfitt had been their professional and he had obviously done a great deal of work with the juniors. Known as the 'Underwood of the north', Clarence was perhaps even brisker than the famous England left-armer and, many might say, even more lethal on a helpful wicket. What immediately impressed me was that every time I went to the ground, there were always children playing cricket on the outfield. I had the feeling therefore that this was a club with a really good long-term future.

The captain, Neil Burnett, was an Arbroath lad but had gone to play for Aberdeenshire to better himself. Now he was back. He is a good player, bats well and is a useful medium-paced bowler who was capped by Scotland. Yet he never quite broke through to the international squad on a permanent basis, partly, perhaps, because he lacked opportunity and partly because he lacked that extra yard of pace as a bowler. He might also have worked a little harder on his fitness, but then, that is a familiar story. I may sometimes seem somewhat hyper-critical of some players because they do not work hard enough either on their game or indeed on their fitness – and it may be that I should temper that view – I know that the amateur may have family responsibilities as well as a job to hold down.

Perhaps because I made cricket my full-time occupation – my profession – I expected too much of the amateur players but my time in Scotland probably taught me that I had to come to terms with this dichotomy and find the right balance between the ideal and reality. For those playing in the Scottish Counties competition, there was an additional burden in the relatively long distances they sometimes had to travel compared with their counterparts in the Western Union and East League.

There were plenty of good players on the county circuit and at Arbroath we had some very talented youngsters. Murray Clarke, a young wicket-keeper, I recognised immediately as someone who had really good hands. He was also, in the hallmark of all wicket-keepers, always busy and a somewhat unorthodox batsman.

The legacy I inherited from Clarence Parfitt was a healthy situation. He had worked hard with them, spent many hours with them – and it showed. Clarrie is a big, imposing man, an effervescent personality, but central to his character is his real love for the game of cricket. I have always had tremendous admiration for him as a bowler. He imparts real spin, spears the ball in at batsmen and is deadly accurate. He works on the basis of if they miss, he hits! He was eminently capable, because of his accuracy, to bowl to a 7-2 field and I'm quite sure, if he had wanted to, even to a 9-0 field!

He was probably the most effective spinner ever to grace Scottish cricket grounds but he had that ability, so essential in a professional, to relate to the kids in his charge. Yet he can be a volatile man. There was an occasion when it fell to me, as the captain of the Scottish team, to tell him that he had been left out of the final XI for a Benson & Hedges game. He was not at all pleased but after some straight talking between us, he accepted the decision and still wanted to remain a member of the squad. The fact was that at nearly 50 years of age, he could not make the contribution I thought so vital to our cause in the field, or indeed with the bat.

Clarence had of course played for Bermuda in the Mini World Cup and I am quite sure that had he come to the UK as a young man, he would have made a tremendous impact upon the game at any level. His 'arm' ball was, as I sometimes found to my cost, lethal and it was utterly fascinating watching him bowl at the experienced county pros. I remember one game in particular, an early-season friendly against Worcestershire at New Road. I persuaded him to let me pack the off-side field and the pros could hardly score a run off him. He tied them down completely.

New Road was also a happy venue for me. It was in one of those early-season warm-up games that I was able to show off my own talents to that boyhood hero of mine, Basil D'Oliveira, by then the coach at Worcester. I hadn't seen Basil in years.

We lost a few early wickets to the pace of Neal Radford and the swing of Phil Newport. Newport had just joined the county and he was a remarkable bowler. In spite of the fact that he seemed to deliver the ball from such a chest-on action, he still managed to make it go away from the right-hander. I was to play with him for Boland in subsequent years. In the event, I managed to reach three figures, latterly farming the bowling to shield our tail-enders, an innings which gave me a great deal of pleasure and satisfaction. That game also gave me a close look at Richard Illingworth, a bowler I admired because, like me, he seemed prepared to work so hard at his game, an effort which later rewarded him with Test caps for his country. I was also to come across him when he played for a while in South Africa.

And of course there was Graeme Hick. He had such a reputation and I can remember bowling at him and experiencing the power he unleashes when he really goes for his shots. Oddly enough, on that occasion he was hit on the helmet by our Peter Duthie, who not even the most ardent Greenock fan would claim to be particularly brisk, a taste perhaps of what the young Rhodesian was to find himself contending with when he finally qualified to play for England. He is, of course, a tall man who stands up straight at the wicket and who has an inclination, almost an instinct, to come naturally on to the front foot from where he certainly does hit the ball with enormous power. However, as we all know, he has looked less certain when the ball is flying round his chest or ears. Yet he is a good puller and hooker. I am inclined to think that he has to make up his mind more positively what to do – either duck the short-pitched stuff, or get inside it and hook and pull. I enjoyed bowling to him but must confess that he did get hold of me on one or two occasions and it was just a question of the fielder going to fetch the ball!

But it was the century that gave me so much satisfaction. It was as if I was showing Basil that the faith he had placed in me as a 15-year-old, when he wanted to take me to the UK almost as a surrogate son, was somehow justified. If I was pleased with my knock I can tell you he was even more pleased, and after the day's play, he simply couldn't stop talking about the time he had 'discovered' me as a teenager and how pleased he was to see me succeeding in the game. I felt that in some way I had paid back the man's faith in me that day.

I think at this stage any vague ambitions I might have had about playing county cricket had faded. However, much to my surprise, I was approached in 1989 by Derbyshire. Initially, I had played for Scotland as an overseas player but later, when I had served the qualification period, I assumed that I could be registered as a home-based player. We went down to Derby and we looked at houses and were all prepared to sell the little semi-detached house I had by then acquired in Bo'ness in central Scotland. It came as something of a surprise because by then I was not too far off 40 years of age, very late indeed to start a county career. But of course Kim Barnett was well aware of my credentials, having played with me at Boland, and he clearly felt I could do a job for them, not only as a spinner but as a middle-order batsman as well.

Everything seemed to be signed, sealed and settled but then came the snag. The TCCB decided that I was only qualified to play for Scotland and thus would have had to be registered as an overseas player for Derbyshire. I was baffled by the decision and indeed there were suggestions that we could take legal action against the TCCB just as Alvin Kallicharran had done. However, I decided not to follow this course of action – much to the disappointment of Kim Barnett. Scotland had been good to me, the SCU had helped in every way possible and so I decided to continue to throw in my lot with them. Derbyshire did try to get the TCCB's decision reversed but it was all to no avail. It certainly provoked much food for thought in my mind. I still wanted to reach for that goal of Test cricket and things in South Africa were particularly unsettled with riots, houses being burned down – enough to make my wife, Conita, and I think very seriously about our long-term future.

But playing for Scotland had already brought to reality previously undreamed of achievements. I had, for instance, played at Lord's for Scotland, at the very Mecca of world cricket. Imagine that tiny little scrap of a coloured boy from Stellenbosch, brought up on street cricket and then on the dustbowls we had to play on, walking through the Long Room at Lord's and out on to that hallowed green turf. And who could possibly have predicted that the occasion would be the annual clash between the MCC – the 'auld enemy', some said – and Scotland?

The first time I played at Lord's was in 1984. It was another of those pinnacles, almost unbelievable. Imagine me bowling and batting at Lord's of all places! It could probably have only happened through my following a career in cricket in Scotland. I revelled in it, not so much in my own personal performances out there but simply to be there. If only Les Bergstedt, the schoolmaster at Luckhoff High who first taught me something about cricket, complete, as he always was, with that MCC coaching manual tucked underneath his arm, could have been there to watch his 'wonder boy', the boy for whom he had initially had to get hold of smaller pads and bats. How happy he would have been. Subsequently I was to lead Scotland out on to that hallowed turf as their captain. Proud moments indeed.

However, back to earth and the domestic scene. Arbroath, astonishingly, in that first season I was with them, carried all before them and won the County Championship at the first time of asking: quite an achievement. I think that they had got into the habit of winning – a good habit, needless to say – and that they simply carried on from the successes they had achieved with Clarence in harness in the Strathmore Union.

I had fitted into the team well. There was a useful seam attack in the Plomer brothers, Neil Burnett and with the left-arm medium pace of Aron Trivedi and my own variety of spinners, we had a well-balanced attack. More to the point was the way they responded to my coaxing to bowl tighter lines, to concentrate on line and length and of course as a fielding side they had the great advantage of youth and enthusiasm. The batsmen also tightened up, were less inclined to play loose shots and throw their wickets away and it was altogether a splendid team performance and a very happy dressing room in which to be.

So I had kept my track record intact, going to a Championship victory at the first time of asking. Even more encouraging was the promise of a young teenager by the name of George Salmond. Even then he was a real athlete, speedy with a good arm and a tremendous pair of hands. He was a good, positive batsman and a really nice guy to boot. I had seen him come through the Scottish Under-19 team, for which I had taken responsibility. He was always a batsman who wanted to play shots but in those early years, and still perhaps now, he was inclined to want to play everything on the front foot. He was a very willing pupil. We worked hard at the nets, trying to get him to play more off the back foot, to cut and pull, and I had him moving back and across in the Iain Philip mode, rather than just lunging forward automatically.

The joy with George was that he was willing to put in the time and work hard to improve his game – in fact they don't come much keener than him. And he has that asset of fitness. He is also a level-headed guy and, in my view, a real credit to his parents who, I know, have given him tremendous support and encouragement – a really nice family. If you have parents who care so much, then you are off to a flying start. I remember all too clearly the encouragement I had from my own family. George has had a few trial games with county teams in England and with his fitness, his high standard of fielding and his willingness to learn and work, I believe he has all the credentials to make it in the professional game.

I am equally sure that if he was able to play overseas – and I would love to see him come out to South Africa – the experience would stand him in great stead. I saw him play a superb innings at Lord's in 1990 when he and Bruce Russell literally won the game for us in a tremendous century stand in just 14 overs, a stand which included some amazingly fleet-footed running between the wickets. He had an unbeaten 56 and it was an innings fit to grace any game at HQ. In 1992, he came within a whisker of recording two centuries in the annual three-day game against Ireland at Forthill, Broughty Ferry. Having scored a century in the first innings, he had reached 95 in the second when he was caught on the boundary going for the 6 that would have brought him his second century.

In my second season at Arbroath, we failed to hang on to our title. Perhaps we never quite managed to sustain the highs of the previous season and there again, perhaps the other teams treated us with rather more circumspection.

At the end of the 1990 season, I decided to move again. Arbroath were looking to negotiate a longer-term contract and at that time, knowing that the wind of change was beginning to blow back home and also being aware that I did not have much time left in the game, I was reluctant to commit myself for a long period. In addition, I had found the travelling from my home in Bo'ness a little irksome and when West Lothian, five minutes away from where I lived, approached me, I decided to throw in my lot with them.

I had become friendly with a South African businessman, Clive Davidson, who had a restaurant, the Champany Inn, close by and who had agreed to sponsor the West Lothian club for a couple of years. I must admit that I was a little uncertain about my own future at this stage, and was looking towards the possibility of seeking a job which would carry me beyond my playing days. And there was some uncertainty about Scotland's future at international level. There also seemed to be a possibility that the Benson & Hedges, which had become the focal point of the early part of the Scottish season, might be changed so that our participation would be reduced.

I felt very frustrated about this because by 1990 we had built a real team and were really achieving. I felt that what I had worked so hard for was beginning to yield dividends. In addition, several of our players were now travelling abroad for the winter, gaining experience in other cricket environments. Iain Philip was still travelling to Western Australia, his opening batting partner, Bruce Patterson, was playing in Tasmania, Bruce Russell played in New Zealand, as later did Jim Govan after his spell with Northants, and Alastair Storie was playing in South Africa. Furthermore, most of these players were now setting a new trend by playing as professionals – home-grown professionals – in the Scottish leagues, all of which added the ingredient of confidence to the national team, the kind of confidence which was to serve us so well during what I believe was the most successful period in Scottish international cricket history. And knocking on the door were several young players, some of whom were also sampling cricket overseas as a part of their cricketing education, such as Craig McKnight of Poloc and Mike Richardson of West of Scotland.

The format of the Benson & Hedges was duly amended in 1993 when the qualifying rounds were eliminated and it became a straight knock-out. Thus from having four guaranteed games a year, Scotland's participation was reduced to one. That I believe was a retrograde step for the good of the game as a whole but at least it galvanised the SCU into positive action: they applied, somewhat belatedly in my opinion, to become associate members of the ICC and enter for the Mini World Cup, something which I believe they should have had the vision to do long before.

Of even more direct concern to me was the gradual emergence of South Africa from the great clouds that had shrouded our development in a national as well as in a cricketing sense. That wind of change was blowing ever harder and I found myself looking more optimistically at our future and more pointedly at my own future. I had to look beyond the pure playing side of my life to the longer term but now it seemed that we might once again, after so many years in the wilderness, take our place in the world cricketing community and it was just possible that I might have a part to play in that.

My move to West Lothian was also rewarding in the extreme even if, in the end, we failed – only just – to take the County Championship. There were some good players at Boghall: Gordon Hollins, the captain, was a solid batsman who had added a very effective brand of off spin to his repertoire, to which talents he added the virtue of being a courageous close fielder; David Fleming was a wicket-keeper-batsman who played several times for Scotland and then fell out of favour. Then we had Gavin Hamilton, a 17-year-old bowler of genuine pace who was later to join the Yorkshire Cricket Academy and play club cricket in South Africa, and Kenny Scott, who had been something of a teenage prodigy some years before and who I remembered scoring a magnificent double century for Scotland 'B' against Durham University, had returned, as had all-rounder David Orr. I always thought that Kenny Scott and David Simpson from Ayr were two of the most outstanding batting talents produced in Scotland.

In 1991 we played some tremendous cricket. Jock Raeburn a real Trojan and now in the veteran class, wheeled away relentlessly and behind the scenes people like Bruce Dixon, Jim Wilson and George Strachan worked tirelessly for the club and to improve the ground.

We were convinced that in 1992 we could make a real bid for the Championship. But it was a bad season weatherwise and I believe it was the weather which eventually cost us the chance of winning the Championship. Forfarshire were the eventual winners. We had played out a draw at Forthill earlier in the season and I came in for some pretty hefty criticism for my part in that draw. We had been set quite a target and they placed most of their fielders in the deep and then seemingly expected us to give our wickets away.

We thought we had turned the tables on them at Boghall. They had established a small points lead by the time they visited us late in the season and, batting first, we had a really good start. I had a century and when they batted we had them in early trouble only for the rain to come down and virtually extinguish our Championship chances. I felt sorry for the whole membership because they had made such a concerted effort to put behind them a number of lean years.

This time, I was not to keep my record but if I took a great deal of pride from helping to steer all those clubs to Championship success, with that one exception of West Lothian, I have also been the first to recognise that it was always a team effort. Apart from my own personal performances out in the middle, the keys to success lay in the creation of the right atmosphere. In all those teams, Poloc, Stenhousemuir, Arbroath and West Lothian, there was a good spirit and a willingness to work to a common goal, to play for each other. If I played my part in organising and motivating those teams, it was the players themselves who really made things happen. If I reaped a personal harvest of satisfaction in each case, equally, I also reaped a rich harvest in seeing the Scottish team weld itself into a unit that was prepared to take on all comers.

The performances in the Benson & Hedges in 1990 against Notts and Northants and again in 1991 when we so nearly beat Sussex at Hove proved that real progress had been made. At Hove, we took them right to the wire, chasing a total of 226 with George Reifer and I going really well. Then George was caught on the deep cover boundary and when we needed only 12 to win off the last 2 overs, we thought we had it in the bag. Then I made one of those mistakes that haunt you. I received a long hop from Ian Salisbury, tried to hit it out of the ground, got a top edge and was horrified to see the ball lob gently into David Smith's hands at mid-wicket. In the end we needed 4 to win off the last ball and Tony Pigott demonstrated his professionalism by spearing in a yorker to bowl David Haggo. So near, yet so far. If I had connected properly... if I hadn't tried to hit the cover off the ball... if I hadn't given a catch that my grandmother could have taken. Cricket is a game of ifs sometimes.

There is, quite naturally, another side to the coin. We also took some good hidings as well. Essex always gave us a hard time of it, never more so than in 1992 when they ran up a record score at Chelmsford.

Perhaps, on such occasions, our self-belief was somehow undermined, our confidence at an unusually low ebb.

However, the opportunity of playing against such star-studded sides must in the end benefit the players. The more you play against top-class opposition, the better your own standards will be.

Yet there is that other element: competitive cricket. The days of friendlies are, in my opinion, over. Now, when Scotland take the field, it must be to play in truly competitive matches and that is why I would like to see Scotland playing against other ICC associate member nations. If Scotland gain entry to the ICC in 1994, I hope that they will play in the next Mini World Cup and that they will begin to play meaningful internationals, both one-day and perhaps three- or even four-day games against other international sides such as Holland, Bermuda and Kenya.

The way cricket is developing on a worldwide basis, I am sure that sooner or later there will be a kind of second (and perhaps a third) division of international cricket and Scotland have every right to be involved in such a development. Why shouldn't Scotland's cricketers have just the same opportunity as the rugby, hockey, squash, badminton, bowls and for all I know tiddlywinks players of playing true international sport? Currently, the Irish game apart, it is only when the touring sides come to Scotland that people get the chance to sample cricket of an international flavour. The crowds certainly turn out to see the Australians, the Indians and the Pakistanis and I'm sure they will turn out in force to welcome the South Africans in 1994.

I have personally enjoyed some successes against such touring teams. I was particularly proud of my innings of 74 against the Indians in just 89 balls at Titwood and especially pleased about the 17 runs I took off Kumble's last over. It is curious that I should ultimately make my official Test debut against them in South Africa and that Mr Kumble should become my first Test wicket. If we lost, we nevertheless gave a good account of ourselves.

Titwood was a good venue for me. In August 1991 we played what I must admit was a fairly weak MCC side in a game which certainly went into the record books. In reaching a first-innings total of 537 for 5, we broke the all-time record total for Scotland and Iain Philip, in scoring a magnificent 234, broke the individual batting record. He and Alastair Storie created a new record for any wicket with their opening partnership of 301 and then, to cap it all, Iain and I broke the record for the 4th wicket with a stand of 143. My 102 not out in 66 balls was also the fastest century for Scotland. We won by the proverbial mile!

My decision to come to Scotland back in 1980 was an important one for me. I could not have begun to dream what rewards I could attain by choosing to begin my professional career there. It is quite a course to chart if you think about that whippersnapper of a 'wonder boy' beginning his life in the dustbowls of Stellenbosch, travelling 6,000 miles to play on the green, green grass of Scotland, and playing at such places as Lord's, Old Trafford, Trent Bridge and Northampton. I wore the thistle with great pride. I made so many friends, learned so much about the game of cricket and, in retrospect, about myself, that I will be eternally grateful to my adopted country which became the birthplace of two of my own children. That lovely country – and it is a country, by the way – is my second home and it gave me and my family so much. I hope sincerely that I was, in some measure, able to give something back. Lang may yer lums reek!

● ● ● ● ● ● ● ● ● ● ● ● ● ● ● ●

BOB WOOLMER

Formerly of Kent and England, Bob Woolmer has built for himself a reputation as one of the leading coaches in the game. He coaches Warwickshire CC and after many winters both playing and coaching in South Africa, he is now coach to Boland.

'I first came across Omar in 1981 when I joined Avendale, a club in Cape Town. He was one of the better cricketers around and on the fringe of being a regular in the Western Province side. As a left-arm spinner, in those days he certainly gave the ball plenty of air, perhaps too much in some circumstances, but when I learned of the difficult course he had charted for himself, I thought it was quite incredible given the pressures he had had to withstand when he went to play in what was regarded as "white" cricket.

'There was no doubt of his love for the game and of his will to succeed. But perhaps just as importantly, he also had as good a temperament to succeed as anyone you would wish to meet. Coming from the kind of background he did, an educational background which was decidedly impoverished, he had to fight the forces of "no normal sport in an abnormal society" which still very much prevailed in some parts of the country. However, sport, and especially cricket, was trying to break the shackles and Omar Henry was one of those people who broke away from the political force which was trying to hold on for the bigger fight.

'Omar became the leading light in this movement simply because he was the best. Others, such as Jock Mahoney and Dickie Conrad, were good cricketers but Omar was the one who really came through and took the big step. He went on and eventually represented his country. Therefore he came through all phases of the rebirth of South African cricket. Remember that the coloured cricketing community had no schools cricket, no good grounds, no infrastructure, no coaches – nothing was structured.

'My own experiences underlined the disparities and the political climate. I found that the facilities the coloured community had at their disposal were appalling and I had to take some criticism for devoting time to coaching coloured youngsters. But it was all part and parcel of the political climate of that time.

'At Avendale, we were able to produce a considerable number of youngsters so they had something to hold on to. We were lucky to have Mike Stakol as a really tireless fund-raiser who made it all happen.

'I suppose that having made the trek to South Africa since 1970 and having seen the immense changes which have taken place, I have experienced many heady days, taking the game into townships and seeing it taken to new areas. Omar was one of those people who had the determination to make it. He had a strength of mind as well as a strength of purpose; he was always a tremendous fielder but in his early days he perhaps bowled too erratically. But there is no substitute for experience. He struggled to command a place at Western Province and then went to Boland. But it was when he played for Free State that he really turned the corner. Perhaps, had Western Province given him the chance, he would have reached the heights much earlier. I wonder how much better he might have been had Province persevered with him in the early years.

'I always felt that if they had invested in Omar in a coaching sense, he could have made it then. There can be no doubt that if you are lucky enough to reach international level, your confidence rises and that is transmitted in your game. Thus he has continued to get better over a long period of time and certainly his appearances against the rebel Australians provided him with a base from which he could become a better, more confident player.

'One little story I can tell about Omar illustrates that he is a fighter. Avendale were playing Claremont. They needed 2 to win with 9 wickets down and their number 11, who certainly didn't fancy it, at the wicket. I said to Omar, "We have got to get this guy out. Do we surround him with fielders or what?" Omar just said, "Get the fielders out and I'll toss one up and he'll hit it in the air."

'I thought it was something of a risk. He said, "If we lose, we lose and if we win, we win." In the event I put in a short leg and a silly point, stayed at slip myself and posted most of the others on the boundary.

'Omar threw this ball miles in the air and I thought it would never pitch. The batsman started to swing, lost his footing, got a top edge and the ball found the top edge, lobbed over the keeper's head and landed in my hands at slip.

'He had the confidence to do it and in that respect he is a player of courage.

'If sometimes Omar can seem to be a little single-minded and, on occasion, persists in following his own beliefs to the exclusion of other opinions, he has shown that by and large he has been right and he has thoroughly deserved the success he has achieved.'

THE CRICKETING ROLLERCOASTER

During those years in Scotland, years which added new dimensions both to my game and to my personal life, I was returning home to South Africa at the end of each UK season. I had already become involved in coaching at Avendale of course and had in effect taken the step of trying to earn a living entirely from cricket. I was still playing for Western Province, albeit mostly for the 'B' team, but the confidence I gained from my first full season as a professional in Scotland really gave me a boost. When I returned from Scotland after that first adventure, I felt sure that my career was poised to take off. As it happened, on the personal front too, my life was going to change considerably.

During that 1980-81 season I did make something of a breakthrough, playing for the Western Province 'A' team in seven out of the eight Currie Cup games. I started reasonably well with a knock of 44 against Eastern Province in the first game, which we won by 10 wickets. However, as a side we simply didn't get going. Natal swept all before them with their bowling attack of Vintcent van der Bijl, Mike Procter, Kenny Cooper and Paddy Clift, winning the Currie Cup at a canter.

The one-day Datsun Shield competition was taken by Transvaal, who beat Eastern Province comfortably in the final. The best we could do was to finish third in the Currie Cup. My contribution of scoring almost 200 runs marked some progress, I thought, but my best innings by far came in the one 'B' team game I played, in which I recorded my first first-class century, against Border in East London, 105. Joining me and also recording his first century at this level was Bossie Clark. He had exactly 100. Needless to say, there was a story behind that maiden first-class century, already recounted. That was the occasion on which I was dropped from the 'A' team during the Christmas game against Transvaal and learned about it from the press.

That first century reflected on the one hand, my growing confidence and on the other, a further significant milestone in my career. I was at the wicket for just under three hours and accumulated a dozen 4s and one 6 in a pretty belligerent knock during which I really did bang the ball all round the wicket. Not bad for a number 8 batsman! It always struck me as being somewhat strange that at home in South Africa I was regarded principally as a bowler, whilst in Scotland, it was my batting which perhaps came out on top.

In retrospect I didn't perform particularly well with the ball during that season, claiming only 8 wickets from 123 overs. In fact I had been given little or no opportunity to test my mettle during that fateful match at Jo'burg. Graeme Pollock took our attack apart for a magnificent innings of 166 – Pollock at his best – and I had hardly been called upon at all. As I have said, I was deeply upset not only about being dropped from the team but by the manner in which it was done. I simply couldn't understand why Eddie Barlow, of all people, had not seen fit to tell me personally. At the time I felt very badly done by and bitter. I felt that I had been betrayed and it certainly showed me, in no uncertain terms, that life can be a bit of a rollercoaster. In cricket, you can be up one minute and down the next. Yet it was, in hindsight, all part of the learning process – not just learning about cricket, but about myself as well. As the record shows, I went off to East London feeling angry but determined. My maiden first-class century followed, as did my restoration to the 'A' team for the next match.

I have always maintained that playing in exalted company helps a player enormously. There is an automatic raising of the confidence factor, especially when one of your team-mates is Eddie Barlow. He led from the front, he was a fitness fanatic and I would go as far as to say he was a real 'street fighter', never giving up, never accepting defeat, always striving for the best. In spite of that tiff we had in Jo'burg, I have to say that he always backed his players to the hilt. That facet of his temperament was never better illustrated than in one of those unfortunate incidents when racism raised its ugly head. That was the occasion on which I was refused service at the Golden Spur restaurant close to Newlands during the New Year match between Western Province and Transvaal.

Typically, Eddie did not mince his words, calling the incident a 'bloody disgrace'. The press reported events thus: 'Henry was refused entry to the Golden Spur restaurant on New Year's Eve after the first day's play of the Currie Cup match. Henry himself passed it off as a misunderstanding [I had, by the way, previously been in the same restaurant without any problems surfacing]. He had, hours before, been performing in front of 13,000 people at Newlands, and was in the company of friends from England when the incident took place. His captain, Eddie Barlow, said that the incident was a bloody disgrace when he heard about it. "I was disgusted, shocked, angry and finally sad and embarrassed as a South African." ' Typically straightforward!

Although I did not make a fuss when the incident happened, I was, I have to confess, inwardly furious and later said so. By coincidence, Dickie Jeeps, the former England international rugby player, was due in town to investigate progress towards normalisation in South African sport. My feelings at the time, not surprisingly, were that he shouldn't even bother to come, nothing much had changed. However, I had, to some extent, become inured to such events.

With the talent we had in that Western Province side, we should have done better, I suppose. In Lawrence Seeff we had a real grafter but an enthusiast and in Peter Kirsten a really great batsman who knew how to milk runs, especially with that famous late cut of his. He scored many runs for Derbyshire and was a brilliant fielder. And then there was Allan Lamb, who had no sense of fear at all, who bubbled with confidence – hyper-active I would call him – and who was a destroyer of attacks. Garth le Roux was a tall, blond quick bowler who had originally, as a schoolboy, bowled off-spinners but later became one of the quickest bowlers in the world. A quick run-down of this galaxy of stars and it is easy to see that I was surrounded by enormous talent. Some of it surely, was bound to rub off on me!

Yet my cricketing life was something of a riches-to-rags existence. If I had become a regular in the Province team, my club Avendale, was still struggling. But we at last managed to win our first match. I should point out that we played on a Saturday to Saturday basis; that is, a game was started on one Saturday and finished the next. That first win came against Pinelands and we ended up needing 120 to win in just 20 overs – 6 an over. I told the players we would go for it and it went down to the wire when we ran a bye off the last ball to record our victory.

It would be an understatement to say that we celebrated that win. There were a few hangovers the next day – not in my case, I might say, because as usual I celebrated by drinking Coke. It was during those celebrations that Julian Hendricks, a good friend of mine at the club, brought along his girlfriend and her cousin, a girl called Conita King, a charming and attractive young lady who immediately caught my eye. Conita was about 18 years old, just out of school and was working at a medical aid company. She came from Landsdown in Cape Town. I invited her to a match the following weekend. But fate took a hand: I was hit on the head during the game and had to be taken to hospital.

The injury wasn't serious – just a touch of concussion – but I soon discovered that my liaison with Conita had ruffled a few family feathers. Remember we were an Afrikaans-speaking Muslim family whilst Conita's family was English-speaking and Methodist. I suppose it was not exactly surprising that her family were a little apprehensive. After all, not only was I a Muslim but it could not be said that I had a particularly secure job.

Professional cricketers could not, especially in the circumstances in which I found myself, claim to be the most reliable people in the world. Perhaps suspicion becomes part of the way of life when a society is so divided and so I can't blame either my own family or Conita's for being hesitant. In the event Conita and I started to see each other regularly nonetheless.

When I returned to Scotland in April 1981, I took with me her work address, simply because her parents still weren't keen on the relationship. In spite of the difficulties, I had a gut feeling that we were destined for each other. Time heals, of course, and in subsequent years, Conita's parents and I have become great friends. On my return from Scotland in September 1981, we were together again and it became clear that our lives would be inextricably linked.

Meanwhile there were sweeping changes at Western Province. Eddie Barlow had left to go to Boland, based in my native Stellenbosch. With him had gone Peter Swart and Stephen Jones, with Peter Kirsten taking over the captaincy. There had also been changes in the administration, Ronnie Delport becoming the new President, Fritz Bing the Vice-President and the coaching falling to new Director Stuart Leary, a name which will be familiar to both cricket and football followers in the UK.

Under this new regime, we were to enjoy a fabulous season. I started in the 'B' team and felt I was playing well. Figures can sometimes be deceiving. In one game at Kimberley, I bowled an exhausting 30-over spell for a return of only 2 for 96, yet I felt I had bowled really well without any luck. By stark contrast, a couple of weeks later at the lovely Constantia ground, against Orange Free State, I had 5 for 34 in the first innings, thanks to some outstanding catches. It was a day on which the rub of the green went my way. In the second innings of the game I hit a lusty unbeaten 43 and then picked up another 4 wickets for 48 to give me a match analysis of 9 for 82. And then I followed up with another 4 wickets against Natal 'B'.

As a result, I was promoted to the 'A' team for the New Year game against Transvaal. Even if at international level, South Africa was very much isolated, enthusiasm for the game still ran high. Over the three days of that match, 36,000 people came to Newlands. It was, needless to say, a tremendous atmosphere in which to play.

Although the game was eventually drawn, it produced some wonderful cricket. Alan Kourie, Transvaal's left-arm spinner, had always performed well at Newlands which, more than most wickets, helped the spinners. He certainly started as if he was going to have another field day, bowling 5 consecutive maidens when he came on. But then Adrian Kuiper and Steven Bruce, playing his first game of the season, gradually got on top of the bowling and added 157. Kuiper scored a fine 62 but Steven was absolutely tremendous and, having hammered a succession of 4s and 6s, was unlucky to miss out on a century, falling 11 runs short with 89. Garth le Roux and I then came together to rub salt into the wounds with an 8th-wicket partnership of 92. I made a very satisfying 53 and continued where I left off in the second innings, smashing a couple of straight 6s into the sightscreen off Alan Kourie. In fact this certainly wasn't his game, for of the 16 6s Western Province scored, he conceded 13! He wasn't a great spinner of the ball but he always seemed to bowl an immaculate length and line.

Needless to say, it was a partisan crowd at Newlands on that occasion and even if we failed to apply the *coup de grâce*, we were on top from start to finish and so the crowd had plenty to cheer about – especially that succession of 6s.

When we faced Natal, with both teams in contention for the Currie Cup title, we got off to a great start, dismissing our opponents for 169 on the first day and sitting comfortably on 92 for 3 at the end of the day's play, having struggled initially. I had a really good day, picking up an early wicket through a catch at short leg by Lawrence Seeff. I finished up with 4 for 22 and included amongst my victims Robin Smith, a man destined to become one of the world's top batsmen yet a player who always seemed to find spin more difficult to handle than pace. I had 22 not out as we established a more than useful lead by reaching 363. There was another 6 over long on in that brief stay at the wicket, by the way! If I failed to take a wicket when Natal batted for a second time, at least I kept their batsmen on a tight rein, bowling 14 overs for just 26 runs. We won by 7 wickets and the Currie Cup was ours.

When I look back on that season, even if I didn't make my way into the team until January, it was still very memorable. To be a part of that Currie Cup-winning team was a tremendously proud moment. You may ask why this was not of more importance to me than the subsequent taste of victory, years later, when I was playing for Orange Free State. Make no mistake, it was a proud moment for me, but I think that there was a little more spice to the Free State triumph. I can't really explain why it seems to have been a more significant win in Bloemfontein but certainly that experience of scoring such a notable victory with Western Province remains one of the most important days of my cricketing life.

Even more dramatic, perhaps, was the victory we fashioned at the Wanderers ground against Natal in the Datsun final which brought us the double. The game was played in that famous Test arena on a specially hot day before 28,000 people who paid a record 150,000 rand to see the action. And it was a game not without its moments of controversy. Two run-outs were given in what most people thought were dubious circumstances, one for each team, which I suppose evens out in the end.

I can't claim to have played a significant role in the victory. However, I did feel I fielded well. We needed to, believe me, for we scored only 178 in our 55 overs. Peter Kirsten's 35 and Adrian Kuiper's hard-hit 38 provided the backbone to our innings although there were an amazing 30 extras in that total, 23 of them leg byes, most of them scrambled with some quick running. The Leicestershire opening bowler, Les Taylor, later to play for England, had 4 for 26. We made early inroads, removing Titch Smith and Chris Rawkins with only 2 on the board. They recovered to 74 but the game was full of ebbs and flows. Barry Richards had 29 and Mike Procter 24, but it was one of those controversial run-outs that tipped the balance when Paddy Clift was the victim. In a thrilling finish, we scraped home by just 2 runs.

The celebrations were somewhat marred by that run-out because the Natal team really took umbrage and refused to take part in the ceremony to award the trophy. If that left a slightly bitter taste in our mouths, nothing could take away the joy of victory.

It was also a very special occasion for me because my father was present, a guest of Johan Rupert, a contemporary of mine and son of Dr Anton Rupert, head of the Rembrandt Group, who has played such an important part in my cricket career. I had delivered papers to their household as a boy and their kindness in inviting my father on that occasion I will always remember. The Ruperts had flown my father from Cape Town to Jo'burg for the game and he had stayed in their house in the city. It was, curiously enough, the first time my father had ever had the chance of watching me play at this level and I always like to think that he was well rewarded, even if I played no significant role in the game. He was, however able to see me collect a winners' medal in one of the country's top cricketing events. That single event, I think, left a lasting impression on my father. Back in Stellenbosch, he could talk of nothing else thereafter.

The Currie Cup and now the Datsun Shield: what proud moments these were for me. The battles had all been worthwhile, the agony and the ecstasy, the trials and tribulations, the kangaroo courts, the ostracism I suffered when, in the words of some, I deserted my 'own kind' to play in mixed-race cricket. This was ample reward for me and it was more than ample reward for my father, who had stood by me over the years, taken some of the flak and yet never wavered in his support. It seemed to be a kind of destiny that we should share the moment – a moment of joy, love and pride.

There were other moments to savour during that season. I fashioned a pleasing performance against a strong South African Universities team. I had 7 for 22 in 16 overs – a bowling spell of which I was inordinately proud, turning the ball quite sharply on occasion and certainly flighting it very well. It was one of those days when I felt completely in tune and in control and amongst the batsmen we were up against were Adrian Kuiper, Roy Pienaar and Hansie Cronje.

There was to be yet another highlight in that memorable season when an English XI led by Graham Gooch came out to South Africa. Predictably, the visit, sponsored by South African Breweries, was very controversial and resulted in several players having bans imposed upon them. In the touring side were such immortals as Geoff Boycott, Alan Knott, Derek Underwood and Dennis Amiss. It is not putting it too strongly to say that the background to the tour involved much wheeling and dealing between such people as Dr Ali Bacher, Geoff Dakin and Joe Pamensky.

I had the honour of playing for Western Province against them and if I didn't exactly make the earth move with my performances, it was nevertheless a privilege to appear on the same field as such internationally renowned cricketers. Once again Newlands was the setting and in fact we very nearly beat the tourists, who were struggling at the end with 8 wickets down and John Emburey nursing a broken hand. Such events were, it seemed to me, further milestones in my career. I was now a full-time professional cricketer, playing through 12 months of the year, living in eternal summers in either Scotland or South Africa. Experiences of playing against such teams could only help advance my career and make me, bit by bit, a better player.

All in all it was a momentous season for me but, more importantly, it proved to be a momentous year in other ways, too. Conita and I got married. She had converted to Islam and our wedding took place in Stellenbosch immediately before I was due to return for another cricket season in Scotland. There were, believe it or not, 500 guests present. It was practically a 'who's who' of Western Province cricket and quite an ordeal for Conita, because the newspapers and television cameras were there. The spotlight was on us and it was quite overwhelming for both of us. My best man was Mike Stakol. Quite unusual, really, because he is Jewish, but he had been a tremendous friend to me and was absolutely thrilled to guide me towards married life. The fact that he was my best man illustrated, in the clearest possible way, that barriers of creed and race are totally artificial. It is what and who we are as people that really counts, not the colour of your skin or the faith you follow.

Within a few days of getting married, Conita and I were on the aeroplane to Scotland. She was, when I look back on it, taking quite a gamble. Marrying a cricketer with no guarantee of any sort of continuity of employment; flying from one end of the world to the other, from heat to the chill atmosphere of Scotland in April. Yet there was some security, or at least that's how it seemed. Western Province, just before Conita and I departed, gave me a two-year contract; I was already on a contract with Poloc Cricket Club in Scotland, and the two together were probably as near to security as you're ever going to get in cricket!

On our return from Scotland, I was soon to be confronted by reality again. If the 1981-82 season had left me feeling that I had made significant progress as a member of the Currie Cup Western Province side which had also pulled off that sensational victory in the Datsun Shield final, then I was soon to be brought back to earth. The impact of the English rebel tour had been such that several of the players, now banned from international cricket, had thrown in their lot with the South African provinces. In Western Province's case, they had captured the considerable talents of Graham Gooch and John Emburey.

There is a dichotomy here because the arrival of such talented international players in South Africa was clearly a fillip to the game here. However, as always, there was another side to the coin. To accommodate such players, someone had to be excluded and that meant some South Africans had to go. With my place in the team heavily dependent upon my spin bowling, the arrival of John Emburey was definitely not good news. Obviously he would be guaranteed one of the spin bowling spots so predictably I once again found myself relegated to the 'B' team.

My response to this disappointing but inevitable consequence was, I'm pleased to say, 'I'll show you!' In the 'B' province games I proceeded to wreak havoc with my bowling, taking a record-equalling 35 wickets in six games. But, well though I bowled in response to the challenge, there really was no way into the team for me. Denys Hobson and Emburey had the spinners' berths well buttoned up. There was little likelihood of them going for a third spinner and whilst I certainly set out to show them that I was still worth a place – and produced the figures to back that – I knew that this would be a season of frustration for me.

Even more frustration arose when the rebel Sri Lankan tour came to town. They were not a strong side and frankly were no match for our boys. But I found myself as 12th man for the so-called 'test' at Newlands. Alan Kourie was picked as the left-arm spinner but after bowling a mere 6 overs, he left the field and I had to field in his place for two full days. Speaking personally, I'm not at all sure that Alan was fit even to start the game and if that was the case then someone else, notably yours truly, should have been given the chance from the start. I've said it before and I'll say it again: no one should go into such a match unless they are 100 per cent fit.

I did, however, play against the Sri Lankans for Western Province – ironically, my only first-team game of the season. The Sri Lankans were, at that stage of their development, simply not up to facing really fast bowling, so they didn't really provide a stern test for us. They were, I always thought, harshly treated. For their pains, they were to receive bans of 25 years, compared with the three-year ban imposed on the English 'rebels'.

Later that season however, there arrived a team of real class, the rebel West Indians, captained by Lawrence Rowe, a batsman of class who had a first-class triple century, no less, to his name. In David Murray they had a real world-class wicket-keeper, and in Colin Croft, Sylvester

Clarke, Hartley Alleyne, Collis King and Franklyn Stephenson a pace attack of real quality and thus, unlike the Sri Lankans, were able to fight fire with fire. Add to those names that of the little dynamo himself, Alvin Kallicharran, whom we knew from his already well-catalogued performances in South Africa, and you knew that this touring team was in a different class.

Needless to say, they played to packed houses in Durban, Cape Town, Port Elizabeth and Johannesburg. It was therefore a thrill for me to be ranged against them for Province in a one-day game at Newlands in which I was pleased with my performance. I had a couple of wickets in my 8 overs which cost 41 runs. Unfortunately, just when I had got going with the bat, I was run out for 14. But this game gave my spirits a real lift. Once again I was rubbing shoulders with great world-class cricketers, having languished for most of the season in the Province 'B' side. Cricket can certainly have its ups and downs!

Yet in spite of the class the West Indians exuded, this, remember, was not their first team by any means. They were in fact the discards from the West Indian tour to Australia, where the first team was whacking the Aussies in fine style. Yet to see those pace men at work was extraordinary. They batted with such exhilaration too. I was, several years later, to renew my acquaintance with Franklyn Stephenson. What a player!

In spite of the added strength provided by Gooch and Emburey, Western Province did not do as well as had been hoped and significantly, they were unable to repeat the double-winning feat of the previous season, coming runners-up in both competitions. There had to be a moral there somewhere!

Transvaal was the team of the season, quite appropriately known as the 'mean machine', a *nom de plume* they carried with them for many years. In the one-day competitions they showed their confidence by selecting only four front-line bowlers when everyone else picked five. Little Alvin Kallicharran and Kevin McKenzie worked the fifth bowler's overs between them. But those four bowlers were quite a team. Vintcent van der Bijl had gone to work in Jo'burg and thus transferred from Natal to Transvaal. He bowled with Richard Hanley, Neal Radford and Clive Rice – not a bad four-pronged attack! And the batting line-up was even more impressive. Jimmy Cook, Henry Fotheringham,

Kallicharran, Graeme Pollock, followed by Kevin McKenzie, Clive Rice and the leading wicket-keeper in the country and a jolly good batsman, Raymond Jennings.

I was actually picked for the Datsun Shield final but we were comprehensively thrashed. They took us for 303 for 5 in 55 overs with Cook, Fotheringham, Kallicharran and Pollock all notching half-centuries. My contribution was to bowl 7 overs – 0 for 43. Then they bowled us out for 194, with my contribution just 9 runs. It was food for thought, that hammering, but for some reason I can't fully explain, I bounced right back. I was sitting in the dressing room after the game when my good friend Bob Sambridge, the reserve umpire that day, together with Alvin, came in and said we should go to the presentation ceremony. Alvin, as usual, was enjoying a beer at the time; I was wrapped in just my towel, having just come out of the shower, and suddenly I turned to them and said, 'One day, I'll play international cricket for South Africa.'

It wasn't just bravado on my part. Something inside me – some kind of steel, in spite of the hiding we'd just experienced – simply filled my spirit and the words just tumbled out, almost involuntarily. Alvin rolled about laughing but I must say that Bob Sambridge took it very seriously. As things were to turn out, he was right! It wasn't that I was being cocky or over-confident. I was readjusting my targets. If I have learned anything during my years in the game it is that you never give up on your aims. In spite of the disappointment of being consigned once again to what amounted to second-team cricket because of the arrival of John Emburey (for whom, by the way, I have always had the greatest respect, both as a man and as a cricketer), inwardly I had gained added strength. I had proved to myself that I was good enough. Now I had to prove it to others – especially to the people who picked the teams.

It goes without saying that when the next South African season came around, the situation was much the same. John Emburey and Denys Hobson held down the spin places and once again I had to settle for 'B' team cricket. For the third year in succession I played in the Datsun Shield final and for the second year running I found myself playing for a losing side, even more comprehensively beaten by the Transvaal 'mean machine' for whom my friend Alvin Kallicharran scored a century, Cook 51, Pollock 49 and Rice 45. John Emburey had 0 for 52 in 9 overs and I was not called upon to bowl, a disappointment to me for if I had been brought into the firing line, I felt confident I could do something. Apart from Roy Pienaar's 84, we had nowhere near enough fire-power to compete. We had been thoroughly taken to the cleaners again. Although I actually played five Currie Cup games that season, my bowling was used extremely sparingly. I was really brought into the team, I suppose, as an all-rounder. I bowled only 57 overs in that 1983-84 campaign, taking just 5 wickets. I accumulated 180 runs with a top score of 79. In comparison John Emburey took only 12 wickets from 244 overs at nearly 46 apiece. Graham Gooch certainly shone with the bat, scoring nearly 600 runs at an average of 52. Add to the bald statistics the fact that the side already had a number of proven all-rounders, and you can see what I was up against.

The innings of 79 came in a victory over Eastern Province at Newlands in a match in which we scored 587 for 7 in our first innings. We had an opening stand of 293 from Graham Gooch and Lawrence Seeff, each of whom scored a century. I had 2 for 31 in 12 overs in Eastern Province's first innings of 373, of which Peter Willey had 111, John Emburey chipping in with 3 wickets. Denys Hobson had 5 wickets in Eastern Province's second innings to wrap things up in an innings victory.

However, even if it was great to be a part of a reasonably successful side, to be rubbing shoulders with the likes of Graham Gooch and John Emburey, it was still very frustrating to me to be in the side and never really get a long bowl. Hobson and Emburey had the lion's share of the spin bowling and I felt my presence in the side was somewhat peripheral. If I was to reach for the stars, this was not the right way to do it. And because I had started my career so late, there was a nagging fear that time was beginning to run out for me. I must be honest and say that I sometimes felt I was not being treated in a straightforward way. It had nothing to do with what was going on on the field – the atmosphere in the dressing room was always great. But I seemed to find it difficult to extract expenses from the administrators. A few little niggles like that were beginning to unsettle me.

This was perhaps the underlying pressure that made me begin to

Above The Luckhoff High School cricket team of 1967, including Omar
Henry (back row, extreme left), show off their season's trophies.
Below Omar with Mike Stakol (right) and Alvin Kallicharran (centre) in
Avendale days.

Facing page Howie Bergins in action for Green Point against Techs in a Protea League senior game in 1979.
Above Dik Abed (left) and Baboo Ebrahim, two leading players in SACBOC cricket.
Below Edward Habane, one of two non-white players included in the South African Invitation side against Derrick Robins' XI in 1975, with other team members (l to r) Peter Swart, Eddie Barlow and Vintcent van der Bijl.

Western Province, winners of the Currie Cup and Datsun Shield in 1981-82.
Back row (l to r): M.J. Nel, S.T. Jefferies, J.D. Du Toit, S.D. Bruce, J. During,
R.F. Pienaar, A.P. Kuiper, K.S. McEwan.

Seated: L. Seeff, D.L. Hobson, R. Delport (president), P.N. Kirsten (captain), K. Funsten (convenor of selectors), G.S. le Roux, S.E. Leary (coach).
Front: O. Henry, R.J. Ryall. (Allan Lamb also played throughout the season.)

Above Omar's first appearance for South Africa against the Australians in 1987. Back row (l to r): D.J. Richardson, R.K. McClashan (12th man), H.A. Page, G.S. le Roux, A.A. Donald, B.J. Whitfield, O. Henry.
Front row: K.S. McEwan, P.N. Kirsten, C.E.B. Rice (captain), D.R. Carlstein (manager), R.G. Pollock, S.J. Cook.
Below Celebrations in the Boland dressing-room after winning the Castle Bowl in 1986.

Eddie Barlow and Omar with a portrait painted by Western Province colleague Richie Ryall, which was auctioned at Omar's benefit dinner. Surprise guest at the dinner was Ted Dexter (below), with Omar and (l to r) Frank Brache, yachtsman John Martin and SABC commentator Trevor Quirk.

Two important administrators.
Left Krish Mackerdhuj (right) has kept a watchful eye on the game for many years.
Below Rashid Varachia (left), president of the South African Cricket Union, discusses the future of South African cricket with English visitor Jack Overy, a member of the emergency committee of the Cricket Council, in 1978.

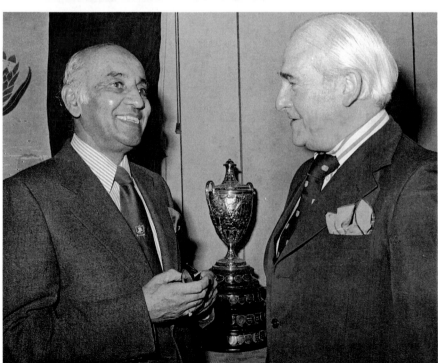

reassess my future. Stephen Jones, with whom I had struck up a great friendship during his days with Western Province and indeed during our days at Green Point together, suggested that I might consider joining Boland, at that time merely a 'B' province team but of course based in my home town of Stellenbosch. Furthermore, Boland had great ambition. They were plotting a course towards recognition as an 'A' province. It was, in the event, to take them much longer to achieve that goal than they, or anyone else, it seemed, could possibly have imagined.

But there many considerations to take into account. A move back to Stellenbosch would inevitably mean that I would have to sever my links with Avendale, a club which had been so good to me. We had, all of us at Avendale, grown up together and Bert Erikson had become almost a second father to me. I had spent six years helping them to build up the club. It was here that, between us, we had given hundreds of underprivileged kids the chance to learn and play the game. It was part of my being, that club. I was nevertheless by now living in Stellenbosch, and Stephen was very persuasive. Not only did he want me to play for Boland, he wanted me to get deeply involved in coaching, especially the coaching of older boys. He himself, it seemed, had a *métier* for coaching the younger kids.

It was all so tempting. I was somewhat dubious about relegating myself to permanent residence in 'B' province cricket. It could be very much a backward step which would, if it went wrong and Boland were not able to gain admission to 'A' Province cricket, sink my international aspirations – those ambitions I had revealed to Bob Sambridge and Alvin Kallicharran in the dressing room after the Datsun Shield final. And I had a contract with the prospect of another contract in the offing, or so I thought. The transition from one administration to another had done me no favours. When it came to the point of renewing my contract with Western Province, whilst I was looking for stability and security, a married man by now, of course, even in the knowledge that John Emburey and Denys Hobson were ahead of me in the queue as first-choice spinners, I hoped to negotiate an even longer-term agreement.

I must say, by the way, that John Emburey was always tremendously helpful. Even playing alongside him, I could learn so much and he was always prepared to give me good, sound advice at the nets. But his very presence was one of the things which seemed to be impeding my progress. I simply wasn't getting the bowling I wanted.

Perhaps it was naive of me to think that with Emburey and Hobson in harness, I could expect a better contract. But the real blow to my pride came when the cricket manager, John Cummins, bluntly told me that it was felt I was not good enough to play Currie Cup cricket. A contract was on offer but it was not the kind of contract I was looking for. It offered me little security; furthermore it seemed to suggest that my prospects of keeping a place in the Currie Cup team and perhaps getting the opportunity to firmly establish myself were evaporating before my very eyes.

All this must be set against the background of my own improving standards of play, and the satisfaction expressed by my captain, Peter Kirsten, who openly told me that he was very satisfied with my performances. I knew that I was playing well and felt convinced that, given the chance, I could really establish myself in the 'A' side.

It was hardly a vote of confidence in me, was it? After making so much progress, they were wanting to hire me only on a one-year basis. It was not, as I saw it, a rung in the right ladder. I really believed that with Denys Hobson's increasing work commitments, my chance to establish myself as a front-line spinner was just around the corner. I had, I felt, served my apprenticeship and now I was being told that I was not really good enough.

I took it a step further by speaking to the President, Fritz Bing, but I made little or no progress. So when I left for what turned out to be another enormously successful season with Poloc in Scotland, the question was still unresolved. I felt somewhat confused by the uncertainty which now suddenly surrounded my future and during the South African winter, whilst I was playing in the Northern Hemisphere, I had numerous telephone conversations with the people at Newlands with promises being made but, in the end, not being fulfilled.

When the contract arrived in Scotland, it did not square with the conversations I had had with Fritz Bing. I was determined that, whatever the consequences, I had to provide for my family and it was at this point that I decided to throw in my lot with Boland. So I rang Stephen Jones and a contract was agreed.

It is worth at this point in the story explaining the idiosyncrasies of the structure of South African cricket. Boland had originally been a sub-province of Western Province but eventually gained 'B' section status in its own right. Eddie Barlow had pushed them into the 'B' Section, which is made up of senior province second teams and provinces to which 'A' Section status has not been granted. But it all qualifies as first-class cricket. These 'B' Section teams play in what was known as the Castle Bowl competition.

I was only too well aware that I was taking a step down the ladder but it was a risk I felt I had to take. If I can strike a comparison, it may be clearer to say that the Bowl competition resembled the minor county competition in England before the full-time county second XIs were pulled out and it became exclusively a minor counties league. So you had out-of-form 'A' province people playing as well as up-and-coming cricketers trying to establish themselves. Make no mistake, it was good cricket, if not representing the highest level of the game in South Africa. But it was classified as first-class. It may be a little invidious to strike a comparison with what Durham achieved in becoming a first-class county after years of trying, because English county cricket is of course entirely professional. Province cricket is not. Most players are not full-time. However, there was something of a parallel between the aspirations of both Durham and Boland at the time.

I was, of course, going home and furthermore there seemed to be a real chance that Boland could break through into the top echelons of the game. Eddie Barlow's time there, needless to say, had made quite an impact. He makes an impact wherever he goes. So there was a decided feeling of optimism.

Stephen Jones, as Director of Cricket for Boland, offered me the job as player (I was to be vice-captain) and Director of Coaching and I took the plunge. My job entailed being Stephen's second in command in team matters, added to which was a total responsibility for coaching programmes in the province as a whole. It is strange how things come full-circle, for I returned to Boland in 1993 to organise a cricket academy. That, however, I shall deal with later in the book.

We had a school system in which we had under-11, under-13, under-15 and under-19 teams, but of course at that juncture there was no unity amongst the racial groups. Our finances were decidedly thin on the ground. We did manage to pick up some sponsorships but it didn't amount to much, so it was always something of a struggle. We got into the very grass roots of the game and, if it was an uphill battle we did, quite soon, begin to tap local resources to such an extent that within a few years we had a number of players in the side who had come through the system. With meagre finances, it was the only way forward for a relatively impoverished province. To further underline the value of that work, in the fullness of time, we had laid the ground well enough for four or five kids from Boland to make it to South African Schools level, progressing through the Nuffield scheme, which is for under-19 cricketers and brings together young players from all over the country.

Thus when I returned from Scotland in September 1984, new challenges lay ahead of me. Suddenly my career was changing direction again and even if I might have seemed to be stepping down a grade, at least I now had an established position. No more uncertainty; the challenge of organising coaching on a substantial scale – and I was as near to security as I could hope for in my chosen career.

The latter commodity had become rather more important now that I had become a father. Conita, you see, had presented me with my first daughter, Shireen, born in Glasgow – a South African 'jock'!

● ● ● ● ● ● ● ● ● ● ● ● ● ● ● ● ●

ALI BACHER

'I have always admired Omar Henry both as a cricketer and as a man. As a coloured player, whilst many of his colleagues remained in SACBOC, he came across to the South African Cricket Union, a courageous decision on his part and one which brought, almost inevitably in those difficult days of the mid-70s, accusations that he had "sold out".

'However, he also earned a great deal of credit and support from both sides of the community, for the dignity he always preserved which, in due course, made him a splendid ambassador for cricket in this country. He has worked long and hard at his game and deservedly reached the very top, gaining his Springbok colours.

'Omar is a team's, a captain's delight. He is an all-rounder in the fullest sense of the word because he has constantly disciplined himself to undertake any task that is found in a cricket man. I have seen him bat, bowl, field, defend and attack with distinction and character at all levels of the game, a player of real ability. In fact he has, I believe, been a much better cricketer than many people think and in his latter days with Orange Free State, he blossomed into an outstanding player of maturity, a marvellous example to everybody.

'I have mentioned discipline with regard to Omar because I believe this has been the key to his success - discipline and dedication. Cricket is not an easy game to play, and certainly in South Africa you have to reach a very high standard to get to, and remain, at the top. South Africa has had another kind of distinction, however, this time a dubious one. If you are a person of colour, then achievement comes that much harder because the odds are stacked that much higher against you.

'Only Omar knows just how difficult his career has been but as a cricketer I know how much work and effort he must have put into his game to overcome the underprivilege that he has faced.

'The fact that he chose the South African Cricket Union route meant that he had to face extraordinary pressures from some members of his own community and when he weighs up the agonies and the ecstasies, I would like to leave him this thought: Over the past number of years, SACU introduced thousands of underprivileged youngsters with a view to broadening the base of cricket, giving these children new opportunities through cricket and improving race relations in South Africa through cricket. Now Omar himself is dedicating himself to this cause.

'He has, throughout, been the light at the end of the tunnel, the role model for a new generation of cricketers – the man very much in the middle.'

SPRINGBOK
AT LAST!

The situation when I began my new job with Boland in Stellenbosch was curious. We had serious aspirations of becoming a fully fledged 'A' province although the financial situation was hardly encouraging. And, of course, we had a major university on our doorstep. However, Stellenbosch University was affiliated to Western Province, in spite of the fact that it was very much at the heart of Boland.

In South Africa, the universities are an important nursery for first-class cricket and we therefore tried hard to persuade the university to throw in their lot with us. The carrot was that the South African Cricket Union had indicated that if we won the 'B' Province Section, we had every chance of being elevated to 'A' province status. However, the university decided to stay where they were.

Boland had already won the 'B' Province Section under the guidance of Eddie Barlow. Our playing headquarters were based at the Stellenbosch Farmers' Winery ground, a really pleasant ground with a good wicket. The Farmers' Winery were eager to see us progress and had guaranteed to us that should we gain 'A' status, they in turn would up-grade the ground and put in chalets which would serve as corporate hospitality units for sponsors.

The coaching regime we set ourselves was demanding. Boland is a widespread area, previously known as Western Province Country Districts, a farming and wine-growing area covering a widely scattered rural population. We covered many a long kilometre as we trekked from one end of the district to the other, often staying away overnight and simply carrying on the next day, visiting schools and clubs either by day or in the evenings, up to Malmesbury, nearly 80 kilometres north of Cape Town, east to Worcester, 80 kilometres in the other direction, south to Strand on the other side of False Bay, penetrating every populated corner of this scattered community, or so it seemed. Our mission was to find talented youngsters, no matter what their race, creed or colour, and then implant a coaching regime to ensure that such talent could be properly developed.

Stephen Jones produced a 100-page document which set out the structure that was needed to achieve our goals, detailing the procedures we would have to put in place. I could not help thinking that I was beginning once again to follow in the footsteps of my boyhood hero, Trevor Goddard, who, years earlier, had engaged himself upon a similar mission. Stephen was an absolute bundle of energy, completely dedicated to the task, and I was swept along by the tide, carried along by the sheer enthusiasm of the man and the mission. We worked as a team and at times I felt like some ancient explorer, visiting places which I had never visited before, entering areas where rugby had established a strong grip but often where cricket had never been developed. It was pioneering work and although sometimes Conita was not too happy about the amount of time I was spending away from home, I was fired with a new zeal. If I wanted a challenge, well, I certainly was confronted with one now.

As important as enthusing the kids themselves was the need to organise the teachers, to keep them on the right tracks. Some might say we were making bricks without straw but, believe me, there was progress to observe, plus factors which galvanised us into even greater efforts. And of course, in between we had to also concentrate on our cricket, on drawing together what talent we had and making the best of it. Perhaps the other dimensions of the job took some sort of toll. I suppose that was inevitable because we were always trying to squeeze quarts from pint pots in terms of the time available to us to work on our own cricket.

Consequently our first season could at best only be described as moderately successful. I scored only 163 runs in 9 innings at an average of 18 with a highest score of 50. However, there was an immediate bonus for me in terms of my bowling. No longer was I the tail-end charlie of the spinners and as a result I bowled 174 overs and took 22 wickets at 20.9 apiece. It wasn't that I was turning in match-winning performances, bowling sides out; more that knowing I was expected to bowl long spells, I rediscovered the rhythm that is so important and consequently I was back into my old groove of nagging accuracy.

We had recruited Kim Barnett from Derbyshire and Gordon Parsons, the Leicestershire medium-pacer, who against Transvaal 'B' produced a wonderful spell on the famous Wanderers ground, in which he had 9 for 72. Stephen was hardly able to bowl his left-arm quickies because of a back injury but he really worked hard on his batting and became a fine middle-order batsman.

Our coaching work was rewarded when we produced the first non-white player to represent South African Schools, Salieg Nackerdien, from Paarl, not far from Stellenbosch, a left-handed bat who was also a good fielder. I actually remembered him coming to practise at Newlands as a 15-year-old and recall being very impressed with him then. He played for a coloured club called Young Peoples. I have always thought that he was a very talented player. Later, he was to prove me right.

Even if sport was now open, cricket at schools was certainly still played on a racial basis. There were still those who were preaching the gospel of no normal sport in an abnormal society. However, one way round it was for coloured club sides to play against white schools, and Salieg began to expand his playing experience in this way. He was an outstanding prospect and eventually made it into the Boland side. There were some extremely promising white cricketers who also began to emerge, like Gielie Vermeulen, Carl Spilhaus, a wicket-keeper-batsman, Marius le Grange and Louis Coen, now playing for Eastern Province, all of whom went to teachers' college and thence by bursary to the university with the condition that they played for us. Louis's case illustrates the difficulty we were working under. He wanted to play at the highest level and in the end had to leave Boland in order to play Currie Cup cricket.

With Stephen Jones I shared many moments of emotion, both highs and lows. We had become acquainted in club cricket, had played together in Western Province 'B' cricket and thereafter in the 'A' team. Like me he had had a spell overseas in both England, where he was pro for Haslingden in the Lancashire League, and then in Holland, where he became a coach. We had our moments together on the field, particularly when we set a new record for Boland – and in South African first-class cricket – in a 6th-wicket partnership of 259 against Border at East London in the 1987-88 season. I had a century whilst he went one better with a double 100. He is currently the coach for Border.

From a fairly modest beginning, we really managed to make things tick at Boland and I really felt stable in my career, travelling to Scotland as a professional at the end of each South African season and returning to Boland each September. More significantly, perhaps, a good deal of my life was taken up with coaching: coaching club players and, of course, the international squads in Scotland, and coaching in Boland when I returned home. And I had another addition to the family: Reyhana, unlike her sister, was born in South Africa, in Cape Town. The extra confidence I gained from the stability that Boland gave me, plus my success in Scotland and playing for Scotland against the first-class English counties, was certainly reflected in my performances. In my second season with Boland, I scored 374 first-class runs at an average of almost 25 with a top score of 117 and took 38 wickets at under 20 apiece. It was a tremendous season for us and we carried all before us, winning the Castle Bowl and, so we thought, paving the way to Currie Cup cricket. It was not to be, however.

In spite of all the assurances, we were not to be promoted to the top echelons of South African cricket. The authorities reneged on their promises and we remained anchored as a second-class cricketing province, much to everyone's disappointment. Cited against us was a weakness in administration and finance, yet we were confident that, given the opportunity, these were facets of our operation which could be put right. Politics, of a cricketing kind, was at work.

In the following season, 1986-87 – a very significant one for me, as I shall reveal – I averaged 38 with the bat and picked up 20 wickets, followed that up in 1987-88 by averaging 34 and capturing 36 wickets, and in my last season averaged 28 and had my best-ever season with the ball with 41 wickets. So these were good years for me. However, after winning the Castle Bowl in 1985-86, we plummeted from top to bottom, having on the way – and in no small measure due to the failure of the authorities to elevate us – lost several key players.

Meanwhile, elsewhere in the world, events were stirring up the cricketing establishment. Kerry Packer had poached many of the world's top players for his World Series television bonanza and we in South Africa, indirectly, were destined to benefit from that. As I have said before, whilst the enthusiasm for cricket in South Africa remained high, doubts had surfaced about the quality of the game here. Apart from the few rebel tours, there were no means of measuring the standard of our players compared with those of the rest of the world. South Africa, not just in a cricketing sense but in sporting terms as a whole, remained in isolation and although there had been a considerable leavening of the bread, so to speak, and an integration of cricket across the races, there were still massive chasms in terms of equality of opportunity. Coloured and black cricketers had so many obstacles placed in front of them, not least sometimes by the obduracy of those who kept on insisting that they would not condone normal sport until radical change was effected at political and social levels to clear society of the abnormal conditions in which we lived.

I remained optimistic that eventually the spirit of liberalisation would win through, that the politicians would have to bow to pressures both within and from without to save South Africa from economic slide and social chaos, even civil war. I have always been, I think, an optimist! There were those chinks of light which kept us in touch with the realities of world cricket and in my third season with Boland, at a time when my own career was really burgeoning, a second Australian rebel tour was scheduled following a successful first venture in 1985-86. The side, led by Kim Hughes, who had been deposed from the captaincy of his national team, was to visit South Africa and play a series of unofficial 'test' matches. If I dwell on this tour rather than its predecessor, the reasons should be obvious, for this time I became involved in a playing sense and was to make a real breakthrough. Perchance to dream? Now at last perhaps an opportunity to test my mettle and, I thought, a faint possibility that, providing I maintained my form, I might just do enough to persuade the selectors to look at me.

Could I, in the nicest way, make Alvin Kallicharran laugh on the other side of his face? Could I fulfil that ambition of playing for my country even though I was by now in my mid-30s? Age, however, the figure on a birth certificate, is irrelevant. I had never flagged in my pursuit of physical fitness. I was in peak condition during that season and, I venture to suggest, playing some of the best cricket of my life. So the impossible dream might not, after all, be that impossible. I was filled with eagerness and optimism.

The team coming to South Africa was, by the rebel nature of the tour, not Australia's strongest. Nevertheless, it was a pretty impressive side. Steve Smith and John Dyson from New South Wales, both of whom had recorded double centuries in Sheffield Shield cricket were the two main opening batsmen, but the stars of the Aussie tour were Carl Rackemann, who outshone Terry Alderman as a strike bowler, and the tireless John Maguire, who sent down 283 overs during the tour, an average of 35 overs a match. But leg-spinner Trevor Hohns made a decided impact, especially in the third unofficial 'test' match.

The tour was not popular with the cricketing establishment in London. The ICC condemned these adventures to South Africa; they were certainly reported to be unpopular with some Australians and there were certain political connotations Down Under. But here in South Africa, there was little fuss made about the arrival of the Australians.

So this was no third-class team and at the very least it would give us South Africans a measure of our own progress. I had an early encounter with them when the tourists came to Stellenbosch to play Boland and, I think, performed well without necessarily hitting the headlines. In their innings I bowled 10 steady overs to take 2 for 34, picking up the wickets of Mike Taylor and Mike Haysman as they struggled against us to reach a modest 180 for 8. We were in a good position, needing 56 off the last 10 overs to win, but the loss of Stephen Jones for 39 was crucial and even if we ran them mighty close, in the end they edged home by just 2 runs, my contribution, 9.

The following day, however, we gained our revenge when Danie du

Toit and I returned to the fray for a Boland Invitation team. Although I failed to pick up any wickets, conceding 42 runs in my 10 overs, Danie and I added 82 runs for the 6th wicket in just 13 overs, with Danie in tremendous form, striking eight 4s and three 6s in his unbeaten 65. I was pleased with my contribution of 33 which helped to steer us to victory.

But it was a Jekyll and Hyde sort of season. It wasn't that we played so badly and we had some terrific moments, but we just didn't have that extra push to turn possible victories into real wins. My own form, however, was good. Against Northern Transvaal 'B' I had 4 for 41 in 17 overs in the first innings and 4 for 144 off 60 overs in the second innings. Boy, was I tired after that marathon bowling spell. In between I had scored 79 batting at number 9. And I still finished on the losing side!

I also performed well for the Impalas, which is a team drawn from 'B' province sides which then played in the Currie Cup. In the Benson & Hedges Night Series we gave Transvaal a real fright, restricting them to 161 for 3 in their 29 overs (the game was truncated by rain) and I had a very satisfying 2 for 36. Furthermore, when we took up the chase I managed to top-score with a vigorous 37 as we gave it everything we had only to fall 3 runs short.

If, like my colleagues, I was sick to have got so near yet so far, I nevertheless took personal satisfaction from my own performance. However, such performances are soon forgotten when you fail to achieve victory. Yet that night was not just significant for the result, or for my own personal performance. As we were preparing to go out on to the field, a lady journalist burst into the room and announced that I had been picked for the third unofficial 'test' against the Aussies. I was to replace Alan Kourie. I must say that initially I thought the whole thing was a hoax, in spite of the fact that our President, Jannie Momberg, had suggested that I must be knocking on the door. The dressing room simply erupted and Stephen Jones came over and just said, 'You will lead the team out tonight.' The emotion that flowed was simply phenomenal.

The word had reached some sections of the crowd and the reception they gave me was one of those moments I shall never forget. Emotion was running high within me for several reasons. I was about to become the first-ever Springbok produced by Boland, which you have to remember was a 'B' province team, which made the selection in some ways controversial. I was also the first player from the coloured community to be selected for South Africa. But there was a sadness there, too, for my father had not lived to see this achievement – he had died a few months earlier. It was tragic that he was unable to share with me that wonderful moment for he had been behind me throughout my career, had supported me through thick and thin. How he would have savoured the triumph, the reward for all those heartbreaks. Perhaps, in some ways, he did.

In the cold light of the next day, the pride began to surface as the reality began to dawn. But there was no doubt in my mind. I had been in excellent form and I believed sufficiently in my own ability and in my inner strength to satisfy myself that I was there on merit. The telephone in my mother's house was jammed with thousands of calls. All the world, it seemed, wanted to congratulate me. There were letters, telegrams and people, wherever I went, who just wanted to offer me their best wishes.

You see that moment of glory wasn't just for me, it was for the non-white community of South Africa. If cricket by then was open, in everyday life, there remained a gulf between the whites and non-whites. It may sound a bit melodramatic, but I did believe that I was carrying a torch for my people and for the future of South Africa, blazing a trail which others, in time, could follow. I had wanted it all so badly; now my resolve, my determination to plough this furrow, had been fully rewarded and I like to think that equally rewarded were my family and friends. And the tangible rewards, not in monetary terms but in the shape of telegrams and telephone calls from Tom Graveney, for instance, who was in the country doing commentaries for television, and of course from Basil D'Oliveira, I will cherish all my life.

It was inevitable that there would be people who did not support my selection, those for instance, who said that the selectors were guilty of window-dressing, that I was the token gesture towards non-racial cricket. As I have already said, the man I replaced, Alan Kourie, was one of those who criticised my selection and he was severely censured for expressing that opinion. I replied to some of the press critisism and said quite bluntly that it would be wrong if my selection had been based upon politics rather than cricket, but I was able to cite the rich vein of form I had found and suggest that I had been picked on merit and for no other reason. I believe that my subsequent performance in the 'test', not to mention my later achievements, were proof of the pudding. I had no doubt at all that I was there on merit but, I suppose inevitably, during the ensuing years the accusation that the selectors were making political gestures was repeated. You have to learn to live with these things, to shrug them off, otherwise you would get nowhere.

Nevertheless, all these comments represented a tiny minority. The vast majority of people believed, as I believed, that I deserved to picked. Of course, I was aware of the responsibility that rested on my shoulders. I had achieved what no one else had achieved; I was, in a sense, the pioneer, the pathfinder, the first player from the coloured community to make the breakthrough to the top. If inwardly I was in awe of that responsibility, I was able to approach that first 'test' match with a positive attitude and with self-belief.

Alan Kourie's outburst was probably a knee-jerk response to being dropped. He had not been in good form and I think his reaction was based largely on the fact that I was, at that time, playing for Boland in the 'B' Section of first-class cricket, whereas he was playing for the all-powerful Transvaal team, the 'mean machine'. Yet I had plenty of cricket experience at the top level during my years with Western Province.

There was no time to dwell on things, however. The very next day I had to go to Jo'burg to get kitted out and then travel to Durban, where the game was scheduled to take place. Ali Bacher, when I met him in Jo'burg to collect my kit, told me that he was absolutely delighted I had been selected. It was a reward for him, too, because he had worked so hard to create opportunities for the underprivileged. He had a soft spot for development in the game and you only have to examine his list of achievements to realise what he has done for cricket in South Africa and, in a more general sense, to bring people together. In some respects my selection may well have been even more significant for him than it was for me because it was the culmination of all that he had stood for. 'This is the moment to show your true ability,' he told me, 'and this is the way forward!'

It goes without saying that there were those on the political extremes who tried to make capital out of the situation. The threats I had experienced all those years ago when I threw in my lot with mixed cricket after the SACBOC kangaroo court, the death threats, the threats against my parents, were repeated and at Dr Bacher's instigation, a guard was placed on my mother's house for the duration of the 'test' match.

I always believed that such threats were nothing more than that, just threats. I don't think I ever believed they were serious. However, there was, in reality, a persistently hard core of really extreme thinking in the political arena. I had always thought that cricket, rather than extreme politics, could be a catalyst for change. Is politics the only vehicle to make you a better person or to bring you greater opportunity or even to create a better society? I felt that I had a chance to show that there were other means and that for me at least, cricket had become that vehicle. There were, of course, those who were not prepared to countenance such a view and who, in my opinion, had buried their heads in the sand.

There were still anomalies to confront. I could stay in the same hotel as the other players, share the same dressing room, share the same emotions in either victory or defeat. I could and would be the centre of attraction to all when I did well and fade to the periphery when I didn't, just like all the other players in the team, white or non-white. But I couldn't, in Durban, go on the same beach as the rest of them. At least, according to the law I couldn't. I can tell you now that in point of fact I *did* go on the beach with them, fully prepared to take the consequences. No one did a thing to prevent me or eject me.

Again, the barriers were coming down and the beach incident reminds me that on one occasion, I took my family to the 'whites-only' beach at the Strand. My children, having spent so much time in Scotland, where they were treated like anyone else, with no race laws to concern them, were worried that we were contravening regulations but we went there and no one said a thing. If they had, we would merely have got up and gone – we wouldn't have argued. It was a different way of confronting an already crumbling system, without belligerence, without rancour, just doing what seemed to be right.

Predictably, Hassan Howa voiced his disquiet about my selection for the 'test' team. If he was something of a dictator, he was nevertheless a man of principle and he was a very clever and strong-willed person. I made it clear to him years earlier that as a cricketer, I had to do my job to the best of my ability, come what may. I believed in the path I had taken; he didn't, and he was entitled to his own opinion. Curiously enough, he sent his children to a white university under permit. I didn't object to him doing that, but I did object to the system forcing him to have to obtain a permit. Education is vital and the artificial barriers then in existence were entirely counter-productive.

In essence, the whole philosophy of apartheid was palpably wrong. I did not look to confront authority; I simply followed my belief – the belief that is part of my faith – that all human beings must be treated equally irrespective of creed or colour.

When I reached Durban a couple of days before the 'test' for practice, the rest of the team gave me the warmest of welcomes. My old Western Province team-mates Peter Kirsten and Garth le Roux were thrilled for me and the captain, Clive Rice, was equally warm in his welcome and congratulations, notwithstanding the fact that I had replaced one of his Transvaal colleagues, Alan Kourie.

There was not a trace of racism. The players treated the whole business as a normal part of the everyday comings and goings of career cricketers. I was no different from them, just another member of the team.

However, in the outside world things were different. An article in one of the South African papers read thus:

'We quote from a report in the London *Sunday Times* on the selection of Omar Henry to play against the Australian cricketers: "While Henry can change in a white dressing room before the big match, he will run into trouble if he goes for a dip in the sea after the game with his team-mates on a white beach. He can play on a pitch in a white suburb, but as a coloured he cannot live there. And while he can coach white boys at white schools, he cannot send his children there." What if the beaches were desegregated, and the Group Areas Act repealed, and all schools opened to all races? Well, says *The Sunday Times,* there's still the problem of malnutrition, poverty, divided families... There are many compelling arguments for the removal of racial inequality, but winning over foreign opinion is not among them.'

Well, that article had a sting in its tail. And along with several other comments it certainly seemed to transpose the background of my selection from a cricketing scenario to one deeply immersed in the politics of the day. I have to confess that I did have my moments of doubt and myself became caught up in the web spun by those to whom political ends were paramount – at the expense of cricket. An edited version of the interview I gave to two London *Sunday Times* journalists was published in the South African press. In it I am freely quoted, on that occasion making, perhaps for the first time in my career, comments on the uphill struggle I had experienced in reaching the pinnacle of playing cricket for South Africa. This is how it read:

'When Henry took his place in the national side it marked the end of a different odyssey from that of his ten white team-mates. They had been carefully nurtured at white schools with good facilities, qualified coaches and all the right equipment. Henry, on the other hand, is the oldest of six children of a Stellenbosch bookbinder. As a boy he played cricket barefoot and watched whites playing at Newlands. "Apartheid kept us back and restricted our opportunities, so I watched white cricketers and stole from them with my eyes," he says.

'A white Afrikaner matron who read an article about him took him to a sports shop and kitted him out at 16. Until he was 23, Henry played in the non-white leagues. One day in 1976, he and some team-mates dropped into a white ground. "We were driving past and, like any sportsmen, we stopped to watch, just for ten minutes."

'But this was against SACB policy and, after he refused to apologise, Henry was banned. He promptly moved to SACU. "I was called a Nazi, a traitor, told I should be put up against a wall and shot – all by people I knew."

'For the next nine years, Henry divided his time between playing in South Africa and the UK. Henry's approach is accepted by few of his community. He wanted to plough back his cricket experience by coaching at his local school for free, "but they didn't want me".

'One man who firmly believes that Henry's selection is just window-dressing is the controversial Hassan Howa, who coined the rallying cry, "No normal sport in an abnormal society." He says: "As far as cricket is concerned, Omar Henry is a 'white person', a coloured playing under special concession."

'Henry's success has been achieved in spite of the many disadvantages faced by non-white cricketers. But even as he took to the field of what should have been the crowning moment of his cricketing career, Henry said it just wasn't worth it. "I can say, even on selection, if I'd known what was in store I would never have played the sport." And he vowed that no son of his would play the sport "in this atmosphere – I just happen to love cricket, but not enough to see my child suffer."

'He is deeply worried about the fate of his two girls as they reach school age. "People are very cruel," he says. "They will blame them for what I did. They may take it out on my kids. The moment that happens, I'll give up cricket."

I think when I spoke to those journalists, I had had enough of the nonsense and was merely giving vent to my feelings. Perhaps it was, for me, a momentary pause, albeit that I was genuinely concerned about the possibility of people taking things out on my children.

To counter-balance that rare moment of bitterness on my part, at least the heading to the article reflected the other end of my emotional spectrum. There I was quoted thus: 'I'm grateful for the selectors' faith in me. This opportunity for me is just great.'

In essence, what they were trying to portray was the truth that a sportsman's life, particularly in South Africa and most especially if you come from the kind of background I had, is not some kind of fairy tale. But these things are all part of the checks and balances of this mad world we live in.

The other side of the coin, written by someone who very definitely did not share Hassan Howa's views – Darrell Thomson – can be shown in the following lines:

'Forget those unkindly jibes of window-dressing. Omar Henry, South Africa's first coloured Test cricketer, did more than enough to prove himself a worthy Springbok on the opening day of the Third Test against Australia at Kingsmead yesterday.

'Keenly aware of the additional responsibilities thrust upon him by his historic selection and the stinging criticism which followed, the slim 34-year-old Bolander yesterday rose to the occasion in great style.

'For a man only too conscious of his situation and watched by an appreciative Kingsmead crowd of more than 10,000 sweltering fans, Henry responded to the call of his captain with a commendable bowling performance that will be recalled as a dream Test match debut.

'In doing so, Henry not only justified the faith placed in him by the Springbok selectors. He also silenced his detractors in the most telling manner possible by claiming 2 of the 3 most important Australian wickets to fall on a pitch hardly conducive to left-arm spin bowling.

'Introduced to the Springbok attack when his team-mates were wilting in the exceptional Kingsmead humidity, Henry needed but 3 overs to grab his maiden Test wicket. And in doing so, he halted in its tracks a threatening Australian 4th-wicket stand between Steve Smith (137) and Graham Yallop (36) to bring his team back into the match.

'At that stage, the two Australians were pushing the score along at a rousing rate to be 148 for 3 before Henry struck in, bamboozling Yallop to play down the wrong line. He was through again 12 overs later to claim the prize scalp of the Australian innings, Smith, when Hugh Page held a fine catch to have the Australians on 220 for 6.'

There were more accolades. For instance, Ray Williams writing in *The Sunday Times* said:

'Newcomer Omar Henry also emerged with flying colours, claiming 2 valuable wickets for 58 runs off 23 tantalising overs of genuine spin.' And Michael Owen-Smith used my 'test' debut to propound the belief that Boland should be elevated to Currie Cup status when he wrote:

'Henry's selection may have come as a surprise to many but this may largely be as a result of the fact that he has been at a disadvantage in terms of opportunity. Boland have only played two first-class matches this season – against Northerns 'B' and Natal 'B' – and Henry has taken 15 wickets and scored a century. What clinched his selection was his 3 for 9 for the Impalas in the historic Benson & Hedges Night Series win against Eastern Province.'

He went on to say that my selection was one more reason for putting Boland in the Currie Cup. 'He is a genuine product of the area in that he grew up and learned his cricket in Stellenbosch.'

I think I proved, obviously to the satisfaction of these journalists and cricket pundits, that I had earned my call-up to the colours.

The whole experience was so tremendous. To be in that hothouse and play in a 'test' match was reward in itself but I really do think I did myself justice. And I was delighted by the way Clive Rice handed me so much responsibility. In Australia's second innings, although I failed to take a wicket, I was asked to bowl 26 overs and bowled so tightly that they took only 44 runs off me. The match was drawn, although after having held the upper hand for so long, the wheels nearly came off in our second innings when, facing a target of 276 at about 4 an over, we were undermined by Trevor Hohns and his leg spin, finishing on a somewhat shaky 143 for 7.

If I thought I had experienced a taste of just how hard test cricket could be, the fourth and final 'test' at Port Elizabeth certainly extended that experience. Apart from the 'hat-trick that never was', I bowled 36.5 overs in the first innings to take 3 for 96, and a further 35 overs – 16 more than anyone else – in the second, 0 for 63 with 14 maidens. It meant that the captain, at least, had plenty of faith in me and I felt sure in my own mind that it completely scotched the stories that my selection was window-dressing, that my appearance was a token gesture on the part of the selectors. A captain does not ask someone selected on that basis to bear the brunt of the bowling as Clive Rice did on both occasions. I had no doubt, the players had no doubt and, in the end, the pundits had no doubt that I was in that side for one reason and one reason alone – merit!

Everyone wants to know about your first wicket in Test cricket. I remember it as clearly as if it happened yesterday. I was bowling over the wicket to the left-hander Yallop, trying to exploit the rough. He kept coming down the wicket but couldn't get me away so I gave the ball a little bit of extra flight. He came at me again but just didn't get to the pitch and lofted it to mid on where Hugh Page took a good catch, running in, a couple of feet from the ground. It was a good piece of cricket and I was, quite naturally, elated, as were my team-mates. I had settled well and had got rid of the butterflies which not surprisingly had fluttered about in my tummy when I first went on to bowl. I had used all the guile I had learned down the years and taken my first Test wicket.

It's funny really that Kim Hughes had already written an article advocating my selection for South Africa following my good performance against the Aussies for Boland. He was one of the first to congratulate me when I arrived at the ground on the first day.

If I was under pressure before the game – pressure from the media, pressure from that section of the community which was not convinced about my credentials – then the part I played in those two 'test' matches boosted my confidence and, in some ways, took the pressure off. If I had felt doubts, those doubts had been blown to the wind. My confidence was also lifted by Clive Rice's approach to things. He is a thoughtful captain and he always discusses the game plan with his bowlers. He expects you then to implement that plan and demands that you follow the strategy. In that I got a long bowl in both those 'tests' and, apparently, fulfilled all that was expected of me by my captain, I was given a further confidence boost. However, I have always guarded against complacency. From such experiences – the highs of life as well as the lows – you must always learn. I learned plenty from those two 'tests' and felt sure at the time that I had not only proved my own mental strength but proved to the world, even the sceptics, that I was certainly not out of place in such company. Not only was I able to learn from my own involvement in the game, I also learned by watching all these great cricketers at first hand.

I felt at the time that I was in the side essentially as a bowler. I was at number 10 in the batting order and must confess, in retrospect, that I somewhat forgot about my batting. That attitude of mind was wrong – something else I learned. I was perfectly capable of batting well against the Aussie attack but I didn't apply myself well enough. In the first 'test', I got out when I played a rather airy-fairy shot, trying to hit the ball on the up off Rodney Hogg and getting caught in the covers. It was a fault in my game at that time. If my mind wasn't quite in gear, I was capable of being a little careless and it wasn't long before I started to chastise myself for it. I knew that I must now ensure that I concentrated *all* the time, not just when I was bowling and fielding.

The second 'test' was notable for the continuous flow of runs. In the first innings Smith scored 77 for the Aussies, Shipperd 53, Rixon 61 and

Kepler Wessels (still playing for Australia at that time) had 135 and I was delighted to pick up his wicket. Always a solid batsman, on that occasion he really got his head down, batting for 361 minutes, facing 295 balls. Again, I used the rough by bowling over the wicket to him and it paid off because he went to cut me, the ball turned just that fraction more and clean bowled him. My second wicket came when I beat Steve Rixon in the air, he played too soon and Hugh Page completed the job at cover. My arm ball was enough to trap Rodney Hogg first ball as he padded up and suddenly I was the centre of attraction, set for a hat-trick.

Enter Rod McCurdy. This time I floated a spinner up, he played forward, nowhere near the line, the ball pitched leg and middle, turned just enough and hit McCurdy on the back foot, plumb in everybody's book – except, and most importantly, the umpire's. The hat-trick that never was.

I must confess I said a thing or two to the umpire, all in the heat of the moment, having appealed twice, the second time from on my knees! I even suggested that his eyesight was not what it might have been. You can't put the clock back but I must have looked somewhat wistful some six months later when umpire Leibenburg confessed to me that after seeing the television replay, he now thought that McCurdy was in fact out. It is never any use crying over spilled milk, but if only...

The run flow continued and we were all treated to an absolutely superb innings from Graeme Pollock, who scored a quite magnificent 144. It was one of those innings it really was a privilege to see. Kenny McEwan also had a century and Jimmy Cook 84 as we went to 533 all out. I had 13 before once again being a little careless and trying to hit the ball on the up. For the Aussies Wessels had a second century in the match and Smith 100 as the game, inevitably, was drawn.

Something else I learned was that even great players sometimes suffer from nerves. Graeme Pollock paced the dressing room endlessly before he went in, could have been out within two balls but then produced the goods. Pollock in full flow is very special. And this event was special, his last Test match and at his own ground at that. The whole dressing room was charged with emotion. My batting experience also taught me a lesson or two. When I went out to join Kenny McEwan, I was greeted by a bouncer first ball from Rod McCurdy, which hit me on the helmet and knocked me over. He just said, 'Get up, you bush turkey!' Kenny Mack told me to just forget about them and concentrate on the ball. When he got the strike Kenny almost inevitably despatched the next ball, another bouncer, to the mid-wicket boundary. McCurdy responded with more and the more he tried, the further the ball went. Kenny McEwan was a superb batsman and again I was privileged to be at the other end watching his mastery over the bowler.

With all those runs scored – 1,321 for the fall of 23 wickets – a draw, as I said, was inevitable. The statistics show that the Aussies scored 455 for 9 declared in their first innings, a total we overhauled by scoring 533. But they ground it out in the second innings to finish on 333 for 4. However, we were jubilant because it meant we had won the series. Although I was not in the team for the first and only decisive 'test' in the series at the Wanderers, which we had won by the relatively narrow margin of 49 runs, I nevertheless felt that I shared in the series victory, that I was a part of the 'test' squad.

There followed the one-day series. I was not included for the first game at Port Elizabeth, where the emphasis was very much on the pace attack. The game itself was regarded as one of the best one-day internationals ever played in South Africa. However, it took a remarkable collapse in the Australian batting to see our boys home. It had looked as if the Aussies were going to cruise to victory when Clive Rice, in the space of a few overs, turned things round and reduced them from 298 for 2 to 310 all out, 8 wickets falling, amazingly for just 12 runs, and South Africa winning by an astonishing 6-run margin when all had seemed lost. Rice with 5 wickets, 4 of them in 11 balls, snatched victory in an inspired spell.

I was brought in for the second game at Newlands which again we won, this time rather more comfortably, by 8 wickets with 4 overs in hand. Rain had intervened but the Aussies batted indecisively, losing 2 early wickets to Allan Donald's bowling. I only bowled 6 overs, but I nevertheless played an important part by dismissing Kepler Wessels when he was just beginning to get going. I gave the ball a little bit more air and he played over the top of it. At 119 for 5 they were in deep trouble but a spirited stand of 57 between Mick Taylor and Peter

Faulkner saw them to the comparative safety of 199 for 7. The rain eventually saw our target adjusted to 188, which turned out to be stroll with Peter Kirsten and Jim Cook in full flow.

I was omitted from the third game, played at Centurion Park, where the Australians came back from the dead to record a 5-wicket win, and failed to earn a recall for the fourth and last game of the series in Jo'burg which we won by 4 wickets. This was Graeme Pollock's last Springbok appearance. What a player! How sad that he was unable to properly fulfil his career on the international stage because of our isolation. If, as I have said, this was by no means Australia's best team, I think we had done enough to show that in spite of the lack of genuine international competition, we were still a force to be reckoned with.

Cricket is so often about peaks and troughs and during that 1986-87 season, I had a rollercoaster existence. Whereas I had, very proudly, become the first Bolander to become a Springbok, at Boland itself we had gone from riches to rags, from Castle Bowl champions with expectations of being elevated to Currie Cup status to wooden-spoonists. I missed two matches because of my selection for the Springboks but was still the top wicket-taker with 15 victims. And I topped the batting averages on 47.83, having scored just under 300 runs, which included an unbeaten century against Natal 'B'. I had become accustomed to the slings and arrows. My departure, in the early days, from SACBOC, and the threats which followed, were renewed, as I have said, when I was capped by the international selectors. In such circumstances, you really have to grit your teeth, grin and bear it. It isn't pleasant and now, of course, I had a wife and two children to worry about. That, perhaps, was the one chink in my armour, the one factor that momentarily gave me cause to question the course I had charted for myself. Yet I knew, even in those moments of doubt, that there was no turning back. Cricket was my living and I knew that I had to make the best of it, now that I had that extra responsibility. Vitally, Conita had no such doubts. As my family had stood by me in those early days, now Conita stood shoulder to shoulder with me, never doubting, always encouraging. She, too, needed all the resolve she could summon up; had to grin and bear it; had to face the slings and arrows. In that respect, I was not alone. And, in other respects, I had the escape route of another season in Scotland.

Before my departure things were beginning to stir. Dr Ali Bacher, a man dedicated to the game of cricket in South Africa, a man with vision and a man determined to cross the artificial racial barriers which, by the nature of things had seen the game develop as predominantly a white sport, was working tirelessly to get cricket into the black townships. His mini-cricket programme may be summarised from the following paragraph published in an article in the *Protea Cricket Annual* of South Africa.

'Based on the Churchillian theory of "give them the tools, and most people build a future for themselves", Dr Bacher, with the help of a small but never-say-die and resourceful team, had, quite literally, thousands and thousands of cricket bats made from South African pine, and even more specially made "soft" balls manufactured by Dunlop – and they were given to children in black townships and indeed throughout the country in the mini-cricket programme.'

The success of this venture culminated in March when he brought together a group of wealthy businessmen whose task was to raise substantial sums of money to take the game even more intensively into the townships. The Chairman of the South African Executive Cricket Club, as they came to be known, Mervyn King, a former judge, was also quoted in the annual: 'We have to address our problems at grass-roots level, and by taking cricket to the children in the townships, we can do a great deal towards making South Africa a better place in which to live.'

All this gave all of us cause for hope. But, much as these endeavours represented positive steps on the part of the country's leading cricket administrator and his merry band of businessmen, the fact – the brutal fact – of apartheid, still remained in place. Furthermore, things were stirring; there was a growing tide of unrest beginning to rise in the country at large. As we departed for another season in Scotland, we were conscious that a new wind of change was beginning to blow through the country. There was, therefore, an underlying current of uncertainty, not just about the political and social future but in our minds at least, about our own future.

We wondered about settling more permanently in Scotland, where our two girls would be free of the stain of apartheid, where they could live freely in an unsegregated society and where they could grow up without the clouds of fear hanging over them. Notwithstanding the fact that I was contracted to return to Boland for the 1987-88 season, it was something which Conita and I thought about very seriously. However, we did return home in September after another good season in Scotland in which my then club, Stenhousemuir, although failing to win the League Championship again, won the Masterton Trophy.

Irrespective of the financial difficulties which were faced by Boland, there was a determination to put the disasters of the 1986-87 season behind us and accordingly the club had signed three professionals from the English game. Kim Barnett was returning, bringing with him Simon Base, a medium-fast bowler, born in England but raised in South Africa, who after a couple of seasons with Glamorgan was to join Derbyshire. He had also played with me for Western Province. The third Englishman was Phil Newport, the young Worcestershire medium-fast bowler I had played against for Scotland and one who was strongly tipped to make it to the English Test team.

So there was a new resolve in Stellenbosch, a determination to rise again to the top and continue the quest for Currie Cup status. It was a challenge which I approached, from a personal point of view, with extra relish. The other thoughts would, for the time being at least, have to be put on the back-burner. There was a job to be done.

•••••••••••••••••

ADRIAN KUIPER

Adrian Kuiper, who is one of South Africa's most talented cricketers, played with Omar when they were both with Western Province and has also shared in many of his triumphs, being a member of the World Cup squad and the squad which went to the West Indies.

'When I started playing for Western Province, we played together for the Province "B" team and he immediately made an impact as a very good spinner, in fact a good all-round cricketer. Unfortunately, it was difficult for Omar to break through into "A" province cricket because we had a really first-class leg-spinner in Denys Hobson and eventually Omar decided to throw in his lot with Boland instead. In hindsight, that might not have been the right decision because soon afterwards, Denys retired from the first-class game and I'm sure Omar would have made the spinner's role in our team his own. However, there was no international cricket at that time, so it may well be that he was right.

'He certainly continued to develop as a fine player, both with Boland, for whom he performed magnificently, and of course in Scotland. Playing cricket all the year round was bound to make him into a better player. I'm sure he learned a great deal from playing in Scotland in the different conditions that prevail there, and I'm equally sure he learned a great deal about himself – a fact which is I think, underlined by his professionalism. Cricket is his life.

'His batting, in my opinion, has improved and matured as he has grown older. He is a good striker of the ball, times it beautifully and of course is very wristy. He is always looking to get on top of the bowlers, never afraid to face a challenge. As a bowler, I'm sure that had South Africa been competing in the international arena, he would have been a regular in the Springbok team long ago, primarily as a very good spinner but also because he can bat and field so well in addition.

'It very often takes one person to show a team that they can win games and Omar is, in my view, a winner, one of a rare breed. He has learned to be a winner through his determination and his willingness to always learn; he is a thinking cricketer.

'Omar is a fantastic person. He has a heart of gold; he is honest and sincere and he and his family I count as really good friends.'

BLOOMING IN BLOEMFONTEIN

The arrival at Stellenbosch of Kim Barnett, Simon Base and Phil Newport was, in itself, a confidence-booster for all of us. With Jannie Momberg at the helm, Stephen Jones continuing as captain and me renewing my responsibilities in the coaching sector, there was a real spirit of optimism abroad. All of us felt that we could put the disappointments of the previous season behind us and really go for it. That goal of Currie Cup cricket was still very much alive and there was a real belief that providing we could repeat the feats of two seasons earlier when we had won the Castle Bowl, our prospects of breaking through to the big time this time were much higher.

It was a bit of a chicken-and-egg situation. A successful side obviously enjoys better support but it is much harder to draw large crowds for 'B' grade cricket and thus much more difficult to raise the kind of money needed to support a successful team with all the infrastructure you need in administration and, most importantly, the development programme we wanted to build so that in time, we could produce more home-grown talent for the future. Quite naturally, people are much keener to watch games in which the stars in the country are playing. And of course, that didn't just mean the South African stars but the host of overseas players then beginning to decorate the domestic game in South Africa in increasing numbers.

So this was to be the season of a really big push and we started it well with two straight wins over Griqualand West in the preliminary round of the Nissan Shield. In the round robin section we gave Eastern Province a really hard game, in fact taking them to the very last over before they edged home, thanks largely to Kepler Wessels. At one time I thought we were going to do it when I picked up the wickets of Kenny McEwan and David Richardson after Phil Newport and Simon Base had really tied things down early on, but Kepler's experience saw them home. Yet it was a really battling performance on our part and seemed to set the standard for the rest of the season. It wasn't all plain sailing, however, because the wheels came off for us in the next Nissan Shield game, when Natal gave us a sound thrashing by the massive margin of 198 runs. Yet the resilience of the team was such that we bounced back from that to take Northern Transvaal all the way with a much better performance, even if we lost at the death to exit from the competition.

We began our Bowl season well by beating Western Province 'B' in Stellenbosch in a game in which neither side topped 200 in any of the four innings. However, that game served to illustrate what an important part in our progress the three imports would play. Kim Barnett's 45 in our second innings stopped a dangerous slide; Simon Base had 3 wickets in each innings for us, Phil Newport 4 in the first innings and I had long bowls in both innings, picking up 3 wickets in each.

We followed that up with a great win over Eastern Province 'B' in what turned out to be a splendid game for me. The Province side was very experienced, eight of their players having been regulars in the 'A' team during the previous season. Young Wayne Truter provided the backbone of our first innings with a splendid maiden first-class century but the rest of our top-order batting was a little fragile. I found myself going in with 6 wickets down for just 100. We had no alternative but to dig in and rebuild the innings. It may not have been very entertaining but that is one of the joys of cricket: you can never predict the course a game will take. Together we ground it out, adding 124 in a 6th-wicket stand which turned things round for us. Wayne's patient innings of 107 took 319 minutes and he faced 272 balls. In some respects, my innings was out of character. My stay at the wicket lasted 252 minutes, during which time I faced 224 balls and hit only nine 4s in my 91. I was very pleased with that knock, though, for it showed that I had gained enough maturity to really get my head down when necessary. We reached a respectable 312, which from a rocky 100 for 6 was a splendid recovery.

Simon Base and Phil Newport were soon nibbling away at the Province batting and bit by bit we got right on top. I managed to nip in with a couple of wickets and in spite of resistance from their tail, we nevertheless rolled them over for 136 to make them follow on. Again Base and Newport made the early breakthrough and Province were reeling on 19 for 4 when I was brought into the attack. The only resistance came from Barry van der Vyver and Adrian Birrell, who rescued them from 46 for 6 to 139 for 7, but once I had Birrell caught by Danie du Toit, we had the game in our pockets and had recorded an astonishing victory by an innings and 15 runs. I was really pleased with a return of 5 for 41, 7 in the match, and that obdurate 91 which had provided us with the base for victory along with Wayne Truter's century.

On a rain-affected wicket against Border, however, we slumped to defeat in another low-scoring match – the highest innings total of the game was Border's first innings of 124, Simon Base again proving that he was a really great acquisition by taking 6 for 28. I picked up the other 4 wickets at a cost of 39. We were, in the event, to exact revenge on Border on our way to the Bowl final, but before that we had another cracking win over Eastern Province 'B', Simon Base again producing a good performance with 3 wickets in each innings. I had 4 wickets in the first innings and 6 for 57 in the second, in which I wheeled away for 31 overs. Kim Barnett led the way with the bat in both our innings, scoring 73 in the first and 51 not out in the second to steer us to an easy 7-wicket victory.

Records tumbled when we went to East London to play Border for the second time. On a really placid, easy-paced wicket, having lost a couple of early wickets, we proceeded to top the 500-mark. It was in this game that Stephen Jones and I went into the record books with a 6th-wicket stand of 259. Stephen had a career-best unbeaten 209 and I reached my highest first-class score of 125, after which, as Border also reaped a reward from the easy-paced wicket, I bowled 41 overs – without reward! Border totalled 310. Simon Base showed real stamina by plugging away for 26 overs to be rewarded with 5 for 68. But we couldn't bowl them out in the second innings and the game fizzled out to a predictable draw.

The highlight of the season came in February, when we took on a strong Transvaal 'B' in the Castle Bowl final, played at the Farmers' Winery ground in Stellenbosch in front of quite a good crowd. Having won the toss and decided to bat, we were given a solid start by Wayne Truter but it was Phil Newport – a much better batsman than he is often given credit for – who set things up for us, and Danie du Toit who applied the *coup de grâce* with a whirlwind 89 in 80 minutes off just 47 balls. At one juncture, these two actually added 50 in 18 minutes. On this occasion I myself didn't trouble the scorers.

Our total of 367 with 89 from Danie, 86 from Phil and a late surge provided by Carl Spilhaus, who scored 44, gave us something to bowl at. Phil wasn't finished for he soon made a breakthrough as we worked our way through the Transvaal batting and he finished with 3 wickets. I bowled in tandem with off-spinner Pienaar Anker, and we each picked up 3 wickets to have Transvaal all out for 168. Stephen decided not to enforce the follow-on in spite of our lead of 199 and with Salieg Nackerdien digging in for a long innings of 70 not out, Stephen Jones took the attack to the bowlers and thrashed a quick 64. I chipped in with a rapid 25 and he was able to declare on 257 for 5 to shut Transvaal out of the game.

Phil Newport struck early again but once again Stephen turned to his spin attack and it was Pienaar and myself who, in essence, wrapped things up with 3 wickets apiece to give us a staggering victory by 259 runs just before lunch on the last day.

It was one of the most devastating victories in Castle Bowl history and now, surely, we thought, the administrators must take us into the Currie Cup. What more proof did they need?

It was a season for the underdogs. In the Benson & Hedges Night Series, the Impalas (which, I remind you, is a team drawn from the 'B' provinces) took on the might of Transvaal, with all their galaxy of stars, and beat them in the Danie Craven stadium in Stellenbosch – the rugby stadium – which has floodlights. Boland was well represented in that Impalas side. Kim Barnett, Salieg Nackerdien, Danie du Toit, Stephen

Jones, the captain, Pienaar Anker and myself were all included. Batting first, we got a really solid start and Stephen Jones, going in at number 7, tore the Transvaal attack apart for us to reach 251 in our 45 overs, at 5.5 an over. You have to bear in mind, though, that as the game was played on a rugby field the boundaries square of the wicket were pretty short. We removed Jimmy Cook early on but Mandy Yachad got going with Louis Vorster until I managed to fool Vorster with a well-flighted ball which bowled him. We chipped away and in the end won by the comfortable margin of 28 runs, 8 of the wickets, incidentally, falling to Boland bowlers.

Benson & Hedges night cricket is an exhilarating experience both for players and spectators alike. In South Africa, the sun sets quickly and, compared with summer in the UK, early, so the second part of the game is played in darkness under the floodlights. We also wear coloured clothing, so these games provide the kind of colourful spectacle which cricket followers in the UK are denied. It isn't to everybody's taste, of course.

Traditionalists might suggest that it is not real cricket. However, the proof of the pudding is in the eating. Night cricket certainly attracts the crowds and the atmosphere is tremendous, with lots of noise and plenty of action. The sightscreens are black because the game is played with a white ball, which is so easy to see from the spectator's point of view.

Impalas went on to beat Orange Free State but we lost heavily to Western Province, for whom Daryll Cullinan had a quick-fire 74 off 51 balls. We all took a lot of stick that evening – once again in the rugby stadium – and I went for 45 in just 4 overs as they amassed 272 for 7. Apart from a fine 66 from Border's Emmerson Trotman, we were never really in the hunt. But we did overcome Northern Transvaal in Pretoria – by the narrowest of margins. The scores were level at 208 for each side, Impalas winning by virtue of losing fewer wickets. I had 3 wickets in Northern's innings and we had reached the semi-finals.

But once again, we found Western Province too strong for us. Adrian Kuiper was the key player with an innings of 76 which had the Newlands crowd cheering until they were hoarse. He is such a good player when he is in good nick, which he certainly was on that occasion.

Previous page Omar, a truly Scottish cricketer.

Above Mike Garnham watches as Omar sweeps during Scotland's Benson & Hedges match against Essex in 1990.

Below The Scotland side which beat MCC at Lord's in 1990. Back row (l to r): D.R. Lawrence (president), A.C. Storie, G. Salmond, M.S. Richardson, J.D. Moir, G.B.J. McGurk, A.B. Russell, A. Bee, N.J. Leitch (scorer). Front row: B.M.W. Patterson, C.L. Parfitt, O. Henry (captain), D.J. Haggo, I.L. Philip.

Happy days in Scotland.
Above Footballing friends from Rangers FC: Ian Durrant, Richard Gough and Andy Goram, who was also a Scottish international cricketer under Omar's captaincy.
Left A chat with Allan Lamb on the steps at Hamilton Crescent, Glasgow.
Below left With Michael Holding before a game against Derbyshire.
Below Remembering old times with John Holder who, before his umpiring days, had played as a professional in Cape Town.

Above Australian welcome at the airport when the South African party arrived
for the World Cup in 1992.
Below Four Springboks in the Orange Free State side that won the Castle Cup
in 1992-93, (l to r) Omar, Allan Donald, Hansie Cronje and Corrie van Zyl.
Facing Page Omar poses for the photographers before his first Test
appearance at Durban in 1992.

Omar in front of the mosque (above) at which he has worshipped since childhood and (below) behind the wicket, reviving boyhood memories of 'Tests' played on this same wasteland.

Facing page The real thing – Omar batting for Boland in their first 'A' Province match against Western Province at Stellenbosch in October 1993.

Above Omar in front of his new office at Stellenbosch. **Above right** Omar's daughters Shireen and Reyhana were flower girls when Allan Donald married Tina. **Below** Omar and family – Reyhana, Conita, Omar, Riyaad and Shireen.

A total of 185 was too many for us and we were eventually all out for 137.

With 346 runs at an average of almost 35 and 36 wickets at just under 20 apiece for Boland in the Castle Bowl, I had reason to be pleased with my season. I felt that I had really consolidated, made real progress, after the highs of the previous season and my first experience of cricket at the highest level, the 'tests'. We had no international cricket during the season so it was important for me to maintain and even improve my form, and with those figures, I had again established myself as one of the top all-rounders in the country.

Our imports had all done exceptionally well. Simon Base, who just a year or two earlier had been playing in league cricket at Fish Hoek but was fast establishing himself as a county cricketer in England, took 35 wickets at 15 whilst Phil Newport picked up 23 at 19. Kim Barnett scored 383 runs at an average of 38 but it was Stephen Jones who topped the batting averages with 487 runs at 46.7. Not bad for someone who in the early part of his career was regarded essentially as a bowler. It all goes to show that if you work hard at this game, it is amazing what you can achieve.

Sadly this was to be Stephen's last season with Boland. And what of our quest for Currie Cup status? Well, I'm afraid our financial situation was an absolute shambles. We were in debt. In fact at one time it seemed we might even have to withdraw from Castle Bowl cricket, never mind claim what we believed was our rightful place in senior cricket. Here we were, triumphant and emphatic winners of the Castle Bowl, at the very top of our own grade of cricket with everything to aim for and a real possibility of Currie Cup cricket, only to see our hopes dashed and our very existence in question.

So it was a very thoughtful Omar Henry who departed from Stellenbosch to resume his career in Scotland. This time, I was going on my own for, in spite of all the difficulties Boland were experiencing, it had been decided to grant me a benefit during the following season. I had my commitments to Scotland so it would be Conita who would have to bear the brunt of getting things organised.

My return in September marked yet another milestone in my career. I was to captain Boland for the 1988-89 season. It meant the parting of the ways for my great mate Stephen Jones and I. He was moving to

Border as coach and the loss of his enthusiasm and experience would inevitably leave a considerable gap in our ranks. It was a back injury which curtailed Stephen's bowling but had we been participating in international cricket, I always felt that at his prime he might have been knocking on the door for a Test place. Simon Base was returning but not Kim Barnett or Phil Newport, both of whom had played for England during the 1988 season. We simply could not afford to retain them.

I should pay tribute to Jannie Momberg. Originally a farmer, he had become a successful businessman and it was really due to him, the finance he personally injected and the finance he attracted, that Boland survived. He departed as Boland's President at the end of the 1988-89 season to concentrate on politics. He is a Member of Parliament, now representing the ANC.

In spite of the fact that I was captain and coach, notwithstanding that this was my benefit year, I ran into some difficulties at Boland. I did not see eye to eye with the Chairman of Selectors, Graham Bam. That clash of personalities was to resurface in time. As far as the benefit was concerned, I was lucky enough to pick up a sponsor, a promotional company called Entercor. Eddie Barlow helped enormously, as did many other people such as Frank Brache. I must say that I shall be grateful to those people for the rest of my life because they provided for me the foundation and security I now enjoy. All in all I made 200,000 rand, the equivalent of about £50,000.

The pressures, as you may imagine, were considerable, captaining and organising practice and training for the team. We had crucially lost Stephen and of course there was no Phil Newport, no Kim Barnett, and some of our other players had moved on. So I really wasn't able to devote time to the development side of my job. Furthermore, the financial situation was so rocky that the monthly cheque wasn't always in on time. However, the benefit went better than I could have dreamed. So many people contributed and expressed their support, no matter how little they were able to give, and in essence demonstrated, in the most practical way possible, their support for me, for what I had done and achieved. It brought home to me the fact that it is a tremendous privilege to be given a benefit in the first place. That it raised so much money – money which was to give me the kind of security I could only have dreamed about – made me feel very humble.

Jannie Momberg had suggested that there would be a new long-term contract for me at the end of the season but, of course, he was to retire and be replaced by Graham Bam. In the event, this radically changed the situation and when, at the end of the South African season, I once again departed to fulfil my contracts in Scotland, there was an aura of uncertainty about my future. My current contract had come to an end and I had received an informal approach from Orange Free State. I merely told them to contact me in Scotland. With Jannie gone and Graham at the helm, I did feel troubled about my future with Boland. There is no point in drawing a veil over things. Graham and I simply didn't get on. Such things happen in life but it certainly undermined me and, above all, it was necessary for me to provide stability for my family. Thus any offer had to be considered.

Whilst I was away in Scotland, I had tried without success to make contact with new President and I even asked Howie Bergins to make contact for me. At last I heard from them. I was playing for Scotland at Lord's when I had a phone call from Conita to say that a telegram had arrived offering me a contract with Boland on a reduced salary. There were no details about whether I was to be captain, nothing about coaching; in other words I had absolutely no portfolio at all. It seemed to me that if I stayed at Boland, there would continue to be a clash of personalities between Graham Bam and myself.

I could not make sense of it, nor could I make contact to clarify things and so I thought it would be better if I severed my contact with Boland. It seemed to be a natural parting of the ways for even if I really, in my heart of hearts, wanted to stay, I didn't think we could work together. I don't feel any malice about it, even though some people suggested that I had taken the money from my benefit year and run. If things are not going to work out, then you are better off looking for alternative options and with Free State expressing interest, with all that implied – a return to Currie Cup cricket for me and a chance once again to play at the top level – I decided that was the direction in which to jump. Nor do I think there is any point in harbouring grievances about such things. In spite of what has happened subsequently, I do not bear any grudges but in the last year, the rift between Graham Bam and myself has become a chasm. That however, I will explain later.

As for the season itself, having lost not only Jones, Barnett and Newport, but also Carl Spilhaus and Pienaar Anker, we were also without the services of Salieg Nackerdien and Simon Base for significant periods through injury: over half the team were in effect missing.

On the plus side, we acquired the Essex player John Stephenson to provide some compensation for the loss of the others. He quickly showed his mettle in the quarter-final of the Nissan Shield with a splendid innings of 80 against Transvaal, but I'm afraid the rest of us could not give him the sort of support he needed and we went down by 52 runs in spite of the fact that Simon Base had 4 wickets and I had 3. We did a little better in the second leg but still lost.

In the Castle Bowl – the bread and butter campaign – we started badly by losing to Western Province 'B'. I won the toss and asked them to bat and in truth, we made an encouraging start. At lunch, they were on 83 for 3 and I had taken a hard return catch to get rid of Adrian Plantema. But John Commins, Gary Kirsten and Laance Bleekers all got into the 70s, enabling them to declare on 305 for 6, and before the end of the first day's play, we were 27 for 2. John Stephenson again showed himself to be a really good player with 63 but again we didn't give him enough support and were well behind. In fact we never really got into the game, although I think I bowled well in both innings. But we were to suffer a 5-wicket defeat in the end.

We held on to force a draw against Natal 'B' and again our batting proved to be fragile. Only Danie du Toit with a typically aggressive innings which included three huge 6s in his 52 and Jaco de Swardt with a composed 60 showed sufficient fight. Richard Illingworth, playing for Natal, gave us a glimpse of the kind of form that made him into a successful Test player for England a year or two later. In the end, Tekkies van Rensburg and myself had to dig in to save the game.

We also lost to Border in a game which we should have won. Ian Howell, the young left-hander, had a dream match, though it was not much of a dream for me when he struck me for a huge 6 over square leg to win the game for Border!

We were to do much better in the return game in Stellenbosch. We had a weakened team but this time we pulled well together. Wayne Truter's 80 gave us a good start with several other batsmen chipping in so we tallied a useful 318. The main resistance came from Emmerson Trotman with 73, but it was great to see Marais Erasmus bowl so well for us. He had 5 for 78 off no fewer than 29 overs and I also bowled well, picking up the other 5 for 59. I also had 64 in our second innings and picked up 4 further wickets in their second innings as we won by just 35 runs, having been given a bit of a fright by Dexter Toppin with 49 and Kenny Watson, who had 34. Their 8th-wicket stand of 52 in 43 minutes had me biting my nails a bit!

I had another 7 wickets in the match against Western Province at Newlands, which we lost by 5 wickets in spite of a fine 100 from John Stephenson, and in general it was hardly a noteworthy season. John topped our batting averages with 360 runs at 36 and I was third with 243 runs at an average of 27. However, I could feel well pleased with my bowling: 37 wickets at an average of 20 apiece. Yet there was only one victory to record and that was a great disappointment after the previous season's exploits. Still, I had to look at things sensibly. We had, after all, lost so many of our star players, the injured Simon Base was not able to bowl anything like the number of overs he had sent down in the previous season and we had a number of rookies in the side.

I look back on the five years I spent at Boland with mixed feelings. We had plenty of high points, winning the Bowl on three occasions. I believe I put a great deal into the job there and indeed learned a lot myself. In spite of the fact that playing for Boland had meant that I was playing in the 'second division' of South African cricket, so to speak, I nevertheless felt that I had made significant progress – enough to be capped for my country, albeit in unofficial 'tests' against the Aussies. The responsibilities I had to take there were also good for me: the coaching, the development and finally, the responsibility of captaincy. It was, in hindsight, a process of maturation for me. In spite of the fact that I was not playing my cricket at the highest level, I continued to build on my game, to get better, to learn the need to get the head down on occasion, to battle it out and restrain my natural attacking flair. And because I had to take increasing responsibility as a bowler, I improved my accuracy and, I hope, my guile. If such self-assessment may imply that I was giving myself a good reference, once again the proof was to be seen when I went to Free State and enjoyed success at the higher level of Currie Cup cricket.

But it was always difficult at Boland. The financial constraints were a massive handicap. They meant that we had an ever-changing team. I am sure it was the lack of financial backing and the weakness of the administration which prevented us from becoming a Currie Cup side. However, it was, as I have already said, a chicken-and-egg situation and I believe the authorities should have had the courage to elevate us after the successes of the 1987-88 season.

It is odd that Boland were eventually granted that status in 1993 when they were arguably even less well prepared for it. However, I am confident that now that goal has been reached, they will gradually become a force to be reckoned with. I hope so – after all, Boland is my home province.

But Orange Free State offered me further challenges. There seemed to be a real drive and ambition about them. They lacked experience, perhaps even an understanding of the game at the highest level, but there was an excellent crop of young players. Allan Donald was already making a name for himself in England with Warwickshire and as a young man had also made an impact against the rebel Aussies here. He was then raw but a bowler of genuine pace and he had learned a lot in England. Corrie van Zyl was probably the most experienced player there. He is a good all-round cricketer who had made an appearance or two against the rebel Aussies. Louis Wilkinson was a natural athlete with lots of natural talent and Hansie Cronje, also a youngster with tremendous natural ability, was a born leader who eventually went on to captain South Africa.

The moment I arrived I knew that the talent in Bloemfontein was there. They had already tasted some success by winning the Benson & Hedges Night Series the previous season, a success largely based on their tremendous fielding. It meant that there was something upon which to build. They had had a stream of names there in recent seasons, all of which had served to lift them and provide ambition in the up-and-coming crop of young players, Allan Lamb, Mike Procter as coach, Ally Kallicharran and Sylvester

Clarke. So there was a platform from which to launch the province.

The importation, from time to time, of these major figures in the game had cost money but it was beginning to pay off. Free State didn't have the traditions of Transvaal or Natal, for instance, but I had the impression that there was a determination to make up for the lack of cricket history and really make an impact. And they had a great feeder school in Grey's College, where Johan Volsteedt was an excellent schoolboy coach, a good breeder of cricketers. Kepler Wessels, Corrie van Zyl, Joubert Strydom, Hansie and Franz Cronje and Allan Donald all came from his stable.

I certainly felt comfortable there from the word go and I seemed to fit in with the rest of the players. They were bubbling with enthusiasm and there was a really good atmosphere in the dressing room, which made me feel at home straight away. However, as seems to have been the case throughout my career, I eventually found myself at odds with someone; this time with Johan Volsteedt who, although a splendid coach, and excellent when it came to technique, nevertheless, in my opinion, lacked the experience of playing the first-class game.

After a reasonably successful first season as far as I was concerned under the stewardship of the experienced Joubert Strydom, Hansie Cronje took over the captaincy in September 1990. Hansie, as I have already said, was and is a really dedicated cricketer, full of ambition, physically very fit and even now only 23. Many people said that he was too young to handle the kind of pressure which is all part and parcel of the game at top level; too inexperienced. But Hansie used that first season at the helm very sensibly. He was, throughout, going through a learning curve and he certainly proved the critics wrong by handling things superbly. He had the desire to be successful; had the drive to drag people along with him. But he was also prepared to listen and absorb the experience that was on offer, work things out and then make his decisions. He was, is and will be an excellent captain for Free State and for South Africa. And the responsibility did not affect his own batting form.

As a professional cricketer, you do tend to become pretty uncompromising. It is sometimes a matter of survival. You tend to develop your own way of doing things. The determination needed tends to make you even more uncompromising. It is both a defence – a protective cloak – and, at the same time, a route you follow as part of the dedication you have to have if you are to ride the ups and downs which are inevitable as you follow the winding route of your career. There have been many examples of how uncompromising attitudes have found their way into the headlines. You only have to remember the controversy of David Gower's omission from the England team. David, one of the really great players in the game, gave the impression of being somewhat laid-back about things whereas Graham Gooch is the epitome of dedication.

In truth, I don't think that Gower's approach is really any less dedicated. It is just that he sometimes seems not to be taking things too seriously. He also has a quirky sense of humour, as witnessed by the famous aeroplane incident in Australia. But I remain convinced that he was as serious about his cricket – his profession – as anyone, including Graham Gooch. However, the different outward approach of these two seemed to create an atmosphere which, although it was certainly exploited by the media, distanced both cricketers, one a past captain of England, the other, at that time, the man at the helm. Rationality in such circumstances sometimes goes out of the window and it did seem quite irrational for Gower to have been left out of the touring party to India in the winter of 1992-93. He had a proven track record against the Indians, plays spin better than most and might just have been the trump card England needed on a tour which turned very sour on them.

Ian Botham is another uncompromising soul whose strong-willed dedication has also probably been misinterpreted. He too fell out of favour with the England selectors and especially with the Gooch-Stewart regime. The same thing, of course, happens in just about every walk of life, but it is no use asking someone to change when it is the very characteristics you want to change that have brought success. And sometimes people in sports management, often quite rightly, want to do things in a particular way, so they want people around them who will conform to that pattern. Again, Ian Botham might fall into the category of not conforming just as much as David Gower. International football managers don't pick players who fail to conform to their vision of the patterns of play they wish to establish. Thus on occasions brilliant players find themselves out in the cold.

It was in my second season at Free State that I found myself briefly out of favour. I do not make excuses but I too can be pretty uncompromising. Throughout my life, I have had to measure up to a variety of challenges, some of which had nothing at all to do with cricket. And if I regard myself as being reasonably flexible, I have to admit that I can also be somewhat unyielding. To succeed in cricket – indeed, in any sector of life – you have to establish a degree of self-belief and if that is sometimes interpreted by others as inflexibility, then disputes and disagreements can follow.

That is what I believe happened in that second season at Free State. I was, I suppose, the most experienced player in the side and Hansie would often discuss tactics with me, seek my views on things. But there developed between Johan Volsteedt and myself some conflict. Our views differed. Unquestionably, we were both motivated by the desire for success, by the desire to win. It came to a head when we were playing against Eastern Province. We had to chase 4 an over on a turning wicket and they had three useful spinners to exploit the wicket. We had a debate about our tactics, Hansie, the coach and myself. I expressed the view that because we would almost certainly find ourselves playing against a spin attack, not only because of the nature of the wicket but also because their seam attack had been affected by injuries, we should ensure that we had wickets in hand when we got to the last 20 overs and, most importantly, that we should keep up the run rate so that we wouldn't have to slog in those last 20 when the fielders, almost inevitably, would be posted in the deep. Johan, however, disagreed. He thought that providing we had wickets in hand, we could chase almost any total. So that was the tactic employed and we got into trouble and ended up struggling to save the game.

There was another conflict of view when we batted too long before declaring, which culminated in the Natal captain at that time, Kim Hughes, setting us a phenomenal target of in the region of 11 an over which we proceeded to chase. I was pushed up the order and when I was padding up the Chairman of Selectors entered the dressing room and told me that they had selected the side for the next game against

Transvaal and I had not been picked. His reasoning was that the wicket at the Wanderers, they had heard, was going to be a green-top. It seemed ridiculous not to take 12 players and make the decision on the day when they had looked at the wicket. But even more profoundly ridiculous was the timing of the statement, telling me this just as I was preparing to go to the wicket in a vain effort to slog 11 runs an over.

It illustrated to me a complete lack of understanding on the part of both coach and selectors of the need for players to concentrate their minds on the job currently in hand. Even if they had waited until the end of the game, I don't suppose I would have been very kindly disposed towards their decision. But the timing was, frankly, what made me really angry.

In spite of this unfortunate intercession, I nevertheless went out and did my damnedest to keep the momentum going but there was a bitter taste in my mouth. It was, on that occasion, my professionalism that carried me through. Years before, when I had suffered a similar fate when playing in Jo'burg for Western Province, I did not have the same experience to ride over the problem and concentrate on the job in hand. At that stage of the season, we were definitely in contention for the Currie Cup and there was a discussion in the dressing room after the game as to how we should tackle the next two games at Jo'burg against Transvaal and then at home against Natal. The debate centred upon leaving some grass on the wicket for the Natal game, enough for our seamers to exploit. At that time, no one knew that I had been left out for the Transvaal match. Indeed, I wasn't even sure that Hansie himself knew. By the time he came to me, I told him that I didn't mind not being in the side against Natal if he wanted to load the side with seamers. Hansie, however, told me that he definitely wanted me in the team as his stock bowler, which in itself seemed to confirm that he did not know I would not be travelling to Jo'burg.

I must admit that I was so disgusted at the treatment I had received, not to mention the fact that apparently the captain did not know about my exclusion, that I failed to turn up for practice the next day. Call it a fit of pique if you like, but that was how I felt. I played for the 'B' team, whilst up in Jo'burg Clive Eksteen, the Transvaal left-arm spinner, was picking up Free State wickets on that green-top. Incredibly, during that

'B' game, the same Chairman of Selectors, Naas Bezuidenhout, came into the dressing room again and this time told me that I was to be in the team for the Natal game!

I suggested that we should have a 'clear-the-air' meeting when we practised in preparation for the Natal game but to my further disgust, Mr Bezuidenhout failed to turn up. Instead, the President arrived and I was taken to task for giving an interview to a press man in which I was apparently quoted – nothing to do with the on-going problems. Even so I got something of a bollocking, not the kind of thing I take very easily. There was some rancour but I resolved to just get on with playing my game, using my experience, continuing to develop my game and making an increasingly important impact on Orange Free State's quest for glory.

That path to glory followed in my fourth and last season for them but when I look back on that second season with Free State in the meantime, in spite of the problems of perception and, I must admit, personality, I think I can honestly say that I made an important contribution to our progress.

My batting – very much my forte in Scotland each year – was now reaping greater rewards in South Africa too. In our first Currie Cup game of the 1989-90 season, I had 88 batting at number 6, against a Western Province attack boasting Craig Matthews, Brian McMillan, Adrian Kuiper, Eric Simons, Dave Rundle and Denys Hobson. Louis Wilkinson had set us up with a splendid career-best innings of 167, but batting with Gordon Parsons, who scored 52, we put the icing on the cake to take a commanding first-innings lead. If the game petered out as a draw, I nevertheless had to shoulder the responsibility of bowling more overs than anyone else; being used, I suppose, as the stock bowler. Louis scored a second century in the next game against Transvaal whereas I had little success with the bat. However, once again I was to bowl 32 overs in their first innings to return 4 for 91, again being used as the stock bowler.

Yet another draw followed at Port Elizabeth, where I scored 59 in our first innings and again shouldered the lion's share of our bowling, capturing, for the nth time, the wicket of Kepler Wessels.

The game from which I was omitted at Jo'burg was drawn and then we faced Natal in Bloemfontein, by which time any title aspirations we might have had had disappeared. Yet another draw ensued. If this all sounds as if we were playing boring cricket, then that would be wrong. The fact was that we just weren't quite strong enough, not penetrative enough sometimes, to apply the killer touch. I really did have to fill the role of stock bowler that season and as a consequence my figures looked ordinary. My 25 wickets cost around 40 each but that conceals the fact that I bowled nearly 50 overs more than anyone else in the side. My batting average that season was just over 26.

In limited-overs cricket, we reached the semi-finals of the Nissan Shield but Transvaal gave us a real thumping in the first leg of the semi with Jimmy Cook at his superlative best scoring a century. We didn't fare much better in the second leg, either, and Transvaal went on to win the final. Our Benson & Hedges campaign was rather ruined by rain. Three of our games were washed out and we were therefore never in with a shout.

We approached season 1991-92 with growing confidence. I tried to put the problems, some might say the personal problems of relating to people in the administration of the Free State, to one side. We had a terrific team spirit in the dressing room and in Hansie Cronje an enthusiastic, thinking young captain. There was a determination amongst the players to achieve success for a province which hitherto had been a bit of a backwater.

But these were also times of change in South Africa as a whole. The political temperature was rising. If things were certainly lacking stability in the country, and this was an uncertain, unsettled period, it was also an exciting time because the tide of change was inexorably moving forward. The infamous Gatting tour and the disruption caused by the Anti-Apartheid Movement was moving goalposts constantly. Slowly but surely, the spirit of reconciliation was beginning to surface, albeit that those heady days when Mike Gatting had to face the wrath of those determined to topple the barriers of apartheid – a confrontation, I might say, which he handled with true diplomacy – produced some very volatile moments which of course hit the headlines all over the world.

The tour which came under Mike Gatting, couldn't, in retrospect, have come at a more unsettled time. Now there was a more united front against the very principle of apartheid. The protests were growing in strength and in confidence; the tide was rolling in and no one could stop it. For the first time, the people were together. And if the protest was, in essence, mounted against the political system, cricket, in spite of the fact that those involved in the game had made tremendous efforts to integrate the sport, to eliminate the racial divides in our society – more I would suggest, than any other sector of life – was still perceived to be a part of that system. So the tour inevitably became a political target for protest and disruption. What the people were demanding, unequivocally, was the dismantling of apartheid, the release of Nelson Mandela, and equal opportunities across the whole community.

Ali Bacher had the foresight not to stand in the way of the protesters. He handled the whole thing so well, allowing the protesters to come into the grounds. And as I have said, Mike Gatting also handled the situation well. For my part, I had made some of my personal feelings about apartheid known publicly. And as much as I wanted to see apartheid dismantled, I still thought that the tour would be of value, especially to South African cricket which, as I have already said, had led the way towards integrated sport, had spearheaded the whole concept of crossing all the racial and political barriers. I believed that in allowing myself to be selected to play against Gatting's team I was continuing to help towards progress, towards change at the highest level. Because I believed that cricket had made giant steps towards dismantling apartheid, I was happy to be selected. I believed in Ali Bacher's commitment to race-free cricket and I admired Mike's courage in facing the mobs and listening to what the people involved had to say.

That the tide of change was rising so rapidly was obvious. Everybody who is an a better position, whether that position has been achieved through race or religion, education, through business or even sport, should reach down. It is hard to imagine the life led by those forced to live in the squalor of the squatter camps. There is an impatience for change and who can blame those people for wanting it to be rapid? The conditions in those camps are terrible. Who amongst us could bear to exist for even a single winter in such appalling circumstances? It is impossible to imagine what it is like to live there unless you have to survive there yourself. I have been there, as a friend of some residents and as a cricketing coach. There is, in spite of the conditions, latent talent within those dreadful camps. But there is so much to overcome before anyone can break out of those circumstances. Perhaps one of the delights I might yet experience is the opportunity to find a really rare talent in such a place and to see that person emerge from what must be regarded as the most improbable background, to better things, as a cricketer and as a person.

It should be remembered that these squatter camps are not a new phenomenon. They were in place when I was a child. They have grown in scale, of course, gradually. Most of the people have probably known better times; many of them will have been removed from some areas during the days of the Group Areas Act which saw my family moved to a township on the edge of Stellenbosch. Some were less fortunate than us. Their houses might have been demolished and then they perhaps found jobs hard, almost impossible, to come by and had to move out of the townships. The recession which has hit South Africa has played its part and there are more jobless people. If economic sanctions against South Africa by the rest of the world were seen as a method of making the country's administrators abandon the evil creed of apartheid, they certainly also had a profound effect on many ordinary people there. Investment dried up, indeed investment was barred to a large extent, and as it declined, so jobs disappeared and more and more people were forced into those squatter camps.

In cricketing terms, the international ban on us forced people here to realise the hard truth that they must open their doors. But it is an enormous battle to change the flow of thought from one of obdurate head-in-the-sand, blinkered apartheid to one of compromise. You have to change attitudes if you are to have any hope of achieving the ultimate goal of harmony right across the board. It is an enormous battle to change hearts and minds. Many people have been forced to the political extremes by the circumstances in which they have found themselves. They now need to be encouraged to be brought back from those extreme positions so that people can compromise and accept one another, be honest with one another and be as one. But how to achieve that after so many years in the wilderness? There is bound to be scepticism, a process of looking over the shoulder, even backbiting. It is going to take a generation, maybe longer, before we are really together as a people.

The prospect of all-out war was, believe me, real enough. I sensed that the only alternative to the violence and the riots which had been boiling up from 1976 onwards was the dismantling of the system. Yet doubts will remain about our ability to go forward without some of the bitterness which has been created surfacing from time to time. As we moved towards the release of Nelson Mandela, and the lifting of the ban on the ANC, and began to see with our own eyes the structure which was slowly being put in place to normalise society, there was a possibility that the isolation our cricketers had experienced might be reaching an end; that perhaps, within my cricketing lifetime, we might – and I just might – take our place in the international arena after more than two decades of almost complete insulation.

My hopes and ambitions were further raised by the fact that Free State brought in Eddie Barlow as their coach for the 1991-92 season. Predictably, he made an immediate impact and from a personal point of view, it was great to be working with 'Bunter' again. First, we annihilated Border in our first Currie – now Castle – Cup game. The major breakthrough back into world cricket meant that we were without Hansie Cronje and Allan Donald. They were in the national squad to tour India. However, Rudolf Steyn's century, another from Corrie van Zyl and a quick-fire unbeaten 64 from me saw us to a first innings total of 464 for 7. Excepting a brave century from Andrew Lawson, Border had no answer to the magnificent bowling of Franklyn Stephenson who, in 22 hostile overs, took 5 for 40. Once again I was used as the stock bowler with 23 overs which yielded me 2 for 39. With so much in hand, we could set out our stall and we worked our way through their batting in the second innings, in which I bowled 31 more overs and took 5 for 56 as we strolled to a 10-wicket win.

With our two Indian tourists back home, we were at full strength against Natal and the combination of Allan Donald and Franklyn Stephenson was enough to make the visiting batsmen struggle, only Arthur Wormington providing stern resistance. The two opening bowlers had 4 wickets each and when we batted our top order really set the standards. No one failed and we obtained a lead of just over 200. After Allan and Franklyn had made the early breakthrough, I was again called on to take on the lion's share of the bowling, taking 4 for 60 to give us victory by an innings and 34 runs.

But then we ran into Kepler Wessels in prime form. He had a century in each innings for Eastern Province at Port Elizabeth. A super century from Hansie Cronje kept us in the hunt and refreshingly, he gambled to declare in our second innings, after I had been sent in to clatter the bowling about, which I did to good effect with 49 off 47 balls, leaving them a target of 289 at about 3.5 an over. If we had taken our chances – we put Kepler down when he was on just 9 and Martin Ventner on 8 – we might have pulled it off but they only needed that second chance and with Kepler not out 147 having faced 214 balls, they strode to a 5-wicket victory.

Worse was to follow when we went to Jo'burg. After being in the driving seat for the first two days of the game – Castle Cup games were now played over four days – with a century from Mickey Arthur and some excellent bowling from our pace trio of Donald, Stephenson and van Zyl, we collapsed in our second innings with Stephan Jacobs and Clive Eksteen rolling us over for 136. But we were not yet beaten. Bradley Player produced an outstanding bowling performance to take 6 for 44 but their later batsmen showed real resolve to edge them home by 2 wickets.

Centuries from Gerhardus Liebenburg and Franklyn Stephenson gave us a healthy enough lead to enable us to brush aside Northern Transvaal by 144 runs but our final game, against Western Province at Newlands, saw Free State make a tactical blunder by not enforcing the follow-on, and having to settle for a two-point win on first innings which cost us the chance of sharing the trophy.

By this time of course, Hansie Cronje, Allan Donald and myself had been absent, far away across the sea representing our country. That, of course, was another pinnacle which I will come to in due course.

We did, however, get our names on the Nissan Shield for the first time. Our win over Transvaal at Bloemfontein set us on our way. Hansie led from the front with a superb innings of 79 in our total of 225 for 8 and with everyone chipping in with wickets, we bowled them out for 176, scores which were almost duplicated when we went to the Wanderers for the second leg, Hansie doing even better with 82. I had a whirlwind 24 in 21 balls at the end of our innings. Our total of 233 was easily too high for our illustrious opponents, who could reach only 177.

We were paired with Border in the semi-finals and I was able to play my full part when, after we had made 212 with Louis Wilkinson scoring a fine 91, I dismissed Lawson, Kirsten and Howell to choke their reply at birth. In the return leg, 100 from Wilkinson and some tight bowling, especially by the seamers, saw us home, although Andrew Lawson made us fight with an unbeaten innings of 99.

The final was, from the point of view of the 15,000 spectators, something of an anti-climax. Our seamers once again did the business, Corrie van Zyl picking up 4 wickets, and Eastern Province were bowled out for a paltry 120. We strode to victory by 6 wickets and the Shield was ours.

The arrival of Eddie Barlow gave me extra impetus. Knowing that he and I were on the same wavelength, I felt really confident that Free State could win a trophy or two. But the real goal had to be the challenge of forcing myself into the reckoning for a place in the Test team. South Africa was agog as the shackles began to be loosened. If I was disappointed to be left out of the squad which made a brief visit to India – Clive Eksteen, the Transvaal left-arm spinner, and Tim Shaw from Eastern Province were chosen ahead of me – I had to face the reality of the fact that I was I was nearly 40, and I knew I would have to play to my very highest standards.

I very nearly didn't play for Free State at all in that third season. In fact, my disputes with Johan Vosteedt and with the administrators had got me the sack. But the spirit in the Free State dressing room was such that the players themselves refused to accept my sacking. They simply said that if the Free State let me go, they would go too. I have never in my long career played with such a team. Not only did they play so well as a unit on the field, they also were a team in every other sense. At that, I cried. That these guys could support me with such conviction was just too much for me. Great guys like Hansie, Allan Donald, Corrie van Zyl, Bradley Player, Louis Wilkinson, Rudolf Steyn and Mickey Arthur and the rest of them all stood firmly by my side. Hansie took the bull by the horns and went to see the President and I was reinstated. So my rollercoaster career continued. Down one minute and now, as the 1991-92 season approached, very much up the next.

Eddie Barlow had a simple approach to the game. He believed in maintaining a scoring rate so that you always left yourself with time to bowl the opposition out. Right from the start, Eddie trained our minds to believe that we could go out there and win. Some say that motivation comes from within. Well, maybe it does, but when Eddie Barlow is around, I can tell you that there is motivation from without as well! My own role in the side was much clearer but it was evident throughout the team that everyone had a clarity of vision that had not been there before. This was a side which was going places, and the following season further triumph awaited us.

Then came the shock. Eddie Barlow stayed just that one season. He wanted his job to be a 12-month long position but the administrators could not or would not make that change. Nevertheless the momentum he gave us was to continue.

But before that decision was made, there was the World Cup into which cauldron South Africa was about to jump, very late in the day. My chances of selection seemed to be enhanced by the fact that our boys, notably the spinners, had not done at all well in India. So there were places up for grabs. Was this my chance?

In a sense, I seized my chance to impress whilst the boys were in India: my performance against Border, I felt, set me up in the very first Castle Cup game of the season. I knew that my 64 not out followed by 5 wickets in the second innings would give the selectors something of a nudge. It wasn't just the figures themselves, it was the manner in which I achieved them.

With Hansie and Allan away in India, extra responsibility rested on my shoulders and that was something I relished. As the season evolved I knew that my performances were showing considerable improvement and I began to feel increasingly confident about my chances, slim though they might be, of being seriously considered for the World Cup. By the nature of things, I felt it likely that the emphasis in the selectors' minds would be on seamers and quickies, but I was equally sure that one spinner would be taken and I set about the task of trying to make sure that the one spin place I anticipated would be available would be mine. The advantage I had over most of my rivals was that I was also performing for Free State with the bat. And that, I felt, could be the key to my possible selection. I had no fears about my fielding because I was really fit.

The crucial game for me was probably the semi-final of the Nissan Shield against Border when I snapped up 3 of the 5 Border wickets to fall. Remember that we are talking, in terms of the World Cup, about one-day cricket and my analysis of 11 overs, 3 for 26 on the flat wicket at Bloemfontein, may well have been the key performance in terms of my inclusion in the squad to go to Australia and New Zealand. After the second leg of the Nissan Shield semi-final in East London, I was driving home to Stellenbosch with my family. We knew the team was about to be announced so we were constantly fiddling with the radio in the car, trying to make sure we were on the right wavelength. We had stopped to eat at lunch-time and heard in the restaurant that the selectors were still deliberating about their choice. As we continued our journey we suddenly heard over the airwaves that the selectors had picked the World Cup squad at St George's Park, Port Elizabeth, and that President Krish Mackerdhuj was about to announce the names.

The previous night Conita and I had enjoyed a meal with Peter Kirsten and his wife. He had not been confident about his selection so I was absolutely delighted when I heard his name announced. Then the magic name of Omar Henry flowed over the airwaves, at which point Conita almost leaped upon me. I slammed on the brakes and stopped, slumped in the seat, whilst my family laughed and shrieked with excitement.

I had been travelling very slowly up to that point. The road was deserted but once I had recovered my composure and wiped the tears from my eyes, I drove like the wind in order to get home as quickly as possible. My mother's telephone apparently never stopped ringing that day.

There were countless calls to congratulate me from everywhere. As it happened, my mother had gone to my sister's in Somerset West and as I had no key to the house I followed her there and a party ensued.

It was a very happy occasion. Another pinnacle in my life. Another trip to the top of the rollercoaster.

As things were to turn out, the World Cup was to be something of a sweet and sour experience for me and the rollercoaster was to zoom back down the hill.

• • • • • • • • • • • • • • • •

HENRY PAULSE

Henry Paulse is the President of Boland Cricket Board.

'Omar Henry is one of the products of apartheid. Because of apartheid, he had to "go over" – to leave SACBOC – and that alienated him in his own community. But he had to take that step in order to develop himself. It proved to be a good step for him, although some might say it was premature from the liberation movement's point of view.

'But now he has returned to share the knowledge and experience that he has gained. And it was right that he should play in Boland's first-ever game in 'A' province cricket because he is a product of local cricket, and, more significantly, the first player from the underprivileged section of the community to go to the highest level in the game and play Test match cricket.

'For him to come back to Boland in order to share the tremendous experience he has gained shows great character and he certainly has a role to play here in developing new young talent. He can make things happen and he certainly has the ability to spot talent and bring that talent on. Because he can speak the language, knows the conditions under which people play and knows the people, he is just the right person to go out there and find the Omar Henries that haven't, so far, been given the chance.'

JANNIE MOMBERG
Former President of Boland and ANC Member of Parliament.

'It has been one of the greatest privileges of my life to have been closely associated with Omar Henry, one of the finest sportsmen I met during my years as a sports administrator.

'Omar was born and bred in Stellenbosch, like myself, and as a youngster, he had to fight to get to the top of the cricket world.

'After playing with success for Western Province for a number of years, he decided to throw in his lot with Boland, and what a happy decision for Boland that was. In his years as an all-rounder for Boland he not only scored hundreds of runs and took dozens of wickets, but the impact he made on Boland cricket as a man will only be determined by history in the years to come.

'Omar Henry loves the game of cricket; he also loves his country. He has richly deserved the successes he has achieved against all the odds and sets a fine example to us all. I am sure he has a major contribution to make to the future of cricket in South Africa.'

THE FINAL TASTE...
SWEET AND SOUR

I was, not unnaturally, full of great expectations as the World Cup approached. My confidence, bolstered by my selection for the World Cup squad, was higher than it had ever been and that showed in my form. I worked even harder, increasing my fitness, practising with even greater zeal. Both physically and mentally I was properly attuned and raring to go. Hindsight is a wonderful thing of course. Had I known what difficulties lay ahead of me, I would not, perhaps, have felt so on top of the world and accordingly my confidence may not have been at such a high ebb.

Before jetting off to Australia and New Zealand, we had a warm-up game against Zimbabwe in Harare. Our northern neighbours were also to travel to the Antipodes as winners of the Mini World Cup, officially known as the ICC Associate Members' Cup. And there was talk of them gaining first-class Test status in the not-too-distant future. However, I think we all knew that they weren't, at this stage of their development, amongst the top cricketing nations in the world and so the game would mainly serve as a means of getting our own approach to the game right.

I was therefore delighted to be included in the team. The gap between the two sides was evident from the outset. Allan Donald's pace was just too much for their batsmen. He beat both Andy Flower and Alistair Campbell for pace, bowling them in quick succession to leave Zimbabwe struggling on 20 for 2. They had reached 54 when Jonty

Rhodes, who was to make quite a name for himself in the ensuing weeks, ran out Wayne James with a direct throw and it wasn't long before I was brought on to bowl. If this warm-up game was, in all honesty, not quite the stern test we were to experience in the next few weeks, we nevertheless took it seriously and I set out to bowl straight, varying my flight but also concentrating on giving the batsmen little or no width. I was pleased with my performance, bowling 10 accurate overs to concede only 27 runs – the most economic of our front-line bowlers – and taking the wicket of the Zimbabwean captain, David Houghton, through a catch by Hansie Cronje.

One thing we most certainly learned was that we had to tighten up when we got down to the real thing. Highest score for them was extras. And of those 30 runs, 19 were wides which brought home to us the narrow margin of error in international one-day cricket. Allan Donald finished with 3 for 29, Tertius Bosch 2 for 44 and Adrian Kuiper, in the side mainly for his batting, gave an early hint that his medium-paced bowling might well be very useful once we got down to business. He bowled 6 overs for just 12 runs as Zimbabwe were bowled out for 170. Although we lost both openers, Kepler Wessels, our captain, and Andrew Hudson, relatively cheaply – we were 30 for 2 – Peter Kirsten's increasingly fluent innings of 64 and a final flourish from Hansie Cronje and Adrian Kuiper saw us home, but not until the last over which should have taught us another lesson in that we really needed to increase our run rate.

And now started the grand adventure. Our arrival in Perth, Western Australia was signalled by a warm welcome which included supporters of the ANC, which was nice to see.

It was a big moment, I'm sure, in everybody's life; it certainly was for me. The heartbeat was perceptibly quicker as we began our whistle-stop progress round Australia and New Zealand and as I had expected, I was singled out to some degree by the media. As it happened, I wasn't the only coloured guy in the party because the selectors had included two others, not as part of the official squad but with an eye to the future. Faiek Davids, who played for Western Province, a medium-pacer and useful batsman, and Yassien Begg, a wicket-keeper, had been included in the party as 'development players', although I personally thought it would have been better if they had been included officially and given more chance to play. Prosaic thoughts on my part, as it turned out.

Now came our first warm-up game on Australian soil, against Western Australia at the WACA. I wasn't in the side for this first game against a very strong WA outfit which included Tom Moody, Geoff Marsh, Mike Valetta, Tim Zoehrer, Martin McCague (later to play for England), Terry Alderman, Brendan Julian and Bruce Reid – almost a Test-strength side.

We started badly with Alderman removing Mark Rushmere and Kepler Wessels early on, went from bad to worse and were only rescued from a batting disaster by Jonty Rhodes and Brian McMillan, who took us from 66 for 5 to 132 for 6. A final total of 157 for 8 was never going to be enough for the bowlers to bowl at. However, Allan Donald and Meyrick Pringle got stuck in and soon the Aussies were struggling too at 83 for 3. Eventually Western Australia, with 7 wickets down, reached their target with 3 overs in hand. But Meyrick bowled really well for 4 for 29 from his 10 overs.

Naturally enough, I wanted to get going as quickly as possible. With such a tight schedule, it is vital to make an early impression and luck can play a big part. Recent history is littered with examples of players on tour not managing to make an early impression and thereafter finding themselves sitting on the sidelines for most of the time. Unfortunately for me, when we arrived at Adelaide for our next warm-up game, rain ruined the first match, against the Australian Cricket Academy. We had scored 205 for 7, Hansie Cronje and Adrian Kuiper both reaching half-centuries, but rain intervened after Bosch and Snell had bowled just 8 overs between them.

The following day the weather relented and we played the Academy again. This time it was Andrew Hudson and Peter Kirsten who got runs but when we bowled, I got my first taste of the trouble I was to encounter later in the tour. The wicket was right on the edge of the square with a very short boundary and when Kepler asked which end I preferred, I said that as the plan was for me to bowl a middle and leg line to a strong leg-side field so as to tuck the batsmen up, it would be better if I bowled at the end which gave me a bigger leg-side boundary. However, I went on at the other end, with an assurance that after a few overs I would be switched. The switch never came, a foretaste perhaps of what was to follow as the campaign evolved. I had a quiet word with team manager, Mike Procter, and he expressed his surprise that I had been asked to bowl to the shorter boundary. My concern was that the difficulties I obviously encountered in having to bowl at the wrong end should not count against me.

I felt a little apprehensive after that episode, uneasy about the captain's attitude towards me. I had made absolutely certain that I had done everything and more than was asked of me, practising assiduously, turning up on time and throwing my all into the cause. There was another incident when the competition got underway. Before the first game, there were two meetings, one for the batsmen and one for the bowlers, and I was excluded from both! I tried hard not let these things get to me. Kepler is a disciplinarian and meticulous about the preparation for games, but I had that slightly uneasy feeling of not really being in the captain's thoughts.

We moved on to Canberra for our next game, this time against Pakistan, and again I found myself left out of a game in which we performed well, Kepler getting the momentum going with the bat and Brian McMillan bowling really well to capture 5 wickets as we beat a side which, by the way, was minus Wasim, by 17 runs.

Next, we were winging our way to Tasmania where at last I was given my chance. Again Allan Donald gave us an excellent start but I was delighted to get my full ration of 10 overs which I felt I used well, taking 3 wickets for 36, the best figures of the day. Chasing a target of 161, Brian McMillan confirmed his all-round status by scoring an unbeaten 40 with Adrian Kuiper on a belligerent 38 not out when we reached our target. This 'all-rounder', needless to say, didn't get in to bat!

Now the campaign proper began in Sydney. South Africa's first official game in the international arena was to be against the host nation, Australia. What a starting point for us!

I must be honest and say that once I had seen the wicket, I knew I would not be in the side. I was content, therefore, when I was left out of the final XI and delighted when things, right from the word go, went well for us. Our boys played really well and Allan Donald should have picked up a wicket with his very first ball. Geoff Marsh seemed to get a touch for a catch behind but the umpire said not out.

If the Aussies seemed set to capitalise on that piece of good fortune with a vigorous opening stand, Adrian Kuiper was to prove invaluable with the ball, having Marsh caught behind and then clean bowling Allan Border first ball. All the bowlers performed well and a target of 170 for 9, we felt, was eminently achievable. Kepler put the issue beyond doubt with a superb 81 not out, Andrew Hudson scored 28 and Peter Kirsten provided an unbeaten 49 as we cruised to an emphatic 9-wicket win. What a start!

But we were soon to be brought back to earth with a vengeance. Three days and many miles later, we were in Auckland to face New Zealand. Eden Park is a rugby ground and the wicket, as Brian McMillan described it, a mud heap. Having seen the wicket, I thought this was my chance. It would turn and I was sure it was a tailor-made wicket for me. But, much to my surprise, I was not in the side. Instead, Bosch came in for Pringle.

We lost, and heavily. Peter Kirsten batted really well and held our innings together with support from David Richardson and Brian McMillan. Peter had a brilliant 129-ball 90 out of our 190 for 9. And just to rub things in, Dipak Patel, New Zealand's off-spinner, was asked to open their bowling, confirming that this was indeed a spinner's wicket. But Mark Greatbatch, with a real swashbuckling innings, and Rod Latham set New Zealand on their way with an opening stand of 114 and the home team quite literally strolled to the most comfortable of wins, by 7 wickets and in double quick time. Peter Kirsten, bowling his off-spinners, was our most economical bowler with 1 for 22 off 7 overs, underlining my belief that this might have been a game in which I should have played. So we had travelled from the high of beating Australia to an abject low. Furthermore, sparks were about to fly.

On the evening prior to the game, my two fellow Muslims – the two so-called development members of the party – had informed me that they had found a Muslim restaurant. We had encountered some problems in terms of food. Unfortunately we had experienced some difficulties in finding halal meat and in fact we had gone a number of days without eating meat at all. I knew that there were plans for the team to dine together that evening but by then I knew I had been excluded so I approached Alan Jordaan, the tour team manager, and explained the situation, saying that if it was required of me to join the team, I would be more than happy to do so. Alan told me that I would be free to go and eat with my two Muslim friends, and that there would be no problems.

However, after the Eden Park débâcle, we were all in the dressing room packing our gear when Kepler suddenly turned on me and let me have a real salvo. He shouted across the dressing room that if I wanted to be a part of the team then I would have to do what he told me to do. 'If there is team meal, there will be a team meal and you will be there,' he shouted. Naturally, I protested, saying that I had sought the manager's permission to eat in a Muslim restaurant. I suggested that he should perhaps sort such matters out with the manager and that I would not be the scapegoat for the team's defeat, especially as I had not played in the game.

It ended up as a shouting match, I'm afraid, and Alan Jordaan and Mike Procter had to intercede. However, it didn't finish there for as we were leaving the dressing room Kepler grabbed me by the shoulder and told me that I had an attitude problem. More heated words were exchanged and I must admit that I was so aggrieved that I told him where to go. I felt I had been treated very unfairly. I suggested to him that it would have been more diplomatic, if he felt I had breached any team discipline, to have discussed it in private rather than in the full glare of the dressing room. It was an acrimonious incident and I'm sure that it had a profound effect on my participation, or rather non-participation, in the rest of the World Cup campaign.

Ironically, I found myself in the team to face Sri Lanka in Wellington two days later. Again we played poorly. Our batting just never got going. The experiment of promoting Adrian Kuiper to open the batting just didn't work and the medium-pace bowling of the Sri Lankans seemed to mesmerise our batsmen, including Kepler himself. He scored 40 in 94 balls and that seemed to set the tone for our innings.

I had to stay calm and focused and forget about the unfortunate incident in Auckland. The press, always quick to seek out a story, had an inkling that something was wrong. They saw that I hadn't been picked to play at Auckland on a wicket which would have suited me, and of course there was the other dimension which, given the chance, the press would exploit. I was, after all, the only coloured player in the squad. All I said to them was that I hadn't been picked and that was that. So it was vital that I cast all these elements aside and got on with the business of proving my worth. However, it did seem that I was cast in the role of the bad apple in the barrel. My selection against Sri Lanka therefore put additional pressures on me and I have to admit that there were a few butterflies flitting around inside my stomach.

Nevertheless, when I went in to bat at the death, I did my best and fashioned 11 runs from 11 balls before being caught on the boundary as Brian McMillan and I scrambled a late stand of 20-odd runs. I was pleased with my spell of bowling, however. Allan Donald had tried to bowl really fast but unfortunately had conceded a number of wides and no-balls as a result. He had captured 3 quick wickets but Roshan Mahanama had stood firm and provided the backbone to Sri Lanka's innings. He was beginning to build a dangerous partnership with Tillekeratne when I managed to squeeze Tillekeratne out. He is a left-hander and he couldn't get me away, eventually heaving at a ball outside his off stump, Mark Rushmere taking a fine catch at mid wicket. My 10 overs cost just 31 runs for that 1 wicket and I felt that I had proved a point, being the most economical of our bowlers. However, I could not prevent the Sri Lankans from going to a 3-wicket win thanks to a sparkling innings from Ranatunga. He and Mahanama each scored 60-odd but our contribution of 25 extras didn't help our cause and I have to confess that even I bowled one of the wides. It was a humiliating defeat for us and the media were certainly looking for reasons. I had been in regular contact with Conita by telephone and she told me that questions were being asked in the South African press. Why was Omar Henry not being picked? Was there dissension in the camp? Was there even a racial undertone to Henry's continuing omission? The fact that I performed reasonably well in what turned out to be my one and only World Cup game only added fuel to the fire.

However, when we moved on to Christchurch to face the West Indies, I was not surprised to be out of the team again. One look at the wicket told me that I would not be picked. It was a wicket for seamers, without doubt. In the event, our boys really bounced back. After poor performances against New Zealand and Sri Lanka, suddenly, they started firing on all cylinders again. Batting first, we made 200 for 8, Peter Kirsten again batting well for 56 and almost everyone making useful contributions, but it was the bowlers who really cut the powerful West Indians down to size, none more than Meyrick Pringle, whose 4 for 11 from just 8 overs was a superb performance. He tore the heart out of the West Indian batting, dismissing Lara – through a stunning catch by Jonty Rhodes off a full-blooded cover drive – Richardson, Hooper and Arthurton and our illustrious opponents were bowled out for 136. What a comeback!

That was the end of our sojourn in New Zealand and now we had to face Pakistan in Brisbane. Predictably I was not selected and we reached 211 for 7 with Andrew Hudson getting 54 and Hansie Cronje a vital 47 not out at the end. Rain reduced the target but again our seamers came up with the goods; this time Brian McMillan took 2 wickets and Adrian Kuiper, having failed yet again with the bat, came up trumps with 3 important wickets, those of Salim, Wasim and Ijaz, to tip the scales our way. It was here that Jonty Rhodes played another trump card and broke an important partnership between Inzamam and Imran. Inzamam had played the ball just behind the wicket on the off side, and set off for a run but was sent back by his captain. Jonty, fielding at cover, swooped and instead of throwing, sprinted then dived full-length to break the wicket before Inzamam could regain his ground – quite spectacular and one of the great moments of the World Cup.

The whole programme was hectic in the extreme: living out of suitcases, practising, on to the next bus, then the plane and off to the next venue. Canberra and Zimbabwe awaited. Tertius Bosch, Mark Rushmere and myself remained out in the cold, hardly having played a game between us. Again, I thought this might be an opportunity to claw my way back into the team. But it was not to be. Any spin that day was to be purveyed by Peter Kirsten, who took 3 wickets, a simple statistic which begged the question of why I had not been picked as the only genuine spinner in the party. Brian McMillan also had 3 and Hansie Cronje a couple as Zimbabwe were bowled out for 183, Kepler with 70 and Peter with an unbeaten 62, knocking the runs off comfortably.

After the game I sought out the manager, Alan Jordaan, and said to him that it now seemed clear I was not going to be picked again. It seemed pointless for me to remain with the party. The press were badgering me for a story, which added to the pressure, and the news from home indicated that there were real rumblings about my continuing exclusion. I really felt under enormous strain. I was still working as hard with the rest of the squad but it seemed increasingly obvious that Kepler did not see a place for me in the team in any circumstances. There was also a tension in the dressing room. Some of the batsmen were uncertain, Tertius Bosch was getting no cricket, Mark Rushmere was getting hardly any opportunities and I felt I was going nowhere and had become excess baggage.

Of the rest of the squad I had talked only to Peter Kirsten, a personal friend, who knew that I was not being treated fairly. But in the circumstances all he could suggest was that I simply bit the bullet.

Alan Jordaan completely understood my plight and the pressure I was now under and he talked to Krish Mackerdhuj, the President of the United Cricket Board. Krish told me that if I was to go back home it would be a sensitive and political issue. He stressed how important it was, from the point of view of the situation back home, and of the whole campaign for me to stay. All I could do was collect my thoughts and grit my teeth and see things through.

I don't know why I was treated in this way. I don't know why Kepler had decided to freeze me out. Could it have been linked to my unhappy experience with Free State, when some people seemed to oppose my presence? Could there have been a link? I did not know but I suspected that there might be. Kepler, somehow, had got it in his mind that my attitude was wrong. Yet all I ever wanted to do was to give my all. Sometimes, I think, people misinterpret dedication and the single-mindedness that is necessary to achieve things in this game. And clearly the fact that I had stood up for myself following that row in Auckland had also been misinterpreted. It seemed I was the scapegoat.

Thank goodness I had something else to do. The M-Net Television people had asked me to do some commentary for the programmes beamed back to South Africa. The management had no objection, so rather than finding myself kicking my heels watching the game against

England at the MCG, I was in the commentary box. Mark, Tertius and I were told that we hadn't been picked for this game because we hadn't played enough. Well, that certainly wasn't our fault! I thought it was pretty farcical to be told that, especially as some of the players who were playing constantly were tired and some were carrying injuries. I continued to work on my game, trying to improve my bowling technique with the help of video cameras.

Again, this was a game which was truncated by rain. After Kepler and Andrew Hudson put on 151 for the 1st wicket we went on to make 236 for 4.

At the end of our innings, Adrian Kuiper at last looked to be regaining some sort of touch with the bat. But our bowling was our strength. Yet the white ball swung much more and sometimes our guys found it difficult to control. In fact, against England they seemed to control it rather better but after rain had reduced the England target to 226 off 41 overs, it was Neil Fairbrother who held centre stage. He played superbly, taking the attack to the bowlers. Alec Stewart provided the backbone but it was Fairbrother – who is, in my opinion, a very fine cricketer, always busy, a sweet timer of the ball, a brilliant runner between the wickets, and a great fielder to boot – who saw England home. I very much enjoyed my stints in the commentary box. At least I was involved and could give my opinions from an informed basis.

At Adelaide against India, after Allan Donald again made the breakthrough, Azharuddin with 79 and Kapil Dev, who hit a rapid 42, took the Indians to 180 for 8 and for once our batsmen got into their stride, Peter Kirsten and Andrew Hudson putting on 128 for the 1st wicket and Kepler stroking the winning runs, the epitome of coolness. Miraculously, we had made it to the semi-final and had to face England again in Sydney in a game which, in the end, was reduced to the realms of farce.

All the England batsmen got runs but this time it was Graeme Hick who set things up with 83. All the bowlers got some stick, none more so than Allan Donald who, it might be noted, had played in just about every game. He was tired and stale, and had our selectors used the full squad and rested some of our key players, such as Allan, as most of the other teams did, perhaps our boys would have been fresher. It was hard to understand why, against teams such as India and especially Zimbabwe, Tertius and I had not been given a run to give some of the others a break. Irrespective of my own desire to play, it would have made so much sense. Tertius had played one game in which he had bowled only 2.3 overs – at least in my one game I had bowled my full 10 overs. What was the point of taking us?

Allan took 2 wickets in that semi but conceded 69 runs. Our innings, from the start, had the momentum, Andrew Hudson scoring a sound 46, Adrian Kuiper at last coming good, thrashing Gladstone Small all over the place with 36 in 44 balls, and Jonty Rhodes taking 43 off just 39 balls. But then it all descended into a comedy. It rained with South Africa needing 22 off 13 balls with 4 wickets in hand. Our boys, naturally enough, wanted to stay on whereas England wanted to come off. The umpires decided to halt play, in spite of the fact that at one time during the England innings when rain had fallen, they had stayed on. The quaint rules of the competition determined that 2 overs had been lost and when the players returned to the field, South Africa needed a ridiculous 22 off 1 ball! It was a dreadful anti-climax to what had been a really courageous showing by us. After so long in isolation, we had shown the world we could still match the best of them on the cricket field.

Even in defeat in such ludicrous circumstances, we were a proud bunch of guys that night. Although my part in the campaign had been absolutely minimal, I had no quarrel with my fellow players, some of whom had become really good friends to me. Some of our players were in tears at the end. We had exceeded all our expectations. The players showed enormous guts and no one more than the captain himself. I bear no grudges. I think he was wrong to treat me in the way he did but he is a man of courage and he is a disciplinarian – and he leads from the front.

Tertius and I had taken different attitudes to our lack of participation. Maybe he was right in that he realised early on that he was destined to play a miniscule part in the campaign and simply set out to enjoy himself. As a matter of fact, he bowled with real hostility at the nets and on one occasion, Mike Procter actually took a relatively new, hard ball off him and gave him a much older ball because he was in danger of injuring some of our own batsmen. Perhaps because I was, palpably, close to the end of my career, I took my exclusion harder. And perhaps my hunger for success is a driving force within me that I find difficult to quell when I am frustrated.

The real irony was that we had beaten the Pakistanis in that early warm-up game and again in the competition itself, and had we taken our rightful place in the final, I felt that we would have gone in with a considerable advantage. And of course, our confidence would have been really high.

If at times there was a tension in the dressing room, which is inevitable when you are playing in such an intensive atmosphere, the spirit amongst us was nevertheless great, whether we were jetting here or there, in the hotels or eating out together. Of the players, I naturally tended to mix with people like Allan Donald, with whom I had become so friendly at Free State, Hansie Cronje, the Free State captain, Andy Hudson and, of course, Peter Kirsten, a longstanding friend of mine since our Western Province days together, and David Richardson, who is a really great guy. All of us stuck together well and I can say that I made a lot of friends during that whirlwind tour.

We are, all of us in South Africa, perhaps vulnerable and sensitive. To have come through what we have come through has inevitably left a legacy of suspicion. The politics of cricket in South Africa has been a veritable minefield and it may well be that one of the things we have to learn is to leave those politics behind us. And we have to be honest with each other, right across the racial boundaries which have been drawn for years.

After that crazy semi-final, almost involuntarily, we did a lap of honour, me included. It was Allan Donald who started it off and you could literally sense the tremendous support and sympathy which existed in the crowd. Again, it was a marvellous euphoric moment.

I found myself on the air again for the final. Pakistan got it absolutely right. They started their campaign slowly but by using their full squad, they ensured that their top players came to the final stages of the competition fresh and on a rising plane. They peaked at precisely the right time and on the day were certainly worthy winners. The Pakistanis wanted the Cup badly and by the time the England team had somewhat fortuitously reached the final, having preceded the campaign with a tour of New Zealand, many of their players were tired and carrying injuries.

There was more emotion when we flew back into Johannesburg. I had never seen as many people – of all races, I should stress – all together as one, waiting to welcome *their* team at the airport and during our official tour of the city centre the following day on board an open-topped bus. The only comparable modern equivalent had been the crowds who welcomed Nelson Mandela when he was released from jail. I had tears in my eyes, and so did most of the guys. It illustrated so clearly how big a part cricket can play in the making of the new South Africa; just how much people want to be a part of this rebirth of a nation and of whatever successes lie ahead of us and want to make their contribution, no matter how small. Even if we had won the World Cup, our welcome home could not have been warmer or more euphoric.

And almost before the dust had settled on the streets of Jo'burg, we were off again, this time for a short tour to the West Indies to play three one-day games and a Test match. Brian McMillan was injured and his place was taken by Corrie van Zyl, my playing colleague at Free State, who was unlucky, in my opinion, not to have been included in the World Cup squad. Otherwise, it was the same squad and if my confidence had been somewhat shaken by my experiences in Australia and New Zealand, I was nevertheless delighted to be making the trip. It was a fresh challenge and this time, I hoped, I would have an opportunity to perform and not be confined to the sidelines.

As England have recently discovered, playing the West Indies in the Caribbean is very different from playing them anywhere else. They had disappointed in the World Cup and indeed we had given them a good beating in New Zealand. But as we were about to discover, once they get to places like Kingston, Port-of-Spain and Bridgetown, they are a very different proposition. To say that we soon discovered how hot it can be in the West Indies is an understatement. In our first one-day international at Sabina Park, we were hit by the full force of the calypso kids – and with a vengeance.

Before we flew out, I had a long chat with Adrian Kuiper. We had always been good friends and I think he was a little embarrassed by the treatment that had been meted out to me during the World Cup. Naturally, he could not overtly criticise the tour management but he did think I had been treated somewhat unfairly. However, he thought it better now to put all that behind us and instead look forward to what lay ahead. He had not enjoyed a very successful World Cup himself; in fact by his own very high standards of batsmanship, he had something of a disaster. He is such a good timer of the ball but he is powerful too, rather, I think, in the Botham mould, and it is my view that he should always be left to play his own game. I think too often we looked to him to lead, whereas he would perhaps have been better left to get on with things himself. He is a tremendously effective one-day cricketer but during the World Cup he was moved up and down the order and, I suspect, became a little unclear as to his role in the side.

He is one of those batsmen who is not afraid to take the aerial route and on his day, he is capable of destroying almost any attack. He is one of the few players who can whack the ball over extra cover – all the way. Ironically, it was his bowling which prospered. If, on occasion, he was expensive, nevertheless his strike rate was phenomenal. He isn't above medium pace but he does swing the ball. Perhaps he hasn't worked on his bowling as much as he might but he certainly played a full part in the campaign with the ball. He is a real gentleman and I have always valued his friendship enormously. He was also a very good rugby player but as a schoolboy he was quite outstanding as a cricketer. He and Danie du Toit dominated club cricket when they were at Stellenbosch University. And in the Lamby mould he is a bubbly character, good in the dressing room, creating a happy atmosphere.

We were pretty tired when we flew out, mentally and physically, but it was necessary for us to undertake the tour because it seemed unlikely that the West Indies would come to us before we had visited them. We are spoiled in South Africa because we do have such good facilities but things are very different in the Caribbean. Practice facilities are sparse. We just had the one net with no back net so we were in effect practising up against a concrete wall at the edge of the ground. The wickets are difficult to read, and brown with cracks. But then on the morning of the match they water them and roll in grass cuttings until they shine almost like glass, making them very difficult for us to assess.

I was picked for that first game in Kingston and I think, in the circumstances, acquitted myself reasonably well, bowling 10 overs for 53 runs which actually turned out to be relatively economical compared with the other bowlers. It was Phil Simmons, the tall right handed batsman, who put us to the sword with an innings of 122 which included five 6s and 12 4s. One of the 6s, off Corrie, soared out of sight over the grandstand and was never seen again. I had one success in that I managed to remove Brian Lara, who, two years later, was to go into the record books with his mammoth 375 against England.

It wasn't, I think, that we bowled badly. Perhaps we bowled too full a length. I didn't feel that the wicket was hard and fast but there is so little movement compared with the grassy wickets in South Africa and I don't think we had time to adjust and work out the way we should play in what were alien conditions to us.

After Allan Donald had dismissed Desmond Haynes – I managed to cling on to the catch in the gully – Lara and Simmons started to get after us. It isn't that you do a lot of leather-chasing out there. With very little grass on the outfield, once the ball has gone past you, you just go and fetch it! And, funnily enough, when Simmons came in, he struggled for a while. I remember he kept coming down the wicket to me for about 3 overs and I kept drifting it into his pads and he just could not get the ball away until he really let rip and crashed me straight out of the ground over long on.

Lara had scored 50 when I had him caught at mid on by Kepler Wessels. I held the ball back fractionally and he was through the shot just that little bit early. I quickly learned that it was essential to bowl straight and give them no width, and more effective to drop that little bit shorter so the ball would gather some pace off the wicket. If my figures were as good as most, I wasn't totally satisfied with my performance. Adrian, however, did it again. He bowled just 5 overs and was taken for 33 runs but in between, he picked up the wickets of Simmons, Richardson and Winston Benjamin. Nonetheless their 287 for 6 always looked to be too many for us.

Andrew Hudson alone looked capable of responding, taking 50 runs off what was a pretty robust attack of Ambrose, Patterson, Benjamin, Cummins and Hooper in 69 balls and collecting 5 boundaries on the way. The only other batsman to offer a real fight was Hansie Cronje with a courageous 42. I batted at number 10 and, with the game by then miles out of our reach, made room for myself to play out on the off side only to have my castle demolished by Winston Benjamin.

It was a very thoughtful South African party which departed from Kingston en route for Trinidad, beaten by 107 runs. But worse was to follow. The first of two back-to-back one-day games at Trinidad's famous Queen's Park Oval, Port-of-Spain, saw us humbled as few other international teams have been humbled. We never really recovered from a disastrous start which saw our top three batsmen from the World Cup campaign back in the pavilion with only 36 on the board. Kepler went to a rather wild shot, caught behind, Andrew Hudson was brilliantly run out – one of three such dismissals in the innings – when Phil Simmons scored a direct hit from point, and Peter Kirsten sliced a catch to third man.

With our backs pinned to the wall, only three batsmen reached double figures: Adrian Kuiper uncharacteristically had to battle for 62 balls as he ground his way to 19, Hansie Cronje, another run-out victim, scraped to 22 and Jonty Rhodes, who took the attack at last to the bowlers, scored 45 before he too was run out. I was involved in the latter incident having gone in at number 9. Jonty called for a quick run but, according to the umpire, failed to beat the throw. Ambrose had a return of 3 for 24. He reminded me so much of Joel Garner bowling from that tremendous height. The ball is somewhere around your chest all the time and if you can't play off the back foot, you are totally lost against him. But there is more to him than just height. He is very fine bowler, one of the best, if not the best in the world today. He can generate real pace when he wants to but is able to bowl within himself and sustain accurate spells. Cummins also had 3 wickets and of course, there were those three run-outs.

Des Haynes and Brian Lara then proceeded to take us to the cleaners. They savaged Allan Donald and, I must say, savaged me as well. They started at a gallop and just accelerated, hitting the ball to all points of the compass with absolute impunity, striking the ball on the up, coming down the wicket at the bowlers. It was mayhem. I went for 41 runs off just under 5 overs and Lara just kept coming at me, hitting the ball inside to out, finishing with 86 off 91 balls as the West Indies raced to a 10-wicket victory, reaching their target of 153 from just over 25 overs!

Des Haynes is such a great batsman. His partnership with Gordon Greenidge surely made them the most feared opening pair in the world. He is technically so good and, as he has so often shown, not only for the West Indies but for Middlesex too, he is capable of holding an innings together. But he can also take on bowlers, as he did on that occasion in Port-of-Spain. When I look at the West Indians, I am constantly reminded of the cricket I played in the early part of my career on matting wickets, which is a game for stroke-makers. They play down the line, often on the up, and providing they are in line on West Indian wickets, which give so little in the way of lateral movement, they can rock forward or back and hit through the line of the ball.

It didn't come as a great surprise to me when I was left out for the last of the one-dayers the following day. I had not bowled well and in any case was not feeling 100 per cent. Instead I was relegated to the drinks waiter role as 12th man and Tertius Bosch was given his opportunity. Even Allan Donald was left out of that game. Yet again, our batsmen were unable to make the rate of progress required. This time Kepler dropped himself down the order and emerged as our top scorer with 45, but a target of 190 was never going to be enough and it was that man Simmons again who took on our bowling with another quite staggering century as they completed the treble at a canter. Meyrick Pringle was the only bowler to escape the mayhem, bowling 5 tight overs for just 6 runs and having the temerity to bowl Haynes for a duck.

By now, I was very much under the weather, having picked up some kind of a bug for which I was given penicillin injections. Unfortunately, I discovered I was allergic to penicillin. So the flight to Bridgetown, Barbados, was an absolute nightmare for me. I was by now covered in a rash and thought that I was busy dying! To make matters worse, after leaving Port-of-Spain, the plane developed a fault and had to return before we eventually made it to Barbados at the second attempt.

It was with bitter disappointment that I realised I was not going to be able to even be considered for the one and only Test match. I certainly had no chance of being fit to play and in fact I was rushed straight to a doctor once we had arrived in Bridgetown. But, in all honesty, I wasn't bowling well anyway. Nevertheless, I did witness what must have been one of the game's greatest Test matches in which, having been flayed in the one-day series, our players bounced right back and fought their way to a winning position, only to collapse to defeat on the last day.

It was a strange experience, though. After the euphoria of the games in Jamaica and Trinidad, which were played in front of packed houses (and a packed house in the West Indies has to be experienced to be believed), the Test was played in front of a very poor crowd, mainly, we were told, because the locals were boycotting the game due to the omission of their local hero, Cummins, from the West Indian side. However, if the atmosphere was untypical, the match itself was totally absorbing. Haynes and Simmons put on 99 for the 1st wicket before both going to Richard Snell, who, as it happened, emerged as our best bowler of the day with 4 for 83. But those 99 runs came off just 22 overs. Brian Lara should have gone first ball but Kepler put him down in the slips. Fortunately it wasn't too costly a miss as he went for 17, but Richie Richardson and Keith Arthurton kept things going in an even-time stand of 92. Our bowlers stuck to their task well and from 240 for 5 the West Indies slumped to 262 all out.

And what a start we had. Although Mark Rushmere was out early, caught in the gully off Ambrose, Kepler took the attack to the bowlers, cutting and pulling savagely in a century stand with Andrew Hudson and had reached 59 when he went to a catch at backward point. Andrew Hudson really took them on, cutting, pulling and driving in a really exhilarating innings, and with help from Adrian Kuiper, he steered us to a healthy lead of 83. Hudson's magnificent innings of 163 was one of the finest I have seen.

Furthermore, when the West Indies batted for a second time, Tertius Bosch made an early breakthrough by dismissing Simmons with only 10 on the board. Lara had a stroke of luck when he dislodged a bail with his back foot after going back and turning the ball to fine leg but the umpire didn't see it. He went on to score an important 64 and Jimmy Adams, against whom I had played in Scotland when he was a professional for Royal High in the East League, took it on from there with a fine unbeaten 79, proving what I had always thought of him, that he had the ability to play at the highest level. Snell collected another 4 wickets and Allan Donald also had 4, and the West Indies were all out for 283, setting us a target of 200. We surely were favourites to win.

However, Curtly Ambrose had something to say about that, dismissing both our openers before Kepler came together with Peter Kirsten. They really set up victory, or so we thought, with a tremendous stand of 96, the captain taking up where he left off in the first innings. Yet the wheels came off on the last day when Ambrose and Walsh snapped up the last 5 wickets for just 17 runs as our batsmen tried to nudge their way to victory rather than maintaining the attack which hitherto had proved so successful. From staring potential victory in the face, we suddenly found ourselves losing by 52 runs!

And that was that. A disappointment for me again. Apart from the health problems, I felt I had not performed well and I feared that my chance of playing in an official Test might have gone for good.

In some ways, perhaps, the fact that I had only one day at home before leaving for Scotland for the last time meant that I had little time to dwell on such matters. Instead, I had to buckle down to the task of playing for Scotland in the Benson & Hedges. I had missed the first two games through my commitments in the West Indies and wished I had missed the next one, frankly. We went to Chelmsford and met a rampant Essex team on a wicket right on the edge of the Chelmsford square.

I think I was somewhat jet-lagged and, with Goochy in an absolutely outrageously unbridled mood, we were taken to the cleaners for a record-breaking 388 for 7 in 55 overs. Gooch got a century and to rub salt in the wounds Neil Foster took us for 62 in 27 balls. I had 1 for 79 in 10 overs! Then, after rain had pushed the game into a second day, we were skittled out for a paltry 116.

Things had to get better from that moment on and thankfully they did: I had a really productive season. When I returned from Scotland, I knew that I might be facing my last season. Furthermore, this 1992-93 season might be the last chance I would have of gaining that elusive Test cap. India were to visit us for a four-match Test series in November and I drew a very deep breath and decided to make one last effort. I had worked hard on my game in Scotland and on my return, kept on working with increasing enthusiasm. I promised myself and I promised my wife that I would make that one last attempt to make it into the Test team.

I started the season well. At Free State, even if we had lost Eddie Barlow, we felt that we had a really great chance of winning the Castle Cup.

We certainly started promisingly, with a 7-wicket win over Border in East London. Louis Wilkinson, who had a fine 115 off just 160 balls, and Hansie Cronje and Corrie van Zyl, who both got into the 80s, set the tone and Allan Donald and I followed up with a quick breakthrough. I was to become the team's stock bowler again that season and in that first game bowled 35 overs in the first innings for 4 for 73. When Border followed on, I took a further 3 wickets in their second innings for a match haul of 7 for 146 off 54 overs.

At Durban in our next game, Franklyn Stephenson lashed the Natal attack for an astonishing 141 after we had started badly and I waved the bat successfully towards the end of the innings for 30 and then bowled 33 overs to grab 6 wickets for 72. In the end Andrew Hudson kept us at bay with a fine innings of 159 not out in their second innings, during which I bowled 46 overs, 19 of which were maidens, to take 2 for 71. If we failed to win that one, nevertheless I had got into a really good groove, dropping on to the spot from the word go.

I had another long stint against Eastern Province in Bloemfontein, where I also performed with the bat, coming in with the score on a perilous 88 for 6 and battling away for three hours during which I faced 134 balls and scored an invaluable 79. With some stoic resistance from Philip Radley and Bradley Player the tail more than doubled our total, but rain and Eldine Baptiste, who scored 154 runs in the match for once out and took 8 wickets, consigned the game to a draw.

The Indians had by now arrived in South Africa and the First Test was imminent. I knew I had performed well enough certainly to be amongst the leading contenders for a place in the Test team. My main opposition would almost certainly be Clive Eksteen and Tim Shaw, but every spin bowler in the Castle Cup had to viewed as genuine opposition. I think my cause was strengthened by the way in which Free State had started the season. We were developing into a winning machine.

It was during the game against Eastern Province, captained of course by Kepler himself, that Allan Donald, Hansie Cronje and myself were picked for the First Test. At last, I thought, I am going to play in an official Test match. I knew full well that it could conceivably be my first and last Test. It was Arthur Turner, the Free State Director of Cricket, who relayed the news to us and needless to say I felt absolutely thrilled. The dream that had lingered within my breast for so many years was about to be to be fulfilled. This, surely, was the icing on the cake. The elation I felt was very much shared by my Free State playing colleagues, who were delighted for me. Late in life, I must admit – I was one of the oldest players to receive a first Test cap in the history of the game – but this was the reward for all those years of trials and tribulations, of good, bad, of humiliation and triumph.

Here was the ultimate challenge. Indian batsmen, notoriously, play spin well and extreme pace less well. They had shown scant respect for our spinners on the short tour to India, but I felt confident because I had bowled so well in those first few weeks of the season. Furthermore, I believed that now I had thrown off the unwanted mantle of the token gesture towards multi-racial cricket in South Africa. I was, I firmly believed, picked entirely on merit. The Indian squad was relatively inexperienced but there were some established 'old heads' like Kapil Dev, Azharuddin and Ravi Shastri. And, unquestionably, there was a huge pool of glittering talent in the likes of Sachin Tendulkar and Pravin Amre.

As luck would have it, my official Test debut was to be made at the same ground where I made my unofficial debut against Kim Hughes' rebel Australians, Kingsmead, Durban. This was indeed an historical occasion: the first home Test for us since the 1969-70 season and the first Test ever between South Africa and India. And of course, I was making history myself by becoming the first coloured player to represent South Africa. As it so happened, there was another piece of history in the making with the introduction of the third umpire and video cameras. Even if I had been through it all before, back in the days of the rebel tours, I must confess that this first Test was a very special moment for me. To be able to say, at last, that I was a Test player meant a great deal to me. No one can ever take that away from me. And, I suppose, no one can ever do it again. It is a funny feeling to be unique! However, I sincerely hope that many more will follow in my footsteps.

As to the game itself, it was quite frankly disappointing. Neither side ever took the initiative. It was a game played with extreme caution, like a sparring session between two boxers. Batting first, we made an abysmal start when Jimmy Cook, such a good player but somehow unable to convert his quality at Test match level, went to the very first ball of the game when Kapil Dev produced a beautiful delivery which nipped away off the seam, found the edge and went straight to Sachin Tendulkar at third slip. So we were struggling from ball one. Kepler held the innings together with a typically gritty century but until Jonty Rhodes joined him, he lacked effective support. Jonty is a jaunty cricketer and at times very unorthodox. In typical fashion, he went after the bowling, scoring 41 before trying to sweep Kumble once too often and nicking on to his pad to silly point.

I'm afraid my contribution amounted to just 3 runs before I pushed forward somewhat inconclusively to give a catch to slip off Shastri. Meyrick Pringle gave our innings something of a final flourish with a couple of 6s on his way to 33 off 27 balls but 254 was, on that wicket, a modest score.

Yet India started their innings badly, stumbling to 38 for 4 with Tendulkar making a bit of history by becoming the first Test player to be 'given out' by the all-seeing eye of the video camera. Inevitably, Jonty Rhodes was the fielder. But then in came Pravin Amre. With his captain, Azharuddin, he brought the Indians back into the game with some resolute batting. Now I had my first bowl in Test cricket. I think the next passage of play was by far the most fascinating in the whole Test match. Amre wanted to come down the wicket to almost every ball. I had to vary the pace, drift it into his pads, hold the ball back or, alternatively, fire it in. It was a real battle of wits and I was in my element. He miscued one just over mid off, and soon afterwards squeezed a ball between me and mid on at catchable height. Then I threw one out a bit wider which he top-edged just out of slip's reach. But he kept dancing down the wicket, sometimes, when he found he had not quite got to the pitch of the ball, finding himself having to kick the ball away with his pads. There was very little help for me in the wicket, so I had to rely on variations of flight and pace. However, there was a little bit of bounce and that helped me. It was a fascinating duel and a really enjoyable experience which tested my mental mettle.

In the event Amre went on to a century before he succumbed, cutting McMillan to Jonty Rhodes at cover. Even then, we found Kiran More virtually immovable. At last I came back into the attack and picked up my first Test wicket, that of Kumble who, after I had completely frustrated him, tried to heave me on the leg side, missed and was bowled. Even better, I also removed Kiran More after a 214-ball innings of 55, trapping him lbw to finish up with figures of 19.1 overs, 3 maidens, 2 for 56. But the Indians had scraped a 23-run lead on first innings.

The fourth day was entirely washed out by rain and that killed the game as a contest, leaving our batsmen with no alternative but to play out time and get some batting practice.

We then travelled to Jo'burg for the Second Test, where I was consigned to the role of 12th man because the wicket was expected to help the seamers. Once again we had a bad start, Jimmy Cook yet again going cheaply. Indeed we were in real trouble at 26 for 4 after Prabhakar picked up some cheap wickets. But Jonty Rhodes and Brian McMillan came to our rescue with some resolute batting, both of them getting into the 90s. Then we suffered a serious blow when Meyrick Pringle was hit in the eye by a bouncer from Srinath which somehow got through his helmet visor, and he took no further part in the game.

There was a century from Tendulkar to admire when India batted but he lacked support and we established a useful lead of 65. But the pace of the game was, frankly, slothful. The prodigious teenager gave us only flashes of his exciting stroke play and in all batted for over six hours. But our batsmen were also pinned down, this time by Kumble, who wheeled away for 44 overs, 22 of them maidens, to pick up 6 for 53. Inevitably the game petered out as a tame draw – hardly a good advertisement for Test cricket!

However, we turned things round in the Third Test at Port Elizabeth when I was back in the team. It was Allan Donald, with some very swift bowling, who set things up for us and then applied the *coup de grâce* in their second innings. Only Azharuddin provided real resistance in their first innings with an obdurate 60 as they toiled to 212, Allan picking up 5 wickets. I had only 11 overs – 0 for 30, but I bowled tidily enough. We didn't fare much better. Kumble again bedded down for a long, long spell, this time bowling 50.3 overs for just 81 runs and 3 wickets. Hansie Cronje provided the backbone of our innings with a maiden Test century, a testament to his temperament if ever there was one.

Hansie is normally a fairly fluent batsman but on this occasion he did what was required of him, scoring 135 in 531 minutes to break the back of the Indian bowling and enable us to establish a lead of 63. I was sent in to literally have a go and managed a 6 and a couple of 4s. I played Kumble as a medium-pacer. I had encountered him in Scotland and knew that he didn't really turn the ball much, mostly bowling top-spinners, so I concentrated on hitting back up the line, then using my feet to him when he bowled it a bit slower. Sixteen is hardly a match-winning score but it was, at that stage of the game, a useful contribution which saw us into the lead.

But then Allan Donald let rip and the Indians were soon in disarray. They lost their 1st wicket with just 1 on the board, their 2nd for 10, their 3rd 1 run later and then stumbled to 31 for 6. Enter Kapil Dev. Very sensibly, he decided that attack was to be the best form of defence and he just threw the bat, scoring a magnificent century. It was the seamers who came in for the most attention. I bowled only 8 overs but very tidily – 0 for 17 – but Kapil just took on the quicker bowlers and his 129 rescued India and made a game of it. Allan Donald had a magnificent game, picking up 7 for 84 for match figures of 12 for 139.

Then Kepler took over. He drove the spinners mercilessly on a flat wicket which enabled him to hit the ball on the up, and although he was dropped a couple of times, he won the game for us on the fourth day by 9 wickets – with a superb innings of 95 not out to take us into a significant 1-0 lead in the series.

And so we now travelled to my beloved Newlands for the Fourth and final Test. I must admit that we took a 'what we have we hold' view of things and another draw was on the cards right from the start. The way this game was played brought widespread condemnation from the press – and not just our own South African media, but from the world's press as a whole.

We batted first and having lost Kepler without a run on the board, subsequently dug in and ground out a first-innings total of 360, if not exactly establishing ourselves on the 'moral high ground' at least ensuring safety! Jonty Rhodes, uncharacteristically, bedded in for a 233-ball innings of 86, his unorthodox approach again frustrating the spinners, Kumble and Raju, who each bowled 47 overs. Brian McMillan was even slower on his home ground. He virtually planted himself for 190 balls for a soporific innings of 52. It was only when Craig Matthews and I got to the wicket that we emerged from our snail-like pace. I had a quick 34 whilst Craig had an unbeaten 28 which induced Kepler to declare with 9 wickets down. We ran like stags, the pair of us, in the end taking one chance too many when I was run out, but at least we had injected some badly needed urgency.

India began even more painfully. It was surprising to me that they didn't try to up the momentum of the game because they were, crucially, one down in the series and a draw was of no consequence to them in that context. Yet that was how they played and so this time I had a long bowl, completing 33 overs in the innings as the Indian batsmen got their heads down and battled it out. Manoj Prabhkar led the entrenchment with 62 in 250 balls. He showed the maker's name, all right, but then occasionally played some quite outrageous shots. I managed eventually to put him and the spectators out of their misery when I got one to turn just that fraction more and found a leading edge to have him held by Kepler at silly point.

Eventually they accumulated 275 and we went in again. But the tempo of the match remained pathetically slow and when Kepler eventually declared our second innings on 130 for 6, the draw which had seemed inevitable from day one brought proceedings, as the *Protea Cricket Annual* put it, to a merciful end with the Indians on 29 for 1!

So I had three official Springbok caps to my name. The final curtain was to fall at Newlands which, I suppose, was fitting, for this was where it had all begun for me. I had done it. That small boy who sat enraptured in the small section of the ground reserved for non-whites and watched devotedly the Trevor Goddards, John Reids and Mike Smiths of the cricketing world had ploughed a lone furrow over many long years, had made his debut for Western Province and unbelievably played on that hallowed turf. I had returned on numerous occasions, of course; I had played there for Orange Free State and now, three weeks before my 40th birthday, I had played a Test match at Newlands. Life is made of dreams but dreams don't just happen. You have to make them happen and if it had taken me all those years, I had, in my own mind, joined my boyhood heroes, had vindicated the struggles and the hardships I had been forced to endure.

There were more high spots to come, more dreams to be fulfilled and the very fact that I had earned those three Springbok caps was to provide me with the inspiration for what was to be one final push in that most memorable of seasons which was, effectively, to represent my final fling in the middle.

• • • • • • • • • • • • • • • •

CONITA HENRY

'I first met Omar when a cousin of mine took me to a disco at the Avendale Cricket Club in Cape Town. In walked Omar, who I hadn't even heard of and, much to my amazement, everyone suddenly became excited. Imagine my surprise when he asked me up to dance when the last record of the evening was announced. However, there was another man who wanted to dance with me. Omar, typically, simply told me that I really wanted to dance with him – and so I did!

'Subsequently he asked me if I would like to come to a game which, in spite of the fact that I had, until then, not been at all interested in cricket, I did. But I didn't even see him. Before I reached the ground he had been carted off to hospital having been hit in the face by a ball.

'However, once he had recovered we did start to see each other, in spite of the disapproval of my parents. I came from a Christian background, you see, and Omar of course was a Muslim. Thereafter we kept in touch with each other, writing when he went over to Scotland,

and when he returned we started to go out on a regular basis.

'Eventually we got married on March 29th, 1982. I had changed my religion. Because he was so involved at the end of the 1981-82 season, for the next two weeks I hardly saw him and then I was whisked halfway across the world to Scotland.

'He had, by the time we met, become something of a controversial character because of the troubles he had when he left SACBOC, and when my colleagues at work learned that I was involved with him, I had some nasty jibes to contend with. And even worse than that were the telephone calls I sometimes had from people who told me, always anonymously, that if Omar went into Cape Town, they were going to kill him.

'But there have been so many happy times, achievements of which he was so proud and, naturally enough, moments which made me feel proud too. I was nearly in tears when he walked out on to the field in his green and gold cap. Equally emotional was the time when we were driving back from Port Elizabeth and his inclusion in the World Cup squad was announced on the radio. I was so excited, crying with joy when I heard his name mentioned.

'The World Cup was of course a tremendous disappointment for him and when he was away, he would telephone me on a daily basis and I knew things were going wrong for him. There were some dreadful things said about Omar and his attitude and that hurt.

'Omar as a man is, I think, sometimes too soft, too forgiving, but then that is his nature. He is such a good man, really. He is also so dedicated to cricket. It hasn't always been easy for me because of course his cricket has been very demanding and sometimes that puts a greater responsibility on me, especially with the children. But this is not a source of regret. I like my cricket, you see, and he is a wonderful husband and father even if he has, perhaps, not seen so much of his children as they have grown up. But then that is a demand which is inevitably placed upon a professional cricketer and you have to have a strong relationship to survive the demands of his career.

'My life with Omar has been fulfilling and certainly very different from what most people would regard as the norm, and for that I thank God.'

A BRIGHT NEW
FUTURE

There were more spoonfuls of sugar for me during that final season with Free State. To add to the three Test caps I had won, within three days of the end of that last Test I was entering the arena again, this time in the most important game Orange Free State had ever played in their 100-year history.

The arena this time was Springbok Park, Bloemfontein. And to add a touch of drama, especially from a personal point of view, our opponents were Western Province. Our Castle Cup challenge had been something of a rollercoaster ride. After a good start to the season, a convincing 7-wicket victory over Border at East London and a first-innings win over Natal at Durban, we had a disappointing draw at home to Eastern Province in a match which I remember well for my rearguard innings of 79 in the first phase of the game. But we had an impressive win over Northern Transvaal at Centurion Park only for Transvaal to beat us during the last Test when Hansie, Allan and myself were involved at Newlands and thus not in the Free State line-up.

The final round of games came with an outside chance of us winning the Castle Cup. The powerful Transvaal team were to face Natal at the Wanderers Stadium and were favourites to take the trophy. And, the way things turned out, who would have bet against them after Province had reduced us to 38 for 4 on the first morning whilst Transvaal were making early inroads into the Natal batting a few hundred miles away?

Happily, it fell to me to mount a rescue operation. Perhaps I had gained extra inspiration from the joy of playing in those three Test matches. I know I was fired up and wanted to go out in what some might describe as a blaze of glory. But I felt good and in some respects, I suppose the situation I faced going in at 6 wickets down for 110, with a real battle on my hands, was tailor-made for me. Fortune, they say, favours the brave. I had a life when I was on 41 but then, with superb support from Bradley Player and, later, Philip Radley and Allan Donald, I managed to transform potential disaster into what turned out to be a match-winning situation with a century of which I was tremendously proud. From the perilous ground of 110 for 6 we went to a first-innings total of 266. Furthermore, we got our act together in the field and bowled Province out for 165 to go into the second half of the game with a more than useful lead of 101, with me picking up a couple of wickets.

Then it was Hansie Cronje who took the game by the scruff of the neck with a quite magnificent innings of 161 not out which enabled him to declare on 303 for 1, having been given great support by Mickey Arthur and Rudolf Steyn.

Meanwhile, in Jo'burg, Transvaal were losing their grip having surprisingly surrendered a first-innings lead of 125 to Natal. But when news came through that they had skittled Natal out for 71 in their second innings and needed therefore only 197 to win, the odds once again had swung in their favour. How fate's twists and turns can change things. We really got stuck into our task in Province's second innings and again I was to be handed the role of leading play-maker whilst, astonishingly, Transvaal's batting was busy collapsing.

I wheeled away for 33 overs in Province's second innings and was absolutely thrilled to capture 5 for 68. We had already heard about Transvaal's collapse and that provided the inspiration we needed to sweep home to victory by 114 runs in an atmosphere so red-hot that it is difficult to describe. We were carried along on the crest of a wave as the news filtered through to us from Jo'burg, with a wildly enthusiastic crowd behind us all the way. What moments these were. Throughout, Hansie kept his cool and I must say that in spite of the tension, our concentration never wavered. Perhaps because I was very much at the centre of the action as I worked my way through the Province batting, there was no time to even think about the fact that fortune was swinging our way. That bowling spell needed immense concentration and I was able to shut out everything around me and focus my mind on what I had to do. I put that down to the fact that I have always taught myself that mental strength is, in this game, of paramount importance. On that occasion I really did practise what I have always preached and my years of experience carried me through.

Euphoria reigned. It was a marvellous moment, what we had all worked so hard for, and it was fitting that our greatest moment should come as Free State prepared to celebrate its centenary.

There was to be one further reward for that tremendous team in which the spirit and the friendship between us was so important. There was no discrimination here, no one in the team who did not play his heart out for the other ten. For the second successive year we won the Total Power Series. What a culmination for me. In Jo'burg we had given Transvaal a real mauling thanks to another super knock of 61 from Hansie Cronje but lost the first leg of the semi-final to Western Province after I had scored 34 to resurrect our innings from 64 for 6 to 153 for 7 at the close.

But the Province batsmen kept things going and we went down by 5 wickets, only to bounce back in the second leg with a dramatic win in which I again starred with 48 off 39 balls, described later as my own brand of mayhem! Allan Lamb and Brian McMillan took them as close as a whisker but we just held on to win by 1 run to make it level over the two games. The next day, we comprehensively won the decider, thanks to some super batting by Mickey Arthur, Hansie Cronje and Louis Wilkinson, to go through to a final against Kepler's Eastern Province, played a week later with home advantage to us.

Our victory in the final was set up by Bradley Player, who claimed 3 vital wickets and Mickey Arthur, who ran out Kepler with a direct throw. Dave Richardson and Eldine Baptiste performed a rescue act and got them to 202 for 6 but Hansie and Rudolf Steyn were rampant and we romped home by 6 wickets with nearly 3 overs in hand.

That 1992-93 season had been a triumphant one for me. I had played in three Tests and even if I had not produced what could be described as startling performances or figures, I felt I had more than held my own, justified the selectors' faith in me and, once and for all, laid that bogey that my inclusion in the side was a token gesture. I knew I had earned my place. And to cap it all, I had played a highly significant part in taking Orange Free State to their first-ever Castle Cup title, excelling myself in that dramatic final game against Western Province.

But it was time to take stock. I had decided not to return to Scotland, my second home. Approaching the ripe old age of 42, I knew I had to settle down and think about the future and, of course, Conita and our three children, for now we had a son, Riyaad, born in Falkirk in 1992 – another 'jock'.

I have seen, in my 42 years, undreamed of changes happening here in South Africa. When you ask me how well cricket is now integrated in the country, I have to say that from the top level down to the clubs it is reasonably well integrated but at the schools, there is still a long way to go. The non-white schools – and in real and practical terms, we are still talking about schools which are not integrated – remain at a tremendous disadvantage. History dictated that under the creed of apartheid, separate development has been a fact of life and it will take years to change the reality of that.

Apartheid created a false world, a fools' world, a short-term paradise for those on one side of the road, and a hell for those on the other. That was a self-inflicted wound to which we must now add the reality of a worldwide recession. To put in place a structure whereby all of our people have the opportunity to learn and play cricket – or any other sport, for that matter – in good conditions, in good stadia, with all the infrastructure that is needed, is going to be very costly. It is therefore imperative that we look at the facilities that are already in place and use them universally. In other words, cricket grounds, rugby stadia, athletics tracks and the rest of them, created for the white community, will have to be shared. At school level that is difficult because in terms of our educational system and the ethos of all sport within that system, integration has not yet happened.

In practical terms, if South Africa is to rise from the ashes of apartheid and the long period of isolation, the effects of which, of course, are evident throughout South Africa as a whole, not just in the sporting community, and which have seriously depleted our economic resources, then some very difficult decisions are ahead of the politicians who will ultimately have the responsibility of guiding us, we hope, to greater prosperity. There is so much to do to rebuild the country, to rid it of squalor, to create a climate of full employment, to rebuild industries which have flagged. And all that rebuilding will place a huge demand upon our financial resources.

Let me concentrate my remarks, for the moment, on cricket. No one is saying, at least I am not, that grounds owned by whites should be handed over to either the coloured or black community or even to some amorphous controlling body. But if we are to have a chance of developing our next generations of cricketers, those facilities will have to be thrown open to all, by mutual consent. I am certainly not saying that now things have changed, that now apartheid has gone, what was yours (the whites', that is), is now mine. But those facilities which are in place must be better utilised by the whole community.

By and large, you see, many of the coloured schools still do not have proper facilities, often no grounds on which to play at all. But in the same communities, there are grounds in what was previously the province of the whites which could be used by the kids from all the schools. This is much more practical than the spending of huge sums, particularly at this stage of our new development, in creating lots of new grounds with turf wickets. Far better that the facilities which already exist are thus thrown open and *all* the kids have the chance of making progress on the basis of their ability rather than on the basis of which schools they go to, whether they have the right kind of facilities to play on or not, and so on.

It is the creation of that ladder of opportunity which is so important. Hitherto, except for those of us who have been lucky enough to find our way through the maze, those vital rungs of the ladder which enable youngsters to progress from schools cricket to club cricket to provincial cricket and then, if they are really good enough, to national level, have not been there for most of the coloured or black kids.

It was with all these thoughts in my mind that I returned to Stellenbosch to begin a new phase of my life. Again, the vital connection was made through the Rupert family. Dr Anton and his son Johan were keen to invest in cricket's future in Boland. Remember that their roots, like mine, are in Stellenbosch. To this end, they wanted to set up a cricket academy. Furthermore, they wanted me to become involved. They asked me to be their Development Director, to bring together a network of coaches throughout the province and set up a comprehensive system which would enable us to identify talent at an early age and bring it to the surface. And that, of course, meant talent from *every* section of the community. My job, therefore, was to construct the ladder, to develop the scheme and start the task of taking cricket to people right across the board, notably of course, to the schools of every denomination, of every creed.

It was, and remains, the most exciting challenge of my life. I have been richly rewarded by the game of cricket, even if there have been plenty of pitfalls on the way and a few decidedly unpleasant moments. But I have battled on in spite of those pitfalls and I have had the chance, denied to many, of taking my place alongside the best. That in itself, for someone with as much passion for the game as resides within my soul, is rich reward indeed. Now I have the opportunity of making that route easier for future generations of cricketers, no matter which part of the community they come from. And just as I have met all the other challenges I have encountered along my journey in the great game of cricket, now I accept the challenge of making it possible for others, with utter delight and with as much dedication as I hope I have shown in my own cricketing career.

It is my belief that if South Africa has in the past produced many great cricketers, in the future it has the potential to produce even more, providing we make that vital effort to serve every section of the community. But first, we must get into the minds and hearts of our children. If a child does not get the encouragement, he will not generate within himself the enthusiasm to continue. The fact is that if you look at the different segments of the South African community, the enthusiasm for cricket is, in any case, very mixed. Black Africans have comparatively little tradition within the game. I knew only one who played to a really high standard – Ben Malamba, who, as a quick bowler, played with Basil D'Oliveira. His sons also went on to play cricket, proof that if the game is introduced to a household, it will follow that others from the same household will play. But then you have to go to the next house and the next. It is no use just putting in place a cricket field and expecting everyone in, say, a township to immediately go out and play cricket. That is where the twin thrust of marketing and education will have to be applied. We have to inject the cricket plasma directly into their bloodstream.

It is therefore vitally important that those in whom is vested the responsibility of encouraging and coaching youngsters from this sort of background themselves have the necessary enthusiasm, the fire in their bellies. It isn't enough just to be proficient coaches. They must be filled with that enthusiasm and they must be able to communicate it throughout the community. If the world expects South Africa to start producing the kind of fast bowlers we know have enabled the West Indies to become such a dominant force in world cricket, then it may be that the world will have to wait. We have a lot of groundwork to do but if we do our job properly, I see no reason why, in time, that should not be the case. The black community also happens to be the poorest part of South African society in general and that represents another tough nut to crack.

The coloured community – those parts of the ethnic group known as 'Cape coloured', whose origins way back, like mine, are perhaps Far Eastern, has produced plenty of good cricketers, but again, poor facilities have stifled progress. Yet they, like the Indian community, who by and large have suffered from the same paucity of proper grounds, turf wickets and so on, have been playing cricket in South Africa for well over 100 years. In that respect, there is a higher starting point.

So the yardstick for each of the ethnic groups is placed in a different position, depending on which group you are talking about. The whites – and I do not resent this – have had all the advantages; now we have to look after all of the different groups and bring them together. I am convinced that the great advantage we have is that the potential, the raw talent, is there. There can be in South Africa's future teams well-built fast bowlers of the West Indian kind; spinners of the style of the Indian subcontinent, wristy batsmen of the same pedigree, whippy quick bowlers in the mould of Waqar and Wasim; and white cricketers in the mould of English or Australian players; for this, above all, is a multi-racial society. But unless we go back to basics and make a real effort to produce a formula which will take the game to the people, no matter which group they belong to, all we can expect is for the odd player to emerge from the different communities.

If we can get into the hearts and minds of people from every ethnic group, if we can not only develop their raw talent but educate them to use their minds and to exercise dedication on their own behalf, the day will come when the South African team has that multi-racial flavour about it. But in the meantime, the political dust will take time to settle; there will be many uncertainties; we have to learn to live together, regardless of the economic disparities which exist and perhaps always will. And there are those of us who now have a new destiny to fulfil, regardless of what has gone before.

In terms of the job I have to do here in Boland, the first task we have to tackle is to imbue the people at grass-roots level with an understanding of what they have to do in terms of cricket. But they must also dig much deeper. They have to identify youngsters with real talent but in order to lay the ground and ensure that such talent as they discover has the will, the means and the background to be able to progress, they must also become acquainted with the background. Sport – and above all cricket – is one of the ways in which some youngsters will find themselves able to escape from what may be very disadvantaged circumstances. Sport – and again I would suggest cricket more than most – is also able to broaden experiences of life: it develops the social skills and pleasure of living together in the team sense yet it is a game which presents youngsters with individual challenges too.

When, many years ago, Dr Anton Rupert launched a similar venture with Trevor Goddard as its co-ordinator, he made a speech in which he said: 'A sound mind requires a sound body. We want to look after Athens but then again, also look after Sparta. We have therefore decided to launch a sports foundation.' That represented real vision back in 1964. It still represents vision in 1994. If we had, as a nation, taken up that challenge then, on a universal scale, to build a country which included everyone, rather than excluding the numeric majority, this country would be a far better place.

Our academy at Boland is, I think, the first of what I hope will be many throughout the country. The credit must go to the Rupert family for continuing the vision shown by Dr Anton all those years ago. The family connection is strong. My father saw me perform at the highest level on only one occasion and that was at the Wanderers ground when Western Province played Natal in that memorable final. He was the guest of Johan Rupert. I did not know it at the time, but during that stay in Jo'burg, my father asked Johan to help make sure that when my playing days were over, there would be a job for me. Johan was as good as his word and thus I found myself here at Boland.

However, nothing in this life seems straightforward and I have found many cross-currents flowing which seemed to threaten to upset my boat; more rough waters with, needless to say, a few personality clashes on the way. Johan's original idea was to attach the academy to the Boland province, base it at Stellenbosch University, where Boland's administration is also based, and integrate it with the province.

At the same time, I was approached to play for Boland. Although it had been my intention to retire from first-class cricket after that stupendous high note at Free State, I agreed to play and set about the task of getting myself fit for the beginning of the 1993-94 season when Boland were, for the first time, to take their place in the top echelons of the game as an 'A' province under the coaching guidance of Bob Woolmer and led by the former Western Province opening batsman, Terence Lazard.

However, in terms of my responsibility in the development sector, as I understood my remit, I was to have an administrator and a free hand to extend our scheme wherever I thought fit. In that context, I was also approached by the University of the Western Cape to help them develop their cricket. This university is situated just outside Cape Town, near to the airport, and therefore outside Boland's boundary. It is, therefore, under the aegis of Western Province. You have to bear in mind that this university is the one to which most of the coloured youngsters go. In South Africa, a university education has to be paid for. There isn't a grant system such as exists in Britain. Thus the University of the Western Cape is far from opulent and it seemed to me that the circumstances presented to me fitted our general overall policy perfectly.

However, although I had gained tacit agreement on the principle of becoming involved at the university from Rupert International, who are my employers, the Boland committee raised strong objections on the basis that the university was part of Western Province and not Boland. And to make matters worse, I found that my academy administrator, Jaco van Rensburg, was being increasingly hijacked by the Boland administration to perform other duties. I cannot claim to be much of an administrator myself but that had been understood from the beginning.

Sadly, some of the personal differences which had emerged when I was playing for and captaining Boland back in 1988-89 resurfaced. Things were made very difficult for me and eventually I had to pull out of my commitment at the University of the Western Cape. I was reluctant to do this but as I was also nominally Boland's Director of Development – a confusing situation because it seemed to imply that Boland were my employers rather than Rupert International – and the effects of those cross-currents began to be felt.

Things had eventually to come to a head. In a joint press release issued in January 1994 by the Boland President, Mr Frans Stroebel, and Chairman Henry Paulse, it was stated, and I quote: 'The parting of the ways between the Boland Cricket Board and Mr Omar Henry must be seen against the following background. With his appointment as Director of the Boland Cricket Academy, Mr Henry was expected to take care of two aspects, namely administration, and coaching and development. The Boland Cricket Board is completely satisfied as regards his coaching and development work.

'Because of Mr Henry's lack of experience as regards administration, the Boland Cricket Board find it necessary to review the post of Administrator and it was decided to discontinue this position. Boland Cricket Board believes that Mr Henry will be able to continue his valuable coaching work in the Western Cape and is indeed in the process of developing such opportunities.

'As far as the Boland Cricket Academy is concerned an exciting opportunity that could lead to the conversion of this academy to a National Cricket Academy is being investigated. The Boland Cricket Board, the Rembrandt Group (Rupert International) the sponsors of the Boland Cricket Academy and Dr Ali Bacher of the South African

Cricket Board will investigate various possibilities in this regard in the near future. The Boland Cricket Board trusts and believes that this National Academy will be established within the borders of Boland.'

Thus the statement ended: sacked, on the face of it, by the people who did not in the first place employ me! I must say that the comments in that statement about my ability insofar as administration was concerned seemed to be somewhat economical with the truth. I was never employed to fulfil that task in the first place and they had hi-jacked my administrator! It was, in my view, a political manoeuvre.

After I appeared in the first few games of the season, the Boland selectors decided to drop me to the 'B' team but I decided to part from them, content to concentrate on the exciting new challenges that have now been presented to me. After all, there are no more ambitions to fulfil on the playing front and as I have learned throughout what some might regard as a somewhat chequered career, every cloud, no matter how dark, has its silver lining.

So I am now Head of Cricket at Stellenbosch University, a job which provides me with the opportunity to embrace development at grass-roots level as well as taking players on to the highest levels of the game. There will be a whole series of courses made available here. We will coach, we will coach coaches; there will be courses for groundsmen, for umpires, even for aspiring cricket administrators and, as you might guess, I will continue to emphasise to future generations of cricketers the need for fitness – physical fitness and, just as importantly, mental fitness.

There is, I'm happy to say, a united approach manifesting itself. Together, the university authorities, Boland Cricket Board and the United Cricket Board of South Africa are creating an enterprise which seeks to drive foward into the future in its goal of satisfying the needs of cricket here in every conceivable aspect of the game and for all sections of the community. This is, I'm certain, the way ahead. We have a watchful, knowledgeable organisation with sound financial support which, as we develop, will have an influence on a global scale. I believe that international cricket needs South Africa as much as South Africa needs international cricket. Here we can begin to put in place the vital stepping-stones for people from every section of the community, for above all this is a community-orientated project.

History tells us that the white English-speaking South African dominated cricket in South Africa. The English-speaking and Afrikaans-speaking whites were the only people to play Test cricket for South Africa but of course they only played their Tests against England, Australia and New Zealand. Significantly, during the apartheid years, no Pakistan, Indian, West Indian or Sri Lankan side ever officially toured South Africa.

The non-whites – the Indian, Muslim and Black communities – played their cricket under a different umbrella, that of SACBOC. They also played Test cricket, but only against Kenya. The International Cricket Conference never recognised this non-white body from South Africa.

It is against this historic background that our new venture must be viewed. We will implement a cricket structure that can create opportunity for every cricket player in South Africa. Finance, facilities, cricket knowledge and coaching are all vital if we are to achieve our objectives, which, in the long term, must be dedicated to the betterment of cricket in South Africa.

It is my personal view that South Africa will only field a truly great side when these needs are addressed. In the meantime, the task is to build a good Test squad for the next ten years and strengthen our domestic game by implanting the kind of structures we are building in Stellenbosch.

But to achieve these goals will require immense efforts to be made by our clubs, schools, colleges and of course, our universities. History again demonstrates that the South African Test scene has been dominated by players with a university background, whereas outside the white community the concentration was only on club cricket.

We will only achieve success if all parties can work together with honesty, sincerity and dedication. The media too has its part to play. TV, radio and the press all have a vitally important role in using their different channels, in all languages, to constantly underline the message. If I can play my part in this ground-swell of progress, then I will be content that all of this will in time overshadow whatever I have myself managed to achieve on the field.

And of course, this must be set against a background of immense change in South Africa itself, when the barriers of apartheid are being rolled back, when a new beginning is being made. There will be teething troubles, of that you can be sure, but we could not be setting up this particular stall, I believe, at a better time. The previous establishment, under the guidance of Trevor Goddard, floundered eventually on the rocks of apartheid. This time, we have a real chance to achieve our goals, right across the community.

The people on the ground have the necessary enthusiasm, and one of my jobs is to maintain it. I know we will trip over some of the hurdles, many of which will, I expect, be placed in our way by the bureaucrats, and initially we cannot guarantee instant success. But for every 100 kids we reach, I'll personally stake my life on the likelihood of at least ten per cent emerging as really talented players – and that figure will then start to rise. If you look at the talent that is, providing we do our job properly, naturally evident in the ethnic mix, plus the talents hidden there, you will see that we will live to see them on display in a South African team.

However, as much as we – and others – prepare the ground and create the opportunity, the bottom line is that those who do emerge will have to grab their opportunities when they arise. Looking back throughout my own career, and almost right to the end, I was always aware that there were huge obstacles in my way. At times it seemed that the opportunity was not there for me to reach the highest level but I stuck to my guns, kept going, always played the game with commitment and dedication and, in the end, doors almost miraculously opened for me. If you don't play cricket with that dedication then why waste your time? You might just as well go and catch fish or devote yourself to something else. Perhaps I have come through a hard school and perhaps that is why I think in the way I do. But to do anything in life without commitment is to only half do it.

Sport is a religion in South Africa; cricket is a religion. Here in Stellenbosch, in my own home town, my spiritual home, we now have 'A' province cricket. Boland has achieved what Durham achieved a couple of years ago, albeit after a very prolonged wait. Perhaps the status we now enjoy here should have come a few years ago when we were such a successful side. Only the game's administrators can answer that. And, in my new capacity, notwithstanding any further developments or changes which may be made in the fullness of time, it is vested in me to produce future generations of first-class cricketers. It is a tremendous challenge and I suspect that it will keep me quite well occupied for the rest of my life.

But if I have put my life into cricket and if there is yet much more to be injected, by the same token, cricket has given me a fuller, richer life than someone from a background like mine could ever have dreamed of achieving otherwise. Cricket has taken me to places I could never have hoped to visit. It has brought me into contact with people from every conceivable sector of life, from the Duke of Edinburgh, whom I met when Scotland played Glamorgan, to the men who emptied my dustbins, who also wanted to talk cricket. Cricket has been a way of life and will always be a way of life for me. The glory of the game is that it demands that you live together within a particular community irrespective of race, religion or anything else and thus it must teach us in South Africa to live in the same way.

Cricket, I firmly believe, has been a catalyst for change in South Africa and the creed of this game which demands that all barriers are removed is one that we would all do well to follow. If we have different beliefs then we should surely always respect the beliefs of others. Cricket demands that; life demands it: tolerance and understanding must be our watchwords.

It is a game apart. It teaches you so much, not just about the sport itself, but about life. I have learned so much about life during my years in this great game. I have made many friends in every corner of the world, and if cricket has taught me nothing else, it has taught me that to play successfully, at whatever level, you have always to remember that you are part of a team. Even as a professional, as a Test cricketer or whatever, you are just one part of a team. It is a case of 'we' not 'I', and that not only goes for cricket, it also applies to mankind at large. I am just a part of that team too.

In my early life, I neglected my education. No one else neglected it, it was my doing and it was my fault, and I wouldn't recommend others to do what I did because education is so important. If the path I chose was stony and difficult, as I grew older and more experienced, as I achieved those seemingly unreachable goals, I became increasingly aware that I was not, after all, alone. There were hundreds, thousands, of people, masses of them, behind me, supporting me, some directly, others indirectly. But there was a growing awareness within me that I was not battling alone. In Scotland they have a phrase to describe the role we all fulfil no matter what our background: 'We are all Jock Thamson's bairns!' And there are times when it is worth remembering that no matter what happens and how bad life sometimes may seem, you will never be the worst off of the human community; nor will you be the richest man, whether in knowledge or finance or whatever. But there is a reason why you are in your particular station in life. You have to find out what role you can play to make life better. And unless you discover your own destiny, you can be in a fools 'paradise.

We are all pieces in a jigsaw. We all have our place in the overall picture. Sometimes it is a struggle to find the right place, the right destiny. But if I had to live my life again, I wouldn't change a single thing. I have enjoyed a rich and productive life, I have the most wonderful family around me and love in abundance and I hope there is more fulfilment yet to come.

But I am aware that I owe debts of gratitude to many people, those who expressed their belief in me like Mrs Schoeman, the Rupert family and not least, my own family. Wherever I have gone, there have been people who have offered me the hand of friendship, in the north of England, in Scotland, and, of course, at home in South Africa. People like Frank Brache, Howie Bergins, Boon Wallace, Jannie Momberg, Eddie Barlow, Stephen Jones, Peter Kirsten, Adrian Kuiper, Richard Swan, Donnie Haines, and indeed enough colleagues down the years to fill another entire book, have all, most willingly, extended helping hands. But above all, it is to my wife Conita that I have to say the biggest thank you. She has travelled with me on the rollercoaster, has had to cope with the violent fluctuations of my life, the ups and the downs. She has had to share the bad times with me as well as the good but through thick and thin, she has always been there.

If I have sometimes been the man in the middle of controversy, very much the man in the middle of the racial tugs of war which have bedevilled South Africa; if I have fulfilled a role as the man in the middle for those thousands of South Africans whose station in life has denied them the opportunity to climb life's ladder and if, through my exploits in the middle of some of the most famous and yet also some of the most insignificant cricket grounds in the world, I have given pleasure and perhaps sometimes inspiration to others, then I am content. No, I was never alone out there in the middle. And of course, my faith has always taught me that God is with me wherever I go. So how could I have failed, with that kind of support? For He too was always with me, out there in the middle.

POSTSCRIPT

BY KEITH GRAHAM

My first encounter with Omar came during his first season in Scotland. I was at the end of my own active cricket career, then captain of Stirling County, and I have a clear memory of the ball disappearing into the outfield when I was bowling my rather flat version of off spin to him. He reached the 90s on that occasion and none of our bowlers were able to contain him, although I do recall that he had two escapes when outfielders failed to hold on to catches on the boundary – off my bowling! That was the only occasion we met on the field itself but I also well remember that we struck up a rapport after the game and we have, I think I can say, been good friends ever since.

It was when I began to cover the international scene for the press and the BBC that I next came across Omar and once again we immediately established a good rapport, often spending hours just talking about cricket during the long journeys we had to undertake during the Benson & Hedges and NatWest campaigns. I think it is true to say that we share opinions on most facets of the game.

If sometimes he is forthright, the determination he has shown in clearing so many barriers during his own long and difficult rise to the top – barriers which, unless you have lived in South Africa, are difficult to fully understand – is also reflected in his unquenchable desire for progress. Hence, on occasion, he does find himself at odds with the administrators. When Omar believes something, he does not shirk from the responsibility of advancing that belief, even if it leads to some conflict. It is not that he is unnecessarily obdurate; instead he is a very positive thinker and a relentless pursuer of goals.

When Omar asked me to help him with his autobiography, I was delighted. He is a man I have admired for a long time both as a cricketer and as a courageous, articulate and very determined human being. He has had to work hard to achieve success, has had to scale massive obstacles in order to fulfil his seemingly impossible dreams. If he will never be regarded as one of the greatest cricketers of all time, I have no doubt that had it not been for South Africa's long period of isolation, he would have become an influential force in world cricket.

Examination of his figures certainly confirms that he has been, statistically and historically, one of South Africa's most successful all-round cricketers. And those figures have been achieved in a very tough domestic arena. South Africans, more than most, play their cricket very competitively.

Omar Henry unquestionably has much more yet to give to the game of cricket, even if the sun is setting on his playing career. And with his record of dedication, you can bet your bottom dollar that he will help produce a new generation of well-motivated young cricketers wherever he is involved.

On a personal note, I would like to express my thanks to Omar, and of course, to his delightful family, for giving me the opportunity to become involved in this book.

I would also wish to pay tribute to Bob Sambridge, who has followed Omar's career closely over many years and without whose groundwork and research this book could never have been written

MILESTONE MATCHES

SOUTH AFRICA vs AUSTRALIA XI
at Durban, January 1987
First appearance for South Africa

MCC vs SCOTLAND
at Lord's, August 1990
Captain for first Scottish victory at Lord's since 1874

SRI LANKA vs SOUTH AFRICA
at Wellington, March 1992
First One-day International

SOUTH AFRICA vs INDIA
at Durban, November 1992
First Test Match

ORANGE FREE STATE vs WESTERN PROVINCE
at Bloemfontein, January 1993
Decisive Castle Cup match

SOUTH AFRICA vs. AUSTRALIA XI

at Durban on 17th, 19th, 20th, 21st, 22nd January 1987
Toss : Australia XI. Umpires : K.E.Liebenberg and L.J.Rautenbach
Match drawn

AUSTRALIA XI

S.B.Smith	c Page b Henry	137	b Page	5
J.Dyson	c Richardson b le Roux	1	c McMillan b Rice	101
K.C.Wessels	c Richardson b le Roux	0	c Richardson b Page	2
K.J.Hughes *	c & b le Roux	25	lbw b Page	9
G.N.Yallop	c Page b Henry	36	(7) c Henry b le Roux	26
M.D.Haysman	c McKenzie b Kirsten	5	(5) b Rice	115
T.V.Hohns	c McKenzie b Kirsten	26	(6) lbw b le Roux	10
S.J.Rixon +	c Richardson b Page	13	not out	42
J.N.Maguire	c Richardson b le Roux	2	run out	2
R.M.Hogg	c Richardson b Page	6	c McEwan b Kirsten	9
R.J.McCurdy	not out	0	c Whitfield b Kirsten	0
Extras	(lb 3,w 1,nb 9)	13	(b 2,lb 14,nb 2)	18
TOTAL		264		339

SOUTH AFRICA

S.J.Cook	b Hohns	44	c Rixon b Hogg	23
B.J.Whitfield	c Rixon b Hohns	59	b Hogg	26
P.N.Kirsten	c Yallop b Hohns	13	lbw b Maguire	33
K.S.McEwan	b McCurdy	101	b Hohns	27
C.E.B.Rice *	c Dyson b Hohns	22	lbw b Hogg	0
K.A.McKenzie	lbw b Hohns	14	b Hohns	3
B.M.McMillan	c Haysman b McCurdy	15	not out	18
D.J.Richardson +	not out	44	c & b Hohns	0
G.S.le Roux	c Rixon b McCurdy	6		
O.Henry	c Yallop b Hogg	7		
H.A.Page	c & b Hohns	2		
Extras	(b 8,lb 7,w 1,nb 7)	23	(b 1,lb 7,nb 5)	13
TOTAL		350	(for 7 wkts)	143

SOUTH AFRICA	O	M	R	W	O	M	R	W
le Roux	13.3	1	33	4	29	5	63	2
Page	17	1	57	2	35	6	87	3
Rice	10	2	32	0	19	4	38	2
McMillan	10	0	57	0	17	3	55	0
Henry	23	4	58	2	26	11	44	0
Kirsten	15	4	24	2	14.4	3	36	2

AUSTRALIA XI	O	M	R	W	O	M	R	W
Hogg	28	5	87	1	16	4	33	3
McCurdy	22	2	76	3	17	3	59	0
Maguire	28	7	74	0	7	3	16	1
Hohns	47.4	13	98	6	17.5	6	27	3

FALL OF WICKETS

	AUS	SAF	AUS	SAF
1st	4	100	7	29
2nd	7	127	11	89
3rd	80	130	25	93
4th	148	177	50	102
5th	198	197	253	115
6th	220	237	260	130
7th	256	309	301	143
8th	256	319	304	
9th	264	341	337	
10th	264	350	339	

MCC vs SCOTLAND

at Lord's Cricket Ground on 22nd, 23rd August 1990
Umpires: R.H.Duckett and T.H.Duckett
Scotland won by 7 wickets

MCC

G.D.Mendis	b Parfitt	57	b Bee	28
R.J.Lanchbury	c Haggo b Bee	13	b Moir	2
S.P.Henderson*	c Moir b Parfitt	25	c Henry b Parfitt	25
R.O.Butcher	b Parfitt	0	c Philip b Henry	21
M.L.Simmons	c Patterson b Henry	5	b Parfitt	13
S.C.Wundke	c Richardson b Sharpe	14	not out	101
G.Sharp+	c Storie b Parfitt	20	b Parfitt	10
M.R.Whitney	b Parfitt	0	not out	8
G.Stead	not out	21		
P.J.Hacker	b Henry	24		
M.E.Allbrook	lbw b Parfitt	6		
Extras	(b 4,lb 9)	13	(b 1,lb 4,w 5)	10
TOTAL		198	(for 6 wkts dec)	218

SCOTLAND

I.L.Philip	b Stead	23	b Stead	83
B.M.W.Patterson	c Mendis b Whitney	0	lbw b Whitney	0
A.C.Storie	c Sharp b Whitney	0	run out	37
G.Salmond	lbw b Allbrook	20	not out	56
A.B.Russell	c Wundke b Allbrook	18	not out	38
D.J.Haggo+	c Sharp b Stead	33		
O.Henry*	c Simmons b Stead	27		
A.Bee	c Wundke b Whitney	26		
M.S.Richardson	not out	16		
J.D.Moir	not out	19		
C.L.Parfitt				
Extras	(b 5,lb 3)	8	(b 7,lb 1,w 5)	13
TOTAL	(for 8 wkts dec)	190	(for 3 wkts)	227

SCOTLAND	O	M	R	W	O	M	R	W
Bee	12	0	42	1	6	2	25	1
Moir	13	5	38	1	7	2	22	1
Richardson	7	1	31	0	2	0	10	0
Parfitt	19	5	57	6	22	4	71	3
Henry	10	5	17	2	18.5	3	85	1

MCC	O	M	R	W	O	M	R	W
Whitney	8	1	14	3	10	3	33	1
Hacker	5	1	19	0	9	2	30	0
Allbrook	18	4	68	3	17	0	73	0
Stead	16.5	3	68	2	17	2	83	1
Wundke	3	1	13	0				

FALL OF WICKETS

	MCC	SCO	MCC	SCO
1st	41	1	2	21
2nd	83	5	35	124
3rd	100	40	66	126
4th	105	54	93	
5th	105	97	110	
6th	139	97	152	
7th	139	155		
8th	139	155		
9th	189			
10th				

SRI LANKA vs. SOUTH AFRICA
at Wellington on 2nd March 1992
Toss : Sri Lanka. Umpires : Khizar Hayat and S.J.Woodward
Sri Lanka won by 3 wickets

SOUTH AFRICA

K.C.Wessels*	c & b Ranatunga	40
A.P.Kuiper	b Anurasiri	18
P.N.Kirsten	c Hathurusinghe b Kalpage	47
M.W.Rushmere	c Jayasuriya b Ranatunga	4
J.N.Rhodes	c Jayasuriya b Wickremasinghe	28
W.J.Cronje	st Tillekeratne b Anurasiri	3
R.P.Snell	b Anurasiri	9
B.M.McMillan	not out	18
D.J.Richardson+	run out	0
O.Henry	c Kalpage b Wickremasinghe	11
A.A.Donald	run out	3
Extras	(lb 9,w 4,nb 1)	14
TOTAL		195

SRI LANKA

U.C.Hathurusinghe	c Wessels b Donald	5
R.S.Mahanama	c Richardson b McMillan	68
A.P.Gurusinha	lbw b Donald	0
P.A.de Silva	b Donald	7
H.P.Tillekeratne+	c Rushmere b Henry	17
A.Ranatunga	not out	64
S.T.Jayasuriya	st Richardson b Kirsten	3
R.S.Kalpage	run out	5
C.P.H.Ramanayake	not out	4
G.P.Wickremasinghe		
S.D.Anurasiri		
Extras	(b 1,lb 7,w 13,nb 4)	25
TOTAL	(for 7 wkts)	198

SOUTH AFRICA	O	M	R	W
Ramanayake	9	2	19	0
Wickremasinghe	7	0	32	2
Anurasiri	10	1	41	3
Kalpage	10	0	38	1
Gurusinha	8	0	30	0
Ranatunga	6	0	26	2

SOUTH AFRICA	O	M	R	W
Donald	9.5	0	42	3
McMillan	10	2	34	1
Henry	10	0	31	1
Snell	10	1	33	0
Kuiper	5	0	25	0
Kirsten	5	0	25	1

FALL OF WICKETS

	SAF	SRI
1st	27	11
2nd	114	12
3rd	114	35
4th	128	87
5th	149	154
6th	153	168
7th	165	169
8th	165	
9th	186	
10th	195	

SOUTH AFRICA vs. INDIA

at Kingsmead, Durban on 13th, 14th, 15th, 16th, 17th November 1992
Toss : India. Umpires : S.A.Bucknor, K.E.Liebenberg and C.J.Mitchley
Match drawn

SOUTH AFRICA

S.J.Cook	c Tendulkar b Kapil Dev	0	c & b Kumble	43
A.C.Hudson	b Kapil Dev	14	c More b Srinath	55
K.C.Wessels *	c Azharuddin b Kumble	118	c More b Srinath	32
P.N.Kirsten	c More b Srinath	13	not out	11
J.N.Rhodes	c Azharuddin b Kumble	41	not out	26
B.M.McMillan	c Prabhakar b Shastri	3		
D.J.Richardson +	lbw b Prabhakar	15		
O.Henry	c Tendulkar b Shastri	3		
M.W.Pringle	lbw b Kapil Dev	33		
A.A.Donald	lbw b Prabhakar	1		
B.N.Schultz	not out	0		
Extras	(lb 6,nb 7)	13	(b 1,lb 2,nb 6)	9
TOTAL		254	(for 3 wkts)	176

INDIA

R.J.Shastri	lbw b Pringle	14
A.Jajeda	c McMillan b Schultz	3
S.V.Manjrekar	lbw b McMillan	0
S.R.Tendulkar	run out	11
M.Azharuddin *	run out	36
P.K.Amre	c Rhodes b McMillan	103
Kapil Dev	c Richardson b McMillan	2
M.Prabhakar	c McMillan b Donald	13
K.S.More +	lbw b Henry	55
A.R.Kumble	b Henry	8
J.Srinath	not out	1
Extras	(b 1,lb 7,w 4,nb 19)	31
TOTAL		277

INDIA	O	M	R	W	O	M	R	W	FALL OF WICKETS				
										SAF	IND	SAF	IND
Kapil Dev	22	6	43	3	19	11	19	0	1st	0	18	68	
Prabhakar	24.4	7	47	2	14	3	47	0	2nd	41	22	129	
Srinath	18	3	69	1	16	3	42	2	3rd	101	38	138	
Kumble	28	8	51	2	16	4	36	1	4th	183	38		
Shastri	11	1	38	2	14	2	22	0	5th	194	125		
Tendulkar					2	1	3	0	6th	206	127		
Manjrekar					1	0	4	0	7th	215	146		
									8th	251	247		
SOUTH AFRICA	O	M	R	W	O	M	R	W	9th	253	274		
Donald	29	6	69	1					10th	254	277		
Schultz	14.5	7	25	1									
McMillan	37	18	52	3									
Pringle	34	10	67	1									
Henry	19.1	3	56	2									

ORANGE FREE STATE vs WESTERN PROVINCE

at Springbok Park, Bloemfontein on 9th, 10th, 11th, 12th January 1993
Toss: Orange Free State Umpires: W.Diedricks and H.de Bruin
Orange Free State won by 114 runs

ORANGE FREE STATE

J.M.Arthur	c Ryall b Pringle	0	(2) c sub b Rundle	71
G.F.J.Liebenberg	c Rundle b Pringle	2		
W.J.Cronje*	lbw b Kuiper	15	(1) not out	161
L.J.Wilkinson	c Ryall b Matthews	41		
P.J.R.Steyn	c Ryall b Pringle	22	(3) not out	56
F.D.Stephenson	c Plantema b Pringle	7		
C.J.P.G.van Zyl	c Ryall b Pringle	16		
O.Henry	not out	104		
B.T.Player	c Lazard b Matthews	24		
P.J.L.Radley+	run out	17		
A.A.Donald	c Matthews b Pringle	3		
Extras	(b 4,lb 4,w 1,nb 6)	15	(b 3,lb 9,nb 3)	15
TOTAL		266	(for 1 wkt dec)	303

WESTERN PROVINCE

T.N.Lazard	b Donald	13	(7) c Player b Henry	12
K.C.Jackson	run out	26	(1) c Radley b Donald	34
A.P.Plantema	b Player	17	(2) c Stephenson b van Zyl	9
G.Kirsten	c Liebenberg b Player	18	(3) c Doanald b Stephenson	105
A.P.Kuiper	c Donald b Stephenson	6	(4) c & b Henry	7
A.T.Holdstock	run out	6	(5) b Henry	0
E.O.Simons	c Cronje b Henry	40	(6) b Henry	50
D.B.Rundle	c Radley b van Zyl	12	not out	14
C.R.Matthews*	b Henry	0	(10) c Steyn b Player	17
R.J.Ryall+	c Radley b Stephenson	10	(9) c Wilkinson b Henry	1
M.W.Pringle	not out	0	b Player	6
Extras	(lb 11,w 1,nb 7))	19	(b 7,lb 24,w 1,nb 3))	35
TOTAL		165		290

W PROVINCE	O	M	R	W	O	M	R	W
Pringle	26.3	8	60	6	16	1	46	0
Matthews	12	2	39	2	13	0	45	0
Simons	19	0	62	0	20	5	46	0
Kuiper	16	5	39	1	12	1	53	0
Rundle	14	3	52	0	22	0	84	1
Holdstock	3	0	6	0				
Jackson					2	0	17	0

ORANGE FREE STATE	O	M	R	W	O	M	R	W
Donald	21	5	38	1	25	9	43	1
Stephenson	22	7	31	2	21	3	64	1
Player	17	5	27	2	17.5	5	40	2
van Zyl	14	8	10	1	20	7	39	1
Henry	21.2	4	42	2	33	10	68	5
Cronje	4	1	6	0	5	3	5	0

FALL OF WICKETS

	OFS	WPR	OFS	WPR
1st	0	49	166	36
2nd	3	63		86
3rd	50	80		108
4th	75	80		110
5th	80	91		216
6th	110	98		238
7th	113	117		243
8th	165	120		247
9th	246	161		282
10th	266	165		290

CAREER RECORD

FIRST-CLASS

TEST MATCHES

Opposition	Venue	Date	Batting	Fielding	Bowling
India	Durban	13/11/92	3		2-56
India	Port Elizabeth	26/12/92	16	2Ct	0-30 & 0-17
India	Cape Town	2/1/93	34		1-86

REBEL TOUR INTERNATIONAL MATCHES

Australia	Durban	17/1/87	7	1Ct	2-58 & 0-44
Australia	Port Elizabeth	26/12/92	13	2Ct	3-96 & 0-63

FIRST-CLASS BATTING (Season by Season)

for Western Province, Boland, Orange Free State, Scotland, South Africa

Season	M	Inns	NO	Runs	HS	Avge	100s	50s	Ct	St
1977-78 WP	4	4	2	34	16	17.00	-	-	2	-
1978-79 WP, WP B	7	11	6	177	44*	35.40	-	-	8	-
1979-80 WP, WP B	6	8	0	56	22	7.00	-	-	9	-
1980-81 WP, WP B	8	12	2	300	105*	30.00	1	-	8	-
1981-82 WP, WP B	10	13	5	281	53	35.12	-	1	9	-
1982-83 WP, WP B	9	14	2	330	54	27.50	-	2	13	-
1983-84 WP	5	8	3	180	79*	36.00	-	1	5	-
1984-85 Boland	6	9	0	163	50	18.11	-	1	6	-
1985-86 Boland, Pres XI	9	16	1	385	117	25.66	1	2	12	-
1986-87 Boland, SA	6	9	1	307	114*	38.37	1	2	4	-
1987-88 Boland	7	11	1	346	125	34.60	1	1	8	-
1988-89 Boland	7	13	2	309	64	28.09	-	1	12	-
1989 Scotland	1	2	0	51	26	25.50	-	-	2	-
1989-90 OFS	10	16	4	288	78	24.00	-	2	6	-
1990 Scotland	1	1	0	23	23	23.00	-	-	-	-
1990-91 OFS	10	18	1	487	88	28.64	-	3	6	-
1991 Scotland	1	1	0	22	22	22.00	-	-	-	-
1991-92 OFS	4	6	1	207	64*	41.40	-	1	1	-
1992-93 OFS/SA	9	11	2	376	104*	41.77	1	2	8	-
1993-94 Boland	3	5	0	119	49	23.80	-	-	2	-

CAREER BATTING AVERAGES (Summary) - Including fielding

	M	Inns	NO	Runs	HS	Avge	100s	50s	Ct	St
Test	3	3	0	53	34	17.66	-	-	2	-
Rebel Int	2	2	0	20	13	10.00	-	-	1	-
All First-Class	123	188	33	4441	125	28.65	5	19	121	-

FIRST-CLASS BOWLING (Season by Season)

Season	Runs	Wkts	Avge	Best	5wI	10wM
1977-78 WP	309	12	25.75	6-31	1	-
1978-79 WP, WP B	608	21	28.95	5-104	1	-
1979-80 WP, WP B	341	21	16.23	4-35	-	-
1980-81 WP, WP B	358	8	44.75	2-54	-	-
1981-82 WP, WP B	695	37	18.78	7-22	2	-
1982-83 WP, WP B	866	41	21.12	6-19	4	1
1983-84 WP	171	5	34.20	2-31	-	-
1984-85 Boland	460	22	20.90	4-41	-	-
1985-86 Boland, Pres XI	809	45	17.97	7-82	4	-
1986-87 Boland, SA	630	20	31.50	4-47	-	-
1987-88 Boland	713	36	19.80	6-57	2	1
1988-89 Boland	855	41	20.85	5-59	1	-
1989 Scotland	174	13	13.38	7-86	2	1
1989-90 OFS	1059	34	31.14	5-66	2	-
1990 Scotland	106	2	53.00	2-54	-	-
1990-91 OFS	1066	26	41.00	4-91	-	-
1991 Scotland	85	1	85.00	1-43	-	-
1991-92 OFS	437	17	25.70	5-56	1	-
1992-93 OFS/SA	865	30	28.83	6-72	2	-
1993-94 Boland	234	2	117.00	2-41	-	-

CAREER BOWLING AVERAGES (Summary)

	Overs	Mdns	Runs	Wkts	Avge	Best	5wI	10wM
Test	71.1	15	189	3	63.00	2-56	-	-
Rebel Int	120.5	39	261	5	52.20	3-96	-	-
All First-Class			10841	434	24.97	7-22	22	3

BEST BATTING
125 Boland vs Border, East London 1987-88
BEST BOWLING
7-22 Western Province vs SA Universities, Cape Town, 1981-82

ONE-DAY INTERNATIONALS

WORLD CUP
Sri Lanka   Wellington   2/3/92   11   1-31

OTHER ONE-DAY
West Indies   Kingston   7/4/92   1   1Ct   1-53
West Indies   Port of Spain 11/4/92   8 *   0-41

BATTING AVERAGES - Including fielding

	M	Inns	NO	Runs	HS	Avge	100s	50s	Ct	St
World Cup	1	1	0	11	11	11.00	-	-	-	-
Other One-Day	2	2	1	9	8*	9.00	-	-	1	-
All One-Day	3	3	1	20	11	10.00	-	-	1	-

BOWLING AVERAGES

	Overs	Mdns	Runs	Wkts	Avge	Best	5wI
World Cup	10	0	31	1	31.00	1-31	-
Other One-Day	14.5	0	94	1	94.00	1-53	-
All One-Day	24.5	0	125	2	62.50	1-31	-

CAREER RECORD FOR SCOTLAND

BATTING AVERAGES

	M	Inns	NO	Runs	HS	Avge	100s	50s	Ct	St
First Class	3	4	0	96	26	24.00	-	-	2	-
B & H Cup	33	33	2	717	62*	23.13	-	6	11	-
NatWest	7	7	2	155	53	31.00	-	1	2	-
Other Games	19	19	4	635	102*	45.35	2	5	13	-

BOWLING AVERAGES

	Overs	Mdns	Runs	Wkts	Avge	Best	5wI	10wM
First-Class	132.4	25	365	16	22.81	7-86	2	1
B & H Cup	351	45	1286	19	67.68	2-17	-	-
Nat West	59	5	219	4	54.75	2-35	-	-
Other Matches	285	63	914	27	21.25	6-54	2	-

In 13 seasons of club cricket in Scotland – for Poloc, Stenhousemuir, Arbroath and West Lothian – Omar Henry scored 14,543 runs (including 28 centuries) and took 811 wickets.

INDEX